SOAS Studies
UNDERSTANDINGS AND PERSPECTIVES

CASTE TODAY

SOAS Studies on South Asia
UNDERSTANDINGS AND PERSPECTIVES

Caste Today

Edited by
C.J. Fuller

DELHI
OXFORD UNIVERSITY PRESS
CALCUTTA   CHENNAI   MUMBAI
1997

Oxford University Press, Great Clarendon Street, Oxford OX2 6DP

Oxford   New York
Athens   Auckland   Bangkok   Calcutta
Cape Town   Chennai   Dar es Salaam   Delhi
Florence   Hong Kong   Istanbul   Karachi
Kuala Lumpur   Madrid   Melbourne   Mexico City
Mumbai   Nairobi   Paris   Singapore
Taipei   Tokyo   Toronto

and associates in

Berlin   Ibadan

First published 1996
Oxford India Paperbacks 1997

ISBN 0 19 564247 3

Printed at Saurbh Print O Pack, Noida, U. P.
and published by Manzar Khan, Oxford University Press
YMCA Library Building, Jai Singh Road, New Delhi 110 001

CONTENTS

SOUTH ASIA: UNDERSTANDINGS AND PERSPECTIVES
GENERAL EDITOR'S INTRODUCTION

The present volume forms part of a project sponsored by the School of Oriental and African Studies, University of London, and initiated during my tenure as chairman of the SOAS Centre of South Asian Studies. It involves many members and associates of the Centre. The intention is to take a number of important terms or concepts, and to discuss each one's different meanings. In each case a volume will be prepared comprising a critical introduction to sum up and reflect upon the state of our knowledge of this concept, plus a number of illustrative essays containing their own analysis, which may or may not agree with that of the introduction. The essays are also intended to be fairly detailed and empirical in emphasis, so as to stand in regard to the introduction in something of the relationship of evidence to interpretation. The project is directed both at specific problems and at a number of fundamental debates on the nature of discourse; and yet it is not intended primarily to generate new theory but rather to make its contribution by approaching questions from a new direction.

Part of the dissatisfaction which lies behind the project is with Eurocentric terminology. This is not because we deny the possibility of there being any universal terms, nor because we think all knowledge produced by Europeans essentially the same and equally corrupted by power. It is because we are impressed by the need to avoid all essentialism, and by the importance, both intellectually and in practical situations, of an appreciation of difference. It is because we are uncertain how larger categories may properly be constructed. Similar concerns are expressed in various ways in many disciplines, and constitute a crisis of interpretation.

We want to start with detailed and concrete studies. Part of our question is: what is it that constitutes 'South Asian' perceptions? We do not think there is—that is, that anyone can provide—an adequate answer to this question as a whole. Moreover we do not intend our work to be merely comparative, especially not between South Asia and Europe, as if the latter were a yardstick. Though we will investigate the question, we are not at all sure that there *are* peculiarly South Asian perceptions, as a type, and we are as interested in differences within the region and over time as in discrepancies between the terminology of our disciplines and that of its subjects. On this basis, we think it worth-while, with regard to concepts in frequent and often uncritical use, to examine the different meanings they have, and then reflect upon the differences. The exercise can be substantive rather than terminological. We question whether the 'virtual reality' of our studies bears any close relation to the complexities of its subjects. We think we can get closer, provided we work with small components. We do so not to be restricted to them out of context, but to use them to focus on larger issues.

Peter Robb
School of Oriental and African Studies, London

ACKNOWLEDGEMENTS

The chapters in this book (except for my Introduction) are revised versions of papers presented at a workshop on 'Caste Today' held at the School of Oriental and African Studies on 12-13 July 1993. The workshop was the fourth in a series held as part of the project on 'South Asia: Understandings and Perspectives' initiated by the Centre of South Asian Studies at SOAS and its then chairman, Peter Robb, who invited me to convene the workshop.

My thanks go first to Peter Robb and all those who presented papers at the workshop. I am additionally grateful to the nine authors represented in this volume for patiently tolerating my editorial deadlines and demands. Besides these nine, papers were also presented at the workshop by Anjan Ghosh, P. Radhakrishnan and Gloria Raheja; their contributions were important, but it was eventually decided that they would publish their work separately. I also thank Katy Gardner, Tony Good, John Harriss, M.A. Kalam, Karin Kapadia, Johnny Parry and David Washbrook for acting as discussants, Burton Stein for chairing part of the workshop, and Karin Kapadia again for letting me consult the detailed notes she made during discussion.

Peter Robb kindly took care of the administrative organisation of the workshop, but much of the work, as well as the production of the camera-ready copy and a great deal of editorial labour were capably performed by Janet Marks of the Centre. I also thank Esha Béteille at Oxford University Press in Delhi for her efficiency and encouragement.

The costs of the workshop were mainly borne by SOAS, but the Royal Anthropological Institute of Great Britain and Ireland is also thanked for its financial contribution.

London, May 1995   C.J.F.

LIST OF CONTRIBUTORS

André Béteille is Professor of Sociology at the University of Delhi

Robert Deliège is Professor of Social Anthropology at the Université Catholique de Louvain and a Researcher of the Fonds National de la Recherche Scientifique

Nick Dirks is Professor of History and Anthropology, and Director of the Center for South and Southeast Asian Studies, at the University of Michigan, Ann Arbor

Frank Fanselow is Assistant Professor of Anthropology at the American University in Cairo

Chris Fuller is Professor of Anthropology at the London School of Economics and Political Science

Raymond Jamous is Directeur de Recherche of the Centre National de la Recherche Scientifique and Director of the Laboratoire d'Ethnologie et de Sociologie Comparative at the Université de Paris X-Nanterre

Helen Lambert is Lecturer in Medical Anthropology at the London School of Hygiene and Tropical Medicine

Adrian Mayer is Emeritus Professor of Asian Anthropology at the School of Oriental and African Studies

Marie-Louise Reiniche is Directeur d'Études at the École Pratique des Hautes Études (5th section), Paris

Sylvia Vatuk is Professor of Anthropology at the University of Illinois at Chicago

Chapter 1

INTRODUCTION: CASTE TODAY[1]

C.J. Fuller

'Continuity and change', the cliché so often applied to modern India, encapsulates a fundamental problem more than a basic truth, because the relation between continuity and change is becoming increasingly complex in the face of the rapid and far-reaching developments so apparent in every domain of contemporary Indian society, including the caste system. Indeed, on the subject of caste, one of the most distinctive of India's social institutions, anthropologists and sociologists have generally been far more confident about structural continuity than contemporary change, and analysis of the relation between them has persistently posed serious intellectual problems.

These problems, moreover, are not narrowly academic ones, because they raise difficult questions about the construction of knowledge by social scientists that have plainly become more contentious in recent years. One of these questions, pertaining to the tendency to privilege continuity and the past over change and the present, is sharply raised by Béteille's response to Dumont's criticism of his article, 'Individualism and equality', first published in 1986 (1991:ch.9). According to Béteille:

> Dumont's lack of ease with modern India is writ large in his work, although it does not shine as brightly as his enthusiasm for traditional India, which is partly an India of his own construction. In this construction traditional India is made of whole cloth.... Modern India, in Dumont's construction, is not made of whole cloth; it is a thing of shreds and patches. (1991:246)

[1] For their encouragement and their criticisms of an earlier version of this chapter, I thank André Béteille, Nick Dirks, John Harriss, Helen Lambert, Adrian Mayer and Marie-Louise Reiniche, as well as participants at seminars in the Department of Anthropology, London School of Economics, and the Centre d'Études de l'Inde et de l'Asie du Sud, Paris.

Nor is it Dumont alone whom Béteille has in mind; he concludes his response by saying that:

I know only too well how generations of Western sympathizers have used their admiration for Indian tradition to mask their allergy to the India of their experience. ... But I belong to the modern world, and I would be untrue to my vocation as a sociologist to disown the world to which I belong. (ibid.:249)

If Béteille's view, which arguably exaggerates modern westerners' allergies, were simply a matter of taste—a preference for the classical rather than the modern—it would hardly matter. But it isn't, for it raises a further question about the connection between scholarship and the contemporary situation, which has become more pressing since the mid-1980s because of the interconnected political crises caused by caste reservation policy and religious militancy. In the wake of the attempt by V.P. Singh's government to implement the Mandal Commission report in 1990, many leading Indian social scientists and other academics involved themselves in public debate over the reservations policy.[2] The relevance of this academic involvement for the study of caste today is not about the rights and wrongs of alternative positions on the reservations policy; it is rather that the public debate as a whole is a very wide one in which many other people, including powerful politicians, are involved as well. Even if the real impact of academics' pronouncements is limited, they are parties to a broad political debate which defines an important dimension of the setting for their work, because the contemporary nature of caste is itself being changed by that debate as it unfolds within its social and political context. The situation is not entirely new, as Béteille in his chapter

[2] Examples of academic involvement in the debate over reservations policy include the exchange in the *Hindu* between Béteille (1990a), Guhan *et al.* (1990) and Radhakrishnan (1990a; cf.1990b); further newspaper articles by Béteille (1990b), Srinivas (1990a; 1990b) and others, which are summarised and criticised by Heuzé (1991); the round-table debate published in *India Today*, 31 May 1991, 33-41, whose participants included Veena Das; some provocative and interesting remarks by Sheth (1991:337-41) on Mandal and Indian sociologists; and two recent newspaper articles by Radhakrishnan (1995a; 1995b), which include some material from his paper for the 'Caste today' workshop.

reminds us by referring to the controversy over Srinivas's address of 1957, 'Caste in modern India' (1962:ch.1). Nevertheless, in the last few years, public political argument over caste has plainly been intensified and, more than ever before (as Dirks also notes in his chapter), anthropologists and sociologists today are studying an institution which is itself being reshaped by a contentious and often confused discourse about it. As Das (1995:25) comments: 'in Indian society one finds controversies of anthropological theory not only mirrored in the ideological conflicts of modern Indian society but also as having provided new spaces for these conflicts to be articulated.' These controversies, of course, are being pursued by foreign scholars just as much as by Indian ones, even if foreigners rarely take part at first-hand in the public debate within India.

None of the above is intended to induce a vacuous 'epistemological hypochondria' (to quote the Comaroffs' phrase) brought on by the recognition that there is no Archimedean standpoint from which the scholar can investigate the 'objective', stable reality of caste. Rather, it is to insist that what caste is and what it means are now in a patent state of flux, and that scholarly discussion of the topic cannot be detached from the discourse of caste engaged in by contemporary Indians. In the chapters collected in this volume, people's diverse and changing understandings of caste and inequality more generally are consistently to the fore, and in this introductory chapter I shall try to set them within their broader analytical context. Moreover, in one way or another, all the contributors to this book share Béteille's concern to understand the modern world, and they therefore recognise that our principal obligation is to write as truthfully, intelligibly and impartially as possible about the ordinary people living today whom we study. Presentism, though, is not a solution if it leads us to neglect contemporary India's relation with its past. This relation is made harder to understand precisely because modern India often does look like 'a thing of shreds and patches', without clearly discernible structural principles, and—as I have already implied in referring to contemporary discourse about it—nowhere is this apparent patchery plainer than in the domain of caste.

The anthropology of 'traditional' caste

The most coherent and powerful theory of caste developed in the anthropology of India is undoubtedly Dumont's, as magisterially set out in *Homo hierarchicus* (1970). As the reader will be familiar with the book, I need not outline its contents, beyond recalling that Dumont's theory of caste crucially depends on axioms—especially about the Brahman-Kshatriya relationship within the *varna* hierarchy—that he derives from early Hindu texts, and that the data explained by his theory come predominantly from ethnographic studies of Indian rural society. The structure of Indian society, as concretely manifested in its contemporary villages, is thus revealed as fundamentally unchanged since ancient times.

The majority of Dumont's critics have, to varying degrees, attacked both his theoretical model and his ethnographic representation of the caste system. The most obvious line of attack on Dumont's model is to question his interpretation of the texts, as has been done by scholars like Heesterman (1971; 1985:ch.1) or Marriott (1969; 1990b), who polemically contrasts ethnosociological approaches with Dumont's 'narrower model of Indian society constructed with some Western categories' (1990a:xiii). In much the same vein is the critique of Dumont's special concept of religion, which largely reduced it to hierarchical values, that has been developed in the large body of anthropological writing on Hinduism produced since the 1970s (cf. Fuller and Spencer 1990:88). My purpose here is not to reassess the criticisms of Dumont's model, but only to observe that it has been disputed by arguing that Dumont has misunderstood the texts, the Hindu religious tradition partly encapsulated in those texts, or both. Because India's ancient past and its structural continuity with the present are under scrutiny, Dumont's critics, as much as he, are therefore predominantly oriented towards traditional rather than modern India, even when they are actually dealing with contemporary material. Béteille (1991:8, 33-5) describes this orientation as the 'book-view' of Indian society, as opposed to the 'field-view', and this chimes in with his criticism of scholarship that eulogises the past and devalues the present. Clearly, a predisposition towards the book-view is partly motivated by contemporary anthropological interest in Hinduism, and because 'traditional' religion is still vital in the lives of most contemporary Indians, it cannot be neglected in any attempt to understand their modern condition. For the analysis of caste, however, the book-view has become increasingly impedimental because it focuses attention on continuities with the past and the scriptural tradition at the expense of the discontinuities that are becoming proportionally more salient. Moreover, the book-view tends to promote a holistic perspective—a preoccupation with pan-Indian structures—which consistently privileges uniformity over diversity. This too has some distorting consequences, to which I shall return shortly.

The most telling criticisms of Dumont's ethnographic representation of the caste system have been inspired by historical research. During the 1970s and 1980s, it became clearly understood that Indian society, and specifically its caste system, as described in the 'village studies' ethnographies of the 1950s and 1960s, were not something ancient that survived in 'traditional' villages. On the contrary, village society was the product of history and particularly colonial history.[3] To summarise all the historical literature that has now been published on this subject is impossible. Fortunately, though, I can draw on the masterly synthesis by Bayly, who rightly observes that both the old idea of timeless India and the newer revisionism which almost claims that colonialism alone made India into a caste society are erroneous. In fact, both in precept and practice, caste as a rigid and hierarchical system had long been

[3] Writing in 1970, Cohn was well ahead of his time in postulating that: 'In some sense it might be argued that the British created the Indian village', and that 'they rigidified some groups and institutions, which formerly had been contingent and flexible', such as castes (1987:195-6). By contrast, in his rethinking of the Indian village in 1975, Srinivas (1987) placed his emphasis on the colonial dissolution of the generally accepted and ubiquitous hierarchical caste system of pre-British India. Cohn's postulate was taken up by Fuller (1977), and although historical research now shows that I exaggerated the discontinuity between the pre-colonial and colonial periods (cf. Fuller 1989), my firmer and more explicit endorsement of Cohn's suggestion, alongside that of other authors, was taken as more or less self-evidently correct in Raheja's survey a decade later (1988:509-10). For Raheja, therefore, the error in my argument was its failure to push the criticism of Dumont's theory far enough.

established at major, Brahman-dominated centres of Hindu scholarship (1988:155-6). Bayly continues:

Yet while most areas of the subcontinent...were aware of the hierarchical and Brahminical interpretation of the universe and responded to it in their own rituals and daily life, there were still in the eighteenth century powerful ideologies working against hierarchy and rigid caste boundaries (ibid.:156).... In the early nineteenth century, however, the spirit of hierarchy and ritual distinction became more pervasive. The British peace speeded the rise of high Hindu kingship, Brahminism, and the advance of principles of purity and pollution in the countryside. (ibid.:157)

Hence hierarchy, based on royal rank or caste purity, became an increasingly pervasive principle throughout society, and 'the Brahmin interpretation of Hindu society which was theoretical rather than actual over much of India as late as 1750 was firmly ensconced a century later' (ibid.:158). 'Traditional' Indian society was not created out of nothing by British rule, but it was in Bayly's apt term 'consolidated' by it. And it was through the combined effect of colonial institutions and discourse, as Dirks argues, that caste was made into a peculiarly rigid social phenomenon detached from political processes, and 'a specifically Indian form of civil society' (1992:76). In his chapter in this book, Dirks returns to a related topic and shows how the evolution of caste in Tamilnadu, especially the development of the opposition between Brahmans and non-Brahmans, is in large part the outcome of transformations which occurred during the colonial period. For India as a whole (and not just Tamilnadu), however, the inescapable conclusion emerging from the historical literature is that the 'traditional' caste system encountered by village studies ethnographers—and generalised to all of India by Dumont—actually acquired its foundational position in the social structure, and much of its apparent stability as regulated by a distinctly Brahmanical preoccupation with hierarchy, during the period of British rule. Latter-day caste society was not in fact 'traditional'—meaning very old—at all.[4]

[4] In his survey of socio-economic historiography, Washbrook reaches conclusions similar to Bayly's and his decisive expression also deserves quotation: 'Much of India's ancient past...may have been made during the

Once again, it is significant that the critique of Dumont pursued by questioning his ethnographic generalisations has been mainly driven by analysis not of the present but the past, albeit the colonial rather than the ancient past. On the other hand, there is a crucial difference between research oriented towards the textual tradition and the ancient past, and research formed or inspired by colonial historiography. Whereas the former is generally holistic in perspective, the latter is normally anti-holistic and consistently emphasises diversity and competition within pre-colonial society. Through the influence exerted by the 'subaltern studies' school of historians, even on their intellectual opponents, great attention has also been paid to alternative ideologies— to 'recovering' the voices of sections of society marginalised or silenced by the colonial-Brahmanical hegemony. Moreover, much of the anti-holistic impetus in this historical scholarship undoubtedly comes from scepticism about the validity of a holistic perspective for making sense of contemporary society, just as reciprocally the uncovering of alternative voices in the past animates the search for them in the present.[5]

Striking the right balance between holistic and anti-holistic approaches is difficult, however. The overwhelming preoccupation with Indian values and structures in Dumont's work meant that diversity was neglected at the expense of uniformity, so that, for example, variant

second quarter of the nineteenth century and, not least, the past of Asiatic Despotism. For the structure of society and economy then taking shape would seem nearer to the ideal-type of Asiatic Despotism than anything South Asia had seen before: a sovereign effecting the claim to possess all resources in his domain, running the economy through his bureaucracy and presiding over a society of self-reproducing village communities, themselves organized around the principles of caste and jajmani' (1988:83).

[5] The large and growing literature of the 'subaltern studies' school is now well-known and detailed citation of it is unnecessary; for a selection, see Guha and Spivak (1988). For one example of debate over the subalternist project (and the critique of 'orientalism'), see the articles by O'Hanlon (1988), Prakash (1990), O'Hanlon and Washbrook (1992) and Prakash (1992). Explicit use of subaltern studies scholarship by anthropologists analysing contemporary material remains unusual; see, however, the 'recovery' of women's voices by Raheja and Gold (1994), which is most interesting and perceptive precisely when the authors explore how north Indian women have no single voice, either of resistance or conformity (cf. discussion of Lambert's chapter in main text below).

notions of caste held among different social groups tended to be ignored. Inasmuch as increasing diversity is itself a salient feature of contemporary change in caste, an excessively holistic approach 's unproductive. On the other hand, partly because of the influence oi recent historical work, there is now a risk of exaggerating diversity within Indian society, as if high and low castes, Hindus and Muslims, or men and women all inhabited autonomous social universes. That plainly is not the case and irrespective of the attention that ought to be given to diversity (or resistance), we should not lose sight of the unity (or ideological dominance) that are also characteristic of Indian society and culture.[6]

Lambert's chapter sheds light on one aspect of this question by discussing variation between men's and women's perspectives on the social significance of caste. Starting from evidence collected in the Rajasthani village of Chawandiya, Lambert re-examines the question of village unity and the related issue of cross-caste ties expressed through fictional kinship; she shows how Dumont's theory, as well as many of the ethnographic sources on which he relied, overemphasised the salience of caste in relation to those other solidarities, partly because the female perspective was neglected. She also argues that 'the treatment of caste and kinship has been coloured by a systematic male bias', and that the significance of locality in relation to caste and kinship only emerges clearly when a 'gendered perspective' is taken. Importantly, though, this is not evidence of truly separate male and female understandings, because women often see their world through a predominantly 'male' perspective, just as men can and do see theirs through a 'female' perspective. A comparable point is made by Raheja (Raheja and Gold 1994:16), who notes that 'in everyday talk, women

---

[6] This point is well-expressed by Vidal, Tarabout and Meyer in introducing a discussion of the Indian concepts of violence and non-violence, when they state that: 'we could be simultaneously at risk of returning to a conception of history and society that is, once again, too fragmented, and actually adopts a perspective closer than might be thought to colonial ideology, in which any unity or coherence in Indian society and culture was flatly denied'. And, as they also say, although non-dominant social and cultural forms must be recognised, 'it is just as crucial that we do not then lose sight of the importance that the dominant ideology can have because it is indeed dominant' (1994:200).

frequently speak from within the dominant discourse, and men may speak in terms set by the more muted discourse associated with women's speech genres'. On the whole, however, Raheja and Gold, more than Lambert, are inclined to insist on women's 'alternative self-perceptions and alternative vantage points on their social world' (ibid.:2), a position that appears more dichotomous than is justified by much of their own evidence (ibid.:29, 147-8). Nevertheless, the research of these scholars and of others (mostly female) who have particularly worked with women clearly demonstrates that the analysis of Indian society has tended to reproduce men's, rather than women's, understandings of it, and that this bias needs to be corrected. Undoubtedly, too, there is a real need for a systematic critique of Indian village ethnography that develops Lambert's arguments further, so that the significance of gender differentiation for the structure of local caste systems can be given something like its true weight.

If we add a potential feminist critique to the historical arguments already discussed, and then include all the other work that has critically reanalysed village ethnographies, little appears to remain of Dumont's ethnographic representation of the caste system.[7] Furthermore, since that representation was mainly built, albeit selectively, from the village studies ethnographies of the 1950s and 1960s, we have to ask whether we actually have any reliable knowledge of caste in the Indian village at that period.

The question is a serious one because, in relation to the subject-matter of this book, any assessment of how caste has changed over the last few decades depends on adequate knowledge of it in the past. Nonetheless, as long as the earlier ethnographies are read with the same kind of critical scrutiny that would be applied to other historical sources, they can supply the data that are needed; taken as a whole, they

---

[7] A specific example of critical reanalysis of village ethnography is the continuing discussion of the so-called jajmani system: see Raheja (1988), Fuller (1989), Lerche (1993), P. Mayer (1993). More generally, however, in both ethnographic monographs and comparative studies, the reanalysis has been pursued in many different directions, ranging from materialist work on agrarian class systems to ethnosociological approaches. Review articles covering the post-Dumontian literature include Fuller and Spencer (1990), Harriss (1991) and Raheja (1988).

include copious, detailed evidence about village society, particularly local caste systems, as well as accounts of ordinary people's concepts and beliefs, which cannot plausibly be dismissed as inaccurate. In other words, even though the ethnographies of earlier years tended to misconstruct 'traditional' caste-based village communities, it does not follow that most of the information contained in them is unreliable ethnographic reportage. Two cases in point, to cite only the village ethnographies written by contributors to this volume, are the monographs on Ramkheri (Madhya Pradesh) in the mid-1950s by Mayer (1960) and on Sripuram (Tamilnadu) in the early 1960s by Béteille (1965). But there are many other sources as well, and as a body of evidence—summarised most fully by Mandelbaum (1970) in an underrated synthesis which is, unlike *Homo hierarchicus*, a work of empirical induction—the ethnography plainly shows that relatively rigid and stable caste hierarchies were central features of village social structure in the mid-twentieth century throughout the plains of India. Undoubtedly, there was a tendency to overstate both the importance of caste in relation to other aspects of the social structure, and the salience of purity and pollution in comparison with other criteria for determining status. Such overstatements were converted with theoretical sophistication into the absolutes of Dumont's theory. Analytical overstatement, however, need not undermine the quality of ethnographic reportage. The answer to the question posed above, therefore, is that the village studies ethnography as a whole provides us with a predominantly accurate record of rural society and caste as they existed at the time of fieldwork, a historical period when the 'traditional' society consolidated by British rule was still largely intact.

In many parts of rural India, things have not yet altered very much. Estimating their numbers accurately is hard, but millions of Indians certainly do still live in villages, mainly ones that are remote from urban influences and have seen little agricultural, infrastructural or educational development, in which there has been relatively little social change during the half-century since independence. In many other settlements, however, considerable change has occurred and caste in particular has become increasingly unlike the institution described in earlier ethnography. It is the empirical fact of social change, as much as contemporary, 'post-structuralist' intellectual movements, which shows us that Dumont's theory is linked to the ethnography of a specific historical period that is now passing away, so that his synchronic structural model has become unconvincingly inappropriate for the analysis of caste today.[8]

Nonetheless, although *Homo hierarchicus* is overwhelmingly concerned with the structure of caste, it does contain an important thesis about modern change as 'substantialisation'. In 1957, Srinivas argued that caste had been strengthened in the context of modern politics: 'the power and activity of caste has increased in proportion as political power passed increasingly to the people from the rulers' (1962:23). Although this strengthening had started in the colonial period, it greatly accelerated after independence in 1947. Partly by generalising from Srinivas and other writers like Ghurye, Dumont sought to identify the process of change in more theoretically exact terms as 'a transition from structure to substance' (1970:226); 'competition' substitutes for 'interdependence' between hierarchically ranked castes, and 'the caste seems to accept equality' which means that 'from the ideological point of view, structure seems to yield to substance, each caste becoming an individual confronting other individuals' (ibid:227). Substantialisation, though, claims Dumont, is

[8] This conclusion about Dumont is apparently inconsistent with my claim when writing about popular Hinduism, that 'hierarchical values and institutionalised inequality are at the heart of both Hinduism and Indian society' (1992:253). In the light of the studies contained in this volume, I now think I previously underestimated the shift away from hierarchical values that is occurring today (cf. Assayag [1994], who criticises my ambivalent critique of Dumont's monolithic structuralism). Yet those values, I would contend, are still at the heart of popular Hinduism, which—unlike other domains of Indian society—has not been so markedly transformed. This contention about religious 'conservatism' raises many questions that cannot be discussed here, but one important point is that the centrality of hierarchical values in popular Hinduism ensures that they are, so to speak, a constant presence in people's lives. Ritual action in particular is the context in which hierarchical relationships—between castes, rulers and subjects, or men and women, as well as between deities and human beings—are repeatedly being constructed, and even when such relationships are not homologous with others outside the religious domain, the former are always present as a model of how the world might or even should be.

still confined to the secondary, politico-economic domain encompassed by the religious ideology of hierarchy (ibid.:228) and hence it cannot amount to a fundamental transformation of the whole system. This claim, which serves to protect the validity of Dumont's synchronic structural model from any ostensibly contradictory evidence emerging from modern change, has become increasingly unconvincing (as I have already implied) in the face of the empirical fact of such change. Yet it is still worth considering how far the substantialisation thesis itself can help us to make sense of contemporary changes in caste. In order to do so, I shall now turn to the evidence on caste today presented in the chapters of this book.

The ethnography of caste today

Partly because he was the author of one of the classic village ethnographies, Mayer's report on the changes that have taken place in Ramkheri over nearly forty years has a special interest. As Mayer shows, caste rank has become much less sharply defined in Ramkheri, at least among the higher castes, and at feasts at which *pakka* food is served rank is barely marked by separate eating lines (*pangat*) nowadays. Caste endogamy, however, is still universally practised, but it is now justified by claiming that the *khan-pin* ('food and drink') or *rahan-sahan* ('way of life') of each caste is distinctive and expressive of cultural differences that should not be mismatched, rather than by suggesting that a purity-based hierarchy of castes should not be undermined. This alteration in the normative basis of caste—from purity as an index of hierarchical rank to difference as a marker of separation—is a matter of degree rather than kind, because 'change has occurred through a realignment of...ideas about rank and equality', with the former becoming proportionally less important in relation to the latter since 1954. Hence there is continuity as well as change, but the pattern of change is consistent with Dumont's substantialisation thesis that, at the ideological level, structure yields to substance and each caste becomes like a collective individual with its own distinctive culture and 'way of life'. Yet this change at the ideological level is simultaneously contradicted at the empirical level by the increasing differentiation of status, power and wealth developing *within* each caste—a development which is itself contributing to the decline of clear-cut caste ranking and hence, paradoxically, to an increasing normative emphasis on difference *between* castes. Substantialisation is, in effect, a self-contradictory process, because as it develops castes actually become more internally heterogeneous.

Mayer's material also suggests that despite the changes that have taken place in Ramkheri, the emphasis on difference between castes can still imply an evaluation of that difference in terms of relative status. Such evaluations, however, are nowadays mainly made in private, not public. Significantly, although the public consumption of *pakka* food scarcely expresses caste ranking today, *kacca* food—the staple diet and always subject to greater restrictions than *pakka* food—is not served on public occasions and is only rarely eaten together by people of different castes at home. As Mayer remarks: 'People may therefore be saying that the old value of caste purity, conveyed by *kacca* food, still exists for them'. This observation strongly suggests that relational hierarchical values, as expressed in purity rules, remain salient in the private, domestic domain even though they have been displaced by substantialist ones in the public domain.

The elimination of hierarchical values from legitimate public discourse accounts, of course, for the claim, already being voiced by villagers in Ramkheri in 1954, that 'there is no caste left'. Much the same claim is heard throughout modern India. Plainly, it is never meant to be a statement of fact and the key point, which is familiar enough, is that the delegitimation of caste inequality in the political and legal arena has had such a far-reaching effect that today, as Béteille remarks, 'anyone who speaks against equality in public is bound to lose his audience' (1991:206). That caste hierarchy can no longer be legitimately defended in public has itself contributed to the emergence of a more or less acceptable public discourse about status coded as cultural difference. Because people cannot openly speak of castes as unequal, they describe them as different; indeed, like people in Ramkheri, they may avoid the terms 'caste' or *jati* and refer instead to 'community' or *samaj*. As Mayer suggests, this change may indicate greater commitment to equality, but it is at least as likely that it does not, for terms like *samaj* are frequently euphemistic and the language of difference can be a coded means to assert the status of one's own caste and to justify inequality among castes. Hence the significance of this language partly lies in the opportunity that it provides to say the publicly illegitimate legitimately, and substantialisation is an ideological shift that simultaneously sharpens the divide between public and private behaviour and expression.

Alangkulam, the Tamilnadu village discussed by Delière, is unusual because it contains only two castes: untouchable Pallars and Valaiyars, a non-untouchable caste which nonetheless has a very low status. In general terms, however, the process of substantialisation as a breakdown in hierarchical interdependence between the two castes is also evident, as is a movement towards social equality and increased competition between them. There is also very little preoccupation with purity and pollution in Alangkulam, although one significant point made by Delière—which is consistent with Mosse's comparative observation (1994:74)—is that the defining feature of the Pallars' former untouchability was their obligation to do 'slave work'; thus servitude, rather than ritual pollution, was crucial to their status and identity. It is interesting, too, that the Pallars—partly because they are not subservient to a large bloc of higher-status or dominant castes— have acquired considerable economic independence and have closed the gap between themselves and the Valaiyars, although they have received no real support from the government's policy of positive discrimination towards the Scheduled Castes.

Delière's observation that the Pallars' inferiority had more to do with servitude than pollution reminds us that caste status is not uniformly understood in terms of relative ritual purity, and Lambert's chapter forcefully emphasises that the meaning and relative importance of caste varies according to context. Thus, for example, she shows that in some contexts people's identity may be primarily constituted by the social unit of the village, rather than their caste, and that in other contexts, cross-caste ties generated by fictive kinship are more salient than intra-caste relationships between 'actual' kin. Moreover, as already mentioned above, Lambert in particular emphasises, clearly and subtly, how the relative salience of caste varies according to gender. Chawandiya, like very many other villages in India, is a place in which 'traditional' ideas and practices related to caste remain prevalent, although by 1995 when she revisited it a decade after her original fieldwork, Lambert was able to see that changes similar to those reported from elsewhere (such as Ramkheri) were occurring: for example, increasing economic differentiation within the larger castes, and relaxation of commensal restrictions among the higher- and middle-ranking castes. Here, though, the crucial point to be stressed is that even—or perhaps especially—in a volume on the subject, caste must not be analysed as if it were an autonomous and monolithic institution with either a uniformly determinant role in structuring society or a consistent set of meanings attached to it.

In urban settlements, as opposed to villages, caste is changing in yet other ways. In Tiruchengodu town in Tamilnadu, described by Reiniche, the Mudaliyar caste has become increasingly powerful during the last half-century. Mudaliyar identity has developed in opposition to the Chettiyars and especially the Vellalars, partly through stereotypes expressive of distinctive caste cultures. At the same time, the Mudaliyar caste's distinctive culture is significantly constituted by its individual members' commercial success, which crucially depends (among other factors) on their ability to master for co-operative purposes kinship and marriage relationships and interactions with other castes. Individual success itself engenders increasing socio-economic differentiation within the caste, and the process of concurrent substantialisation, at the ideological level, and differentiation, at the empirical level, is similar to that found in Ramkheri village, but in Tiruchengodu it is more firmly established. Reiniche's analysis is also important because it unmistakably shows how thriving mercantile capitalism can reinforce, rather than dissolve, cultural distinctiveness among castes so that, in Tiruchengodu, individuals 'who have successfully differentiated themselves and their own lineage segment may embody, and at the same time mobilise, the apparently united front of their caste'.

In different urban contexts, however, caste is changing in different ways. In the first place, whereas merchants, for example, often belong to traditionally mercantile castes, other occupational groups may have no traditional caste base, so that for them, unlike the citizens of Tiruchengodu, individual or family-based economic success does not and cannot embody or mobilise caste unity. This is the position for the professional, middle-class 'intelligentsia' in the metropolitan cities discussed by Béteille. For such people, caste origin is increasingly irrelevant in many areas of life, any moral obligation to follow an ancestral occupation is practically extinct, and caste membership is seen as unconnected with the means of livelihood. Thus even if membership of a particular caste or kin group may in practice be helpful for finding a job, more or less meritocratic qualifications are frequently more important and are normally regarded as the only legitimate ones. Moreover, irrespective of people's attitudes towards the reservation policy for the low castes, caste inequality lacks any public legitimacy whatsoever; indeed, Béteille argues, caste cannot even be coherently described by most of the urban intelligentsia. This does not of course mean that 'traditional' attitudes to caste have simply disappeared; in particular, they are still widely observed in the arrangement of marriages, even if other criteria have become proportionately more weighty, because caste endogamy is still observed by a large majority of people, although it can no longer be enforced by local subcastes which have lost almost all their power of sanction.

In discussing the nature of caste for the urban intelligentsia, Béteille observes that attitudes towards it have become highly ambivalent, and that the meaning and legitimacy of caste—and identities and relationships formed by it—are shifting significantly. Modern urban India, as he points out, remains a status-conscious world, but distinctions of status are nowadays more frequently based on education, occupation or income; moreover, even when caste is invoked, it may be used metaphorically to refer to other kinds of social distinctions, particularly extreme or elaborate ones. Hence—to extend Béteille's argument further than he explicitly does so himself—status distinctions may be expressed in the language of caste, but they may no longer pertain to caste hierarchy, which has lost all its legitimacy, or even to caste as an array of culturally distinct groups, which has become largely irrelevant in comparison with mainly class-based cultural variations. After all, class distinctions are constructed in cultural terms in all modern capitalist societies, and in India the language and practice of caste provide the most potent and pervasive terms. For example, if someone says derogatorily of a colleague at work that he is acting like a 'typical Brahman', this may well be a comment on his assumption of a superiority that actually derives from his high occupational position, not from his caste, which may not even be Brahman. On the other hand, how far caste is used metaphorically for class can itself vary with caste rank for, as Béteille comments, 'the burden of caste may weigh more heavily on the lower- than on the upper-caste person'. Thus members of the urban intelligentsia belonging to high castes can more safely dismiss the importance of their birth and more readily employ caste as an idiom for class than those belonging to low castes, because the latter are more aware of and sensitive to their lowly status within an elite in which they are still a minority. Hence to slight a Harijan colleague as a 'typical Harijan' is likely to be taken—unlike the 'typical Brahman' jibe—as a direct and highly offensive reference to his actual caste. Such variations in meaning and metaphorical connotation exacerbate the already difficult task of interpreting the ambiguous beliefs and practices relating to caste among the populous and influential urban intelligentsia, which Béteille's chapter discusses so subtly and penetratingly.[9]

So far I have been mainly discussing Hindus and I shall now consider the Muslims. As Fanselow and Vatuk particularly stress in their chapters, anthropological discussion of whether Indian Muslims

[9] If we are to believe the acerbic report on New Delhi's super-rich in 'Snobbery: the new status games' (*India Today*, 15 June 1993, 24-30), 'ethnic chic' and the 'real' India are now in style. In this glittering milieu, caste has completely vanished from view as an index of anything and it will surely never return, but an 'authentic' ancestry is nevertheless a useful lever in raising one's status still further: 'But now that you have everything else, lineage suddenly begins to look more tempting. Since you can't buy that, you do the next best thing: buy an antique, some jewellery which looks five generations old, or a sari which you pretend is from your great-grandmother in your ancestral home. And if you are smart, it's some village in what's now Bangladesh or Pakistan, or a remote village elsewhere so that nobody can catch you out'. (p.30)

have caste has often been unproductive, notably because it has paid too little attention to how Muslims themselves see the issue and has failed to recognise that the answer to the question flexibly depends on the context. Moreover, the problem of Muslim caste has commonly been treated in entirely functional or structural terms, whereas it ought to be addressed in relation to the historical processes of Islamisation and the modern formation of Muslim identity. Plainly, throughout India, there are countless Muslim *jatis* or castes that are functionally integrated into the caste system, but this empirical fact in itself tells us hardly anything about how Muslims (or indeed Hindus) understand caste and status among Muslims, or about how such understandings are related to social practice.

The three chapters on Muslims provide interesting and contrasting data on these issues. Jamous describes the Meos of Rajasthan, an endogamous caste with a kinship and marriage system similar to that of Hindu Rajputs. The Meos specifically prohibit parallel-cousin marriage, the ideal Muslim arrangement, and although various Islamic customs are observed in their marriage rituals, these are of a predominantly Hindu kind. For the Meos, though, such rituals are Rajput, not Hindu, and they are both Rajputs and Muslims, even though these identities seem incompatible to many Rajasthani Hindus.

Among the Muslims in southern Tamilnadu discussed by Fanselow, a striking feature is how different groups define themselves in alternative ways, although no Muslims admit to the existence of caste (or associated Hindu customs) within their own group. Rather, caste is only found among *other* Muslims, who are thereby demeaned as less Islamic within the context of status competition among the Tamil Muslim population as a whole. For all Muslims and also Hindus, however, it is today a 'basic, logical equation that one cannot be a real Muslim and have caste, so that to have caste implies that one is not a true Muslim'.

For members of the elite Nawwayat 'family' (*khandan*) of Hyderabad and Madras described by Vatuk, their own status and self-identity are entirely defined within a distinctively Islamic discourse of rank and status, so that even more plainly than for the Meos and southern Tamilnadu Muslims, caste is excluded from the Nawwayats' own understanding of themselves. At least in these cases, it is therefore necessary, as Vatuk observes (following a suggestion by Béteille), to look more broadly at 'fields of inequality'—rather than caste alone—in order to analyse the evidence on status and identity.

The reader may object that it is illogical to discuss communities which do not have caste in a volume on caste today. But that objection would miss the point that an emphasis on the absence of caste among Muslims in India is, to a significant extent, a function of its ubiquitous existence among Hindus. Moreover, from all three chapters, as already suggested, it emerges clearly that the question of inequality and caste among Muslims has to be understood in its historical context. Islamisation and the development of Muslim ethnicity in India during the past century and a half are complex historical processes which cannot be reduced to simplistic assertions about the colonial construction of a separate Muslim identity (van der Veer 1994: ch.2). Nonetheless, it is plain that distinct Hindu and Muslim ethnic identities and 'religious nationalisms' have grown up alongside and in counterpoint to each other; as van der Veer (ibid.:x) expresses it: 'Hindu and Muslim nationalisms develop along similar lines and...the one needs the other'. For Muslims, one component of their growing nationalism has been an increasingly emphatic denial that they have caste, and this started to become important in reaction to the progressive strengthening of the colonial-Brahmanical discourse that made caste definitive of Indian civil society. Increasingly, therefore, as Fanselow argues, caste had to be 'disinvented' among Muslims, and the 'universal denial of caste among Muslims is a logical necessity for their identity as Muslims in a modern world, in which the boundaries between being Muslim and being Hindu can no longer be left undefined'. Particularly during the past decade, communal politics and the rising tide of religious nationalisms have tended to reinforce the Islamisation process, although not necessarily uniformly; as Jamous's data show, the Meo response to the Ayodhya crisis involves an attempt to mobilise themselves as both a Rajput caste and a Muslim community, even though these two forms of identity increasingly imply conflicting values. Nevertheless, among Indian Muslims in general, the notion of a common Muslim identity that is definitely not Hindu is a more and more vital determinant of Muslim ideas about caste—namely, that they do not have it—and about status ranking—which they do have, but not in the form of caste, unless it is negatively invoked to demean other Muslims.

The modern transformation of caste

Throughout modern India, public and political discourse about caste is dominated by the perceived illegitimacy of 'traditional' caste hierarchy, and by the need to overcome the effects of persisting caste inequality. Nowhere is this discourse simple and devoid of inconsistency, but in Tamilnadu, as Dirks's chapter shows, it has probably attained its most involuted and singular form. By tracing the development of ideas about Brahmans and Brahmanism, mainly in the context of the growth of a Dravidianist ideology identifying Brahmans as Aryan 'others', the 'Muslims' of the south, Dirks explores how these ideas were complexly constituted during the colonial period in often paradoxical ways. By analysing the 'cultural politics' of caste, Dirks particularly reveals the inadequacy of explanations for the rise of anti-Brahmanism which focus too narrowly on non-Brahman resentment of Brahman political and economic dominance, and he is also able to explain how those cultural politics remain salient even today, when the old Brahman dominance has virtually disappeared. Put simply, the Brahman versus non-Brahman opposition is now so deeply inscribed in Tamil discourse that caste—particularly as expressed by that opposition—'always seems to be the rhetorical point of overdetermination'. Thus progressive Tamil politicians continue to need Brahmans to attack and some Tamil intellectuals, responding to their own sense of marginalisation within India, fear that Brahman hegemony may be restored under the rule of Jayalalitha, the Brahman leader of the ruling Dravidian party. Caste in Tamilnadu has had and still has an obviously 'strange career'; nevertheless, Dirks not only makes sense of much of this strangeness, but also raises questions about the cultural politics of caste which could be fruitfully explored for other regions as well.

The pecularities of Tamil discourse on caste do not of course mean that caste hierarchy retains its legitimacy in Tamilnadu; indeed, Dravidianism has generated some of the fiercest anti-caste rhetoric heard anywhere in India. Thus in Tamilnadu as everywhere else, the political delegitimation of caste has penetrated all levels of society, so that many ordinary Indians, like people in Ramkheri, say that 'there is no caste left'.

What, then, does exist today? The answer emerging from the ethnography presented in this book is that contemporary understandings of caste—what it is and what it means—are above all a denial, most explicitly in the public domain, of the existence or continuing significance of caste in its 'traditional' form. In other words, the prototype against which these understandings are fashioned is the predominantly Brahmanical ideology of caste as a hierarchical system governed by rules of purity and pollution that was elaborated most fully during the British period, and manifested most completely in 'traditional' society as consolidated under colonialism. It was this 'traditional' society that was investigated in villages by ethnographers in the years after independence, and for very many Indians today life in a caste-based village society is remembered or imagined as their own past, a social and ideological reality that is now on the wane. Furthermore, when the existence and importance of caste are still acknowledged, this often takes the form of a substantialist assertion about cultural distinctiveness ostensibly belieing inequality both between and within castes, although substantialisation is itself accompanied at the empirical level by increasing intra-caste differentiation. Moreover, because cultural distinctiveness retains evaluative implications, it can also provide a coded language to refer to caste inequalities. These inequalities are widely recognised and even approved in private, but normally they cannot be legitimately endorsed in public. What may be loosely described as a substantialised version of caste largely prevails, in one guise or another, in Ramkheri, Alangkulam and Tiruchengodu today; with the qualifications mentioned above, we can therefore agree with Dumont in his identification of substantialisation as a crucial aspect of modern change in the caste system. Among the metropolitan, middle-class intelligentsia, however, caste as constituted by cultural distinctiveness has lost much of its perceived significance as well, and it has tended to become an idiom for status distinctions which are primarily determined by class criteria. Finally, among many Muslims, the principal relevance of caste in any shape or form is that is a Hindu institution only persisting among other, allegedly lower-ranking Muslim groups, although the Meos do still define themselves as both Muslims and Rajputs.

In making sense of the data on caste today, it is useful to reconsider the relation between caste and ethnicity, for Barnett's description of substantialisation as a form of ethnicisation (1975:158-9) has some analytical advantages which have not been sufficiently explored. In Weber's original model, status group stratification develops from perceived differences between styles of life, and if these differences are thought to be based on common descent and are further reinforced by restrictions on intermarriage in particular, status groups become ethnic groups. Ethnic groups in turn can develop into castes: 'the caste structure transforms the horizontal and unconnected coexistences of ethnically segregated groups into a vertical social system of supra- and subordination'. And whereas each ethnic group can 'consider its own honor as the highest one', the caste structure 'brings about a social subordination and an acknowledgement of "more honor" in favor of the privileged caste and status groups' (Weber 1978:934). In general terms, the transformation from ethnicity to caste described by Weber is now proceeding in reverse in contemporary India. The 'vertical social system' defined by hierarchical relationships is decaying and castes are becoming like 'horizontally' disconnected ethnic groups, putatively differentiated by their own styles of life (cf. Searle-Chatterjee and Sharma 1994:19-20).

All this may look fairly obvious because it amounts to no more than a translation into the terminology of ethnicity. The point of the exercise, however, is to scrutinise the material on caste today through a different comparative lens. For example, for the metropolitan intelligentsia described by Béteille, there is a further development in the decaying process that has some parallels, but also contrasts, with ethnicity among urban, middle-class, white Americans. For the latter, ethnic groups have largely ceased to exist as functioning social units determining individual life-chances, as castes have for their Indian equivalents, and ethnicity, like caste, is no longer the main determinant of styles of life that primarily signal class distinctions.[10] Yet 'symbolic' ethnicity (Gans 1979) remains important in urban, middle-class, white America—at least for all the many people who call themselves Italian-Americans, Jewish-Americans and so on—pariticularly because it is perceived as important for personal and familial identity. In this respect, however, symbolic ethnicity differs from its caste equivalent, because ethnic distinctiveness is evaluated positively in modern America, whereas caste division is not, so that urban, middle-class Indians are highly ambivalent about the place of caste in defining their own identities. On the other hand, whereas caste is a powerful cultural idiom for the expression of mainly class-based status distinctions, ethnicity among whites—as opposed to the dichotomy between whites and blacks—is a relatively weak idiom for status ranking in America today. Through this brief comparison, we can see that the changing meaning of caste, as described by Béteille, contrasts with the development of symbolic ethnicity in urban, middle-class America, although in both societies the relevant changes have been primarily caused by similar factors, notably the decline of caste or ethnic origin as a main determinant of economic opportunity.[11]

Obviously, the development of ethnicity in the west, specifically the United States, and the ethnicisation of caste in India are entirely separate processes, but the difference between them—as Béteille (1991:ch.9) insists—should not be exaggerated by baldly asserting that the west is egalitarian and individualist, whereas India is (or was)

---

[10] For black Americans in particular, the evidence is less clear-cut and more controversial; Wilson (1978) argues that even for blacks, race has become increasingly insignificant in determining life-chances, but his argument has been strongly contested, for example by Landry (1987).

[11] Berreman (1972) focuses on the use of ethnic (including caste) categories and stereotypes by urban strangers, and his is a rare example of a study done in India which takes up the classic problem of social interaction in an anonymous, ethnically-plural, urban environment.

hierarchical and holistic. In fact, as we have seen, caste inequality in contemporary India is publicly as illegitimate as ethnic-group or racial inequality in America; furthermore, caste inequality is privately defended and publicly described in coded language much as ethnic inequality is, even though caste provides a far more powerful and pervasive cultural idiom for social inequality than any equivalent in modern America, notwithstanding the racial distinction between black and white. After all, caste equality—unlike ethnic or racial equality—must be a virtual contradiction in terms; Gandhi's famous assertion that in truth all castes are equal because 'A scavenger has the same status as a Brahmin' (quoted in Zelliott 1972:73) has never been credible to any twentieth-century Indian.

The one parallel frequently drawn between caste in modern India and ethnicity in the United States comes from the political field, because, in these two countries, electoral majorities are often built on coalitions of castes or ethnic blocs respectively. This political strategy has been seen by Srinivas and many others as crucial for the survival or strengthening of caste in post-independence India. Treating substantialisation as ethnicisation, however, also helps to draw attention to connections between the politics of caste and religious nationalism (or communalism). As we have already seen, Islamisation and the associated development of Muslim identity are significantly expressed by a collective denial that Indian Muslims have caste, unlike Hindus. At first sight, it looks as if the reinforcement of caste-group solidarity in the political field ought to inhibit the development of a broader Hindu identity, but this is not in fact inevitable. Indian politicians are consistently trying to forge inter-caste alliances in order to build much larger blocs, and in theory this process of alliance formation could continue until all Hindu castes joined together in a single Hindu 'community' opposed to Muslims, Sikhs, or other religious minorities. Such a unification is indeed a major objective of the Hindu nationalist movement, the Vishwa Hindu Parishad, whose rhetoric consistently stresses the need to incorporate Harijans and tribal groups in particular within the 'Hindu nation' (van der Veer 1994: 52, 134-6). In principle too, the Bharatiya Janata Party, which is closely linked to the VHP, is striving to unite all Hindu castes, although in reality many problems beset any attempt to create such a vast alliance, as the BJP pragmatically recognises.

All the same, the strengthening of Hindu communal identity in India today is, at least in part, an extension, rather than a negation, of the ethnicisation of caste. Moreover, the substantialised, ethnic identity of a caste may be reciprocally expressed by emphasising its Hindu identity—by asserting that its distinctive caste culture is itself a manifestation of Hindutva, 'Hindu-ness'. Such a development, whereby the symbols of Hindu identity are transmuted into new symbols of caste identity, appears to have been actively promoted by the BJP in Rajasthan, where Hindutva has been refashioned as a distinctively Rajput set of values (Jenkins 1994:639-41). Something similar is probably occurring among a range of north Indian high castes whose members tend to support the Hindu nationalist movement.[12]

The link between caste and religious nationalism bring me to a final point about ethnicity. No serious scholar who has written about the development of modern religious identities in India—whether Hindu, Muslim or any other—has any doubt that these are historically constructed identities which have depended on a reconfiguration of the meanings of 'Hindu', 'Muslim' and so on during the colonial and post-colonial periods. Thus each of these religious 'communities', like any ethnic group, has no antecedent reality determined by 'primordial' affiliations. Ethnic groups, including religious ones, exist if and only if people believe or assume that they belong to such groups, and others within their society concur. Although modern scholars increasingly recognise that castes have also been historically constructed as groups, they are still inclined to overlook the full implications of this point. Hence the existence of castes as bounded units within a system sustained by an elaborate set of norms and institutions tends to be represented by anthropologists and sociologists as a Durkheimian objective social fact. Finding a definition of 'caste' may be hard, but recognising castes 'on the ground' is not, it seems, because their

---

[12] For the reference to Jenkins's article and pertinent comments on caste and Hindutva, I thank Christophe Jaffrelot.

objective existence is given by a mass of concrete data that do not
depend on the informants' subjective understanding of caste. Or, to put
the same point into Weberian language, the intentions and beliefs
constitutive of social action that may, in shorthand, be called caste
action can be treated as supernumerary, because the identification of
such action, which is ostensibly determined by the objective social fact
of caste, appears to be unproblematic.

It can be charitably argued that in the ethnographic description of
relatively stable, caste-based village societies in the mid-twentieth
century, it was not too seriously distortive to regard the identification of
caste action as unproblematic and independent of the intersubjective
meanings of caste. In describing caste in India today, however, it
certainly is distortive, because the intentions and beliefs constitutive of
caste action are precisely what is at stake. Castes are still being
historically constructed, or perhaps more aptly being 'deconstructed',
as a vertically integrated hierarchy decays into a horizontally
disconnected ethnic array. Under these contemporary circumstances,
although the overall direction of change is fairly clear, the social fact of
caste appears increasingly ambiguous, inconsistent and variable. What
people mean when they identify themselves as members of castes—as
nearly all Hindus still do—or as non-members of any caste—as many
Muslims do—is itself changing in diverse ways, and the same of course
applies to the identification of others. Intentions and belief in relation to
caste therefore become patently problematic to an extent that they did
not before, and this is partly because the deconstruction of 'traditional'
caste entails the collapse of a relatively coherent, internally consistent
ideology, so that a multiplicity of often contested meanings emerges in
its place. Runciman, in his Weberian exposition of social theory, rightly
insists that:

it follows from the fact that meanings are constitutive of human actions
that they must be correctly understood in the primary sense if a valid
explanation, or understanding in the secondary sense, is thereafter to be
arrived at. (1983:41)

The problem faced by the anthropologist of contemporary caste, there-

fore, is not only that the 'primary' understanding of the people themselves is increasingly complex, but also that the explanation of caste
action—and indeed of the very survival of caste as an institution—is
correspondingly complexified as well. The chapters contained in this
volume do not pretend to solve all these difficult problems, but they do
firmly address them and thereby collectively advance our knowledge of
caste as it is in India today.

Weberian sociology, I know, will not be illuminating for every
reader, so let me close by citing a more accessible source, even if it is
unconventional to complete academic arguments with a particular illustration taken from fiction. The illustration, which is more revealing than
any I can easily recall from ethnography, comes from Vikram Seth's *A
suitable boy* (1993), an entrancing work of realistic fiction set in north
India in 1951-2. As I do not want to give away the novel's plot, let me
merely state that a suitable boy has to be found as a husband for the
heroine, Lata, who lives with her widowed mother in a large town.

One of several candidates for Lata's hand is a man called Haresh
who works as a middle manager in a big shoe factory; like Lata, he
belongs to the non-Brahman, but high-ranking, Khatri caste. To Lata's
mother, his caste—and indeed his subcaste—is one crucial fact in his
favour; as she says at one point, she wishes Lata to marry a 'proper'
Khatri—which would exclude Khatris of low subcaste—but she also
says that 'I think that one's own community creates a sense of comfort'
(Seth 1993:548), a sentimental expression of the substantialist notion
that each caste has its own distinctive culture.

To Lata's elder brother, on the other hand, Haresh is a very unsuitable boy. Lata's brother is a highly westernised member of the business elite who lives and works in Calcutta, and he has married outside
his own caste. At one point in the story, he itemises his objections to
Lata's suitor; he cannot speak English well enough, he will probably
not want to send their children to a good school, he comes from a
family of 'small people' who are 'undistinguished', and he could never
move in Calcutta's elite social circles (ibid.:1292-4). In other words, it
is snobbish distinctions of education and social class that mainly make
Haresh unsuitable. Earlier, however, Lata's brother, in a fit of anger,

has expostulated that we cannot have a 'shoemaker in the family'
(ibid.:1128). Haresh, although he works in a shoe factory and knows
how to make shoes, is not by occupation a shoemaker. In north India,
shoemakers are all Chamars or Jatavs, members of the large Harijan
caste that classically epitomises untouchability, and the force of the
insult lies in its implication that Haresh is really like a Chamar.

It is true that when Haresh takes Lata to visit a tannery, she is beset
by 'an atavistic revulsion against the whole polluting business of hides
and carrion' (ibid.:576) and that even Haresh finds it necessary to protest too vigorously about his uncle's opinion that he has become polluted and has 'lost caste by working with leather' (ibid.:577). The polluting taint attached to leatherworking and Chamars cannot be entirely
wished away, despite a conscious desire to do so. Yet the real objections to Lata's suitor within her family are on grounds of class, so that
her brother's insult strikes home because Haresh's class status is compared with the Chamars' caste status, although no mention of Chamars
is actually voiced. It is a patent and subtly complex illustration of the
crucial point that in one context an implied reference to caste may
really signify new distinctions of class, even though in another
traditional ideas about pollution force themselves to the surface.

Ethnographic and other evidence suggests that the characters in
Seth's novel exemplify attitudes to caste which have now become much
more widespread in India than they were in the early 1950s. Whether
Seth has projected on to that period some notions from three or four
decades later is largely immaterial here, because everywhere today
there plainly are people like Lata and Haresh, who consciously reject
the values of caste and yet find that they react viscerally to pollution
and remain very sensitive to any suggestion that they actually are
tainted by it. Lata's mother, an elderly urban woman, has a half-
hierarchical, half-substantialist notion of caste, which is now found
among both urban and rural people throughout the country, while her
brother's preoccupation with class—as metaphorically expressed
through an implied reference to caste—now pervades a much larger
section of the urban middle classes than the small, westernised,
metropolitan elite. In comprehending the diversity, inconsistency and

ambiguity of caste in India today, it is essential to discard objectivist illusions and to insist upon the importance of intersubjective meanings. Our very identification and reportage of the phenomenon of caste, as a system of values and as a determinant of social action—let alone our analysis and interpretation of it—must therefore restore to their necessarily privileged position the complex intentions and beliefs of people like Lata and those close to her.

References

Assayag, J. 1994. '*Homo hierarchicus, homo symbolicus*: approche structurale ou herméneutique en anthropologie sociale (de l'Inde) (note critique).' *Annales HSS* 1994, 1:133-49.

Barnett, S.A. 1975. 'Approaches to changes in caste ideology in south India.' In B. Stein (ed.), *Essays on south India*. Hawaii: University Press of Hawaii.

Bayly, C.A. 1988. *Indian society and the making of the British empire*. Cambridge: Cambridge University Press.

Berreman, G.D. 1972. 'Social categories and social interaction in urban India.' *American Anthropologist* 74:567-87.

Béteille, A. 1965. *Caste, class and power: changing patterns of stratification in a Tanjore village*. Berkeley: University of California Press.

——. 1990a. 'Caste and reservations.' *Hindu*, 20 October 1990.

——. 1990b. 'Caste and politics.' *Times of India*, 11 September 1990.

——. 1991. *Society and politics in India: essays in a comparative perspective*. London: Athlone Press.

Cohn, B.S. 1987 (1970). 'Is there a new Indian history? Society and social change under the Raj.' In *An anthropologist among the historians and other essays*. Delhi: Oxford University Press.

Das, V. 1995. *Critical events: an anthropological perspective on contemporary India*. Delhi: Oxford University Press.

Dirks, N.B. 1992. 'Castes of mind.' *Representations* 37:56-78.

Dumont, L. 1970 (1966). *Homo hierarchicus: the caste system and its implications*. London: Weidenfeld and Nicolson.

Fuller, C.J. 1977. 'British India or traditional India? An anthropological problem.' *Ethnos* 42:92-121.

——. 1989. 'Misconceiving the grain heap: a critique of the concept of the Indian jajmani system.' In J. Parry and M. Bloch (eds.), *Money and the morality of exchange*. Cambridge: Cambridge University Press.

——. 1992. *The camphor flame: popular Hinduism and society in India*. Princeton: Princeton University Press.

Fuller, C.J. and J. Spencer. 1990. 'South Asian anthropology in the 1980s.' *South Asia Research* 10:85-105.

Gans, H. 1979. 'Symbolic ethnicity: the future of ethnic groups and cultures in America.' *Ethnic and racial studies* 2:1-18.

Guha, R., and G.C. Spivak (eds.). 1988. *Selected subaltern studies*. New York: Oxford University Press.

Guhan, S. *et al.* 1990. 'South India and reservations: a reply to André Béteille.' *Hindu*, 27 October 1990.

Harriss, J. 1991. 'A review of rural society and agrarian change in south Asia.' *South Asia Research* 11:16-39.

Heesterman, J.C. 1971. 'Priesthood and the Brahmin.' *Contributions to Indian Sociology* (n.s.) 5:43-7.

———. 1985. *The inner conflict of tradition: essays in Indian ritual, kingship, and society* . Chicago: University of Chicago Press.

Heuzé, G. 1991. 'Troubled anthropologists: the controversy over employment quotas in India.' *Anthropology Today* 7, 6:5-7.

Jenkins, R. 1990. 'Where the BJP survived: Rajasthan assembly elections, 1993.' *Economic and Political Weekly*, 12 March 1994:635-41.

Landry, B. 1987. *The new black middle class*. Berkeley: University of California Press.

Lerche, J. 1993. 'Dominant castes, rajas, Brahmins and inter-caste exchange relations in coastal Orissa: behind the facade of the *"jajmani"* system.' *Contributions to Indian Sociology* (n.s.) 27:237-66.

Mandelbaum, D.G. 1970. *Society in India*. Berkeley: University of California Press.

Marriott, M. 1969. 'Review of L. Dumont, *Homo hierarchicus*.' *American Anthropologist* 71:1166-75.

———. 1990a. 'Introduction'. In M. Marriott (ed.), *India through Hindu categories*. New Delhi: Sage.

———. 1990b. 'Constructing an Indian ethnosociology'. In M. Marriott (ed.), *India through Hindu categories*. New Delhi: Sage.

Mayer, A.C. 1960. *Caste and kinship in central India: a village and its region*. London: Routledge and Kegan Paul.

Mayer, P. 1993. 'Inventing village tradition: the late 19th-century origins of the north Indian "jajmani system".' *Modern Asian Studies* 27:357-95.

Mosse, D. 1994. 'Idioms of subordination and styles of protest among Christian and Hindu Harijan castes in Tamil Nadu.' *Contributions to Indian Sociology* (n.s.) 28:67-106.

O'Hanlon, R. 1988. 'Recovering the subject: *subaltern studies* and histories of resistance in colonial South Asia.' *Modern Asian Studies* 22:189-224.

O'Hanlon, R. and D. Washbrook. 1992. 'After orientalism: culture, criticism, and politics in the Third World.' *Comparative Studies in Society and History* 34:141-67

Prakash, G. 1990. 'Writing post-orientalist histories of the Third World: perspectives from Indian historiography.' *Comparative Studies in Society and History* 32:383-408.

———. 1992. 'Can the "subaltern" ride? A reply to O'Hanlon and Washbrook.' *Comparative Studies in Society and History* 34:168-84.

Radhakrishnan, P. 1990a. 'Some issues overlooked: reply to André Béteille.' *Hindu*, 8 November 1990.

———. 1990b. 'Two steps backward.' *Frontline*, 1-14 September 1990:19-24.

———. 1995a. 'The quota conundrum.' *Hindu*, 19 February 1995.

———. 1995b. 'Reservation politics.' *Hindu*, 26 February 1995.

Raheja, G.G. 1988. 'India: caste, kingship, and dominance reconsidered.' *Annual Review of Anthropology* 17:497-522.

Raheja, G.G. and A.G. Gold. 1994. *Listen to the heron's words: reimagining gender and kinship in north India*. Berkeley: University of California Press.

Runciman, W.G. 1983. *A treatise on social theory. 1: The methodology of social theory*. Cambridge: Cambridge University Press.

Searle-Chatterjee, M. and U.M. Sharma. 1994. 'Introduction.' In M. Searle-Chatterjee and U.M. Sharma (eds.), *Contextualising caste: post-Dumontian approaches*. Oxford: Blackwell.

Seth, V. 1993. *A suitable boy*. London: Phoenix House.

Sheth, D.L. 1991. 'The future of caste in India: a dialogue.' *Contributions to Indian Sociology* (n.s.) 25:331-41.

Srinivas, M.N. 1962. *Caste in modern India and other essays*. New York: Asia.

———. 1987 (1975). 'The Indian village: myth and reality.' In *The dominant caste and other essays*. Delhi: Oxford University Press.

———. 1990a. 'End of the egalitarian dream.' *Sunday Observer*, 11 September 1990.

———. 1990b. 'The Mandal formula for backwardness: caste versus individuals.' *Times of India*, 6 September 1990.

van der Veer, P. 1994. *Religious nationalism: Hindus and Muslims in India*. Berkeley: University of California Press.

Vidal, D., G. Tarabout and E. Meyer. 1994 (1993). 'On the concepts of violence and non-violence in Hinduism and Indian society.' *South Asia Research* 14:196-213.

Washbrook, D.A. 1988. 'Progress and problems: South Asian economic and social history c.1720-1860.' *Modern Asian Studies* 22:57-96.

Weber, M. 1978 (1922). *Economy and society*. Berkeley: University of California Press.

Wilson, W.J. 1978. *The declining significance of race: blacks and changing American institutions*. Chicago: University of Chicago Press.

Zelliott, E. 1972. 'Gandhi and Ambedkar: a study in leadership.' In J.M. Mahar (ed.), *The untouchables in contemporary India*. Tucson: University of Arizona Press.

Chapter 2

CASTE IN AN INDIAN VILLAGE: CHANGE AND CONTINUITY 1954-1992[1]

Adrian Mayer

In this paper I will attempt to identify and assess changes in the nature of caste, and of its significance in the wider social organisation, in a village of central India. The period under review covers 38 years, and my data are drawn from extended initial research in 1954-6 and briefer visits in 1983 (one month) and 1992 (two months).

In 1954, membership of a caste was a pivotal aspect of an individual's social position and identity. It provided a set of rules of behaviour towards people of other castes as well as towards fellow caste members; to some extent it regulated permitted occupations, as well as the possibility of political leadership; and it was legitimated not only by specific historical and mythological facts, but also by its acceptance as a normative feature of society. Constituting a by no means entirely rigid system of caste groups, caste also provided one of the avenues through which change could occur, notably through efforts by members to improve their status or gain political power, but this was a long process with an uncertain chance of success.

However, intimations of more rapid and radical change existed in 1954. Anti-caste legislation, as well as the introduction of new political institutions, provided further avenues for social mobility (and, of course, for a reactive strengthening of caste interests too), and the national ideology which stressed the caste-free equality of its citizens provided a counter-value for those who wished to adopt it. Villagers acknowledged this development when they told me that 'there is no

[1] I acknowledge the assistance of the Australian National University, the School of Oriental and African Studies, University of London, the Leverhulme Foundation and the Nuffield Foundation in funding these studies, and of Gakushuin University, Tokyo, in the writing of this paper, as well as of members of the 'Caste Today' workshop for their comments.

caste left' or that Brahmans alone could now be seen as a distinct caste (Mayer 1960:48). These statements, known to be literally untrue, since the village contained many castes, articulated the villagers' feelings about what the future might hold.

I wish to consider how far this trend has gone, given that it is at once clear that the same castes still exist in the village. My account examines first the morphological and then the institutional aspects of caste. That is, I look first at overt and explicit patterns of caste behaviour, and will then ask how far this behaviour is seen as morally justified. In this way, I will render my data comparable to Béteille's recent analysis of caste amongst urban professional people (Béteille 1991; 1992). I shall also use the distinction I made in 1954 between the external and internal relations of caste. Inter-caste relations existed mainly within the village, whereas intra-caste relations also extended to those villages into which marriages had been made.

Caste and commensality: the position in 1954

Before describing the present situation as regards inter-caste relations, and at the risk of oversimplification, I will set out the picture I gave for the mid-1950s, since this will constitute my baseline for comparison. At that time, the village of Ramkheri contained 25 Hindu castes and two Muslim caste-like groups, ranging in size from two to 181 persons. There was a generally held view that these had an element of rank in their relations. This stemmed especially from each caste's believed-in degree of purity and its adherence to customary behaviour linked to a favoured model. That is, on the one hand, there were criteria linked to a theory of pure materials (used in a caste's diet and its traditional occupation) and on the other an adherence to a way of life based on the classical model of the ranked *varna*—notably the life styles of Kshatriya/Rajputs and 'Vaishyas' expressed especially in non-vegetarian and vegetarian habits of diet and ritual respectively.

The chief way in which differences in rank were expressed was through commensality. For commensal relations covered all castes, whereas other manifestations of rank, such as place of residence, use of wells for drinking water, or touchability, were not comprehensive

Table 1: *Caste Ranking in Ramkheri*

Division 1	Brahman

Division 2			Division 3			
Rajput	Gosain	Tobacco-curer (Kumawat)				Carpenterr (Sutar)
Barber (Nai/Sen)		Potter (Kumhar)	Gardener (Mali)	Smith (Lohar)	Farmer (Khati)	Bairagi
Oil-presser (Teli/Rathore)		Dairyman (Ahir)			Tailor (Darzi/Mehta)	
	Goatherd (Gari)					

Division 4
Bhilala
Mina
Nath
Drummer
(Doli)

Division 5
Weaver   Balai Babaji
(Balai)
Tanner
(Chamar)
Sweeper
(Bhangi)

indicators giving the whole range of differences. Commensal relations were expressed through the taking of food cooked in water (*kacca*) or in oil (*pakka*), the taking of water from common receptacles, and the smoking together of cigarettes or pipes. A caste's eating of *kacca* or *pakka* food from the hearth or hands of another caste betokened that the former was either equal to or inferior to the latter. Conversely, a prohibition on commensal relations meant that a caste considered itself superior or simply separate. Within this broad idiom were further intricacies which I do not need to detail here. Suffice it to say that I was able to draw up a pattern of rankings from my data (Mayer 1960:36), and to express it as in Table 1.

The ranking in the table represents the broad consensus of villagers, and was in fact made up from their responses to my questions about which castes they could eat, drink or smoke with. Because these commensal relations embraced all castes I called the ensemble a hierarchy in the sense of a ranking system subject to a consistent principle—here, the notion of caste purity expressed through food and water.

It is true that, looked at in terms of actual behaviour, this ranking was to some extent a notional one. For much inter-caste commensality had never been tested by actual invitations to eat together. Had this been done some variations might have entered; but I do not think that they would have been major ones. More important, the placing of 14 of the 23 castes in separate but equally ranked divisions within which, again, several castes were equally ranked, recognised that equal separation as well as rank was a principle of organisation. In fact, people told me that inequality was really only between the categories of upper (*uttam*) and lower (*madhyam* or *nic*) castes and that within the former there was broad equality rather than ranking. When to this is added the debate between adherents of meat-eating and vegetarianism, which often ended in the view that these models could not really be ranked, one could ask, as I did, whether the castes in divisions 2 and 3 may not have had a different outlook about ranking: for, 'whereas castes in the lowest and highest ranks both think and say that they are higher than their neighbours, the castes in the middle may think they are higher but say publicly that they are equal' (ibid.:44). I concluded, however, that the situation was not a drastic one of a difference in belief, but rather that 'there is something of each of these two attitudes in almost every inter-caste relation. The problem is to decide just what the proportions of these two ingredients are in any given relation' (ibid.:47).

The table (or indeed the matrix provided by Dumont (1970:86-7) from my data) is in another sense incomplete. Besides not indicating whether the relations in it were theoretical or actual, it does not tell us what happened literally 'on the ground' at an assembly of people for a feast. To know this, we must add the constitution of the eating line (*pangat*): for two castes able to eat food cooked by a third might only do so when leaving a gap of up to several feet between each other (see Mayer 1960:Plate IIIB).

I gave (ibid.:41) the examples of two feasts, and from these and similar data it is possible to abstract the following degrees of commensality. The food served in these feasts, and generally in 1954, included both *kacca* and *pakka* dishes—roasted wheat balls (*batti*) with pulse sauce, and sweetmeats (*laddu*) respectively. Hence, the more restrictive rules were observed. Because the cooks were Gosain, the Brahman priests could only take raw foodstuffs home to cook. Rajputs and what I called their allied castes of division 2 were able to eat this food and sat in the same line to do so: the more marginal castes of the division—the Gari and Teli—would have needed to sit separately, but avoided showing their inferiority by taking raw supplies home to cook. Raw supplies were also given to the castes of division 3, who took them home or might cook their food separately on site (ibid.:Plate IIIA). Castes of division 4 ate the prepared food at the same time as the Rajputs but sat in different eating lines from both allied castes and each other. The Balais and Chamars of division 5 ate separately, being fed later, and the Bhangi collected the scraps and took them home to eat. One can see, then, that the hierarchy was spread out before one on the occasion of such feasts—given, of course, that these were important enough for a range of castes to have been invited. And both rank and separation were shown.

Before considering the situation at my revisits, I should note two factors which indicated the potential for change, and which contributed to the general opinion that a wind of change was starting to blow in the village. The first concerned the efforts of castes to change their positions in the hierarchy itself. The two marginal castes of division 2, the Teli and Gari, tried (unsuccessfully) to enter the category of allied castes by eating in the same line as them (ibid.:48). The Gari's case rested on the fact that another subcaste of Gari (the Ujle), which had given up goat-herding, was in other villages allowed to do so. The case of the Teli showed a more general attempt to raise status as a result of education and enhanced professional status. Besides this, the Bhilala and Balai were trying to disengage themselves from divisions 4 and 5 respectively, using a change of diet as well as historical claims as a basis. The fact that these attempts had not succeeded did nothing to detract from the atmosphere of change which they promoted.

The other factor of change was the introduction of restaurants and teashops in the market town—and erstwhile Princely State capital—of Dewas seven miles away, and the participation of some villagers in government functions at which caste restrictions were not observed when it was time to have food or drink. These contexts had produced a number of villagers who appeared to accept a dual standard of behaviour, ignoring caste restrictions under such circumstances but observing them in village functions. Now, allowance had always been made for commensal behaviour prohibited in the village to be followed in other villages, since it was recognised that each village's traditions were autonomous (ibid.:49). But this had only occurred within acceptable limits, whereas in the town restaurants or at official functions one might be eating next to castes of division 5, which, had this occurred in the village, would have brought an 'outcasting' and fine. In general, then, commensal restrictions within the village in 1954 were pretty generally accepted, and an individual's willingness to breach them had to be expressed privately (of which there were some known cases) or else needed to be outside the village.

Caste and commensality: the position in 1992

The position as it has developed in the past 38 years involves both continuity and change. This also applies to village life in general. Ramkheri's population has grown from 912 to 2,063 (1991 census), shown in both an enlarged and more densely populated village site as well as by a ribbon development of new houses along the approach road. Physically, the village in part looks different with a number of cement and brick houses, although some wards have changed little. Electricity had arrived in 1972, people's dress has changed, and many consumer durables are now in evidence. Again, the area of cultivated land has increased as well as the proportion of irrigated land, and with this the crop pattern has changed. Moreover, a significant number of villagers now work in Dewas, although agriculture continues to be the core activity. This paper cannot examine the general picture, though I shall have something to say about the wider economic and political spheres within which castes exist. Here, I only wish to note, unsurprisingly, a mix of change and continuity in the general as well as the commensal sphere.

In the latter, a distinction is still made between *uttam* and *madhyam* castes, which continues the general idea of rank. But the behaviour of castes in each category has become markedly different. For, whereas there has been a major lessening of commensal distinctions within the *uttam* category, within the *madhyam* category caste distinctions remain much as before. As to the question of dual standards of behaviour, the difference between a person's behaviour as a member of a caste group and as an individual has now entered village contexts, whereas it was formerly largely a difference between behaviour in village and town. Let me first consider the nature of commensal relations when they concern group feasts of a formal kind.

The transformation of commensal relations among *uttam* castes in this context has come about at the material level because formal occasions are now based on the serving of *pakka* food alone (*puri*, vegetable curry and sweetmeats), for the most part cooked by a high-caste professional cook (in Ramkheri usually a Gosain)..[2] The exclusive serving of *pakka* food has meant that one of the major constraints on commensal co-operation has been eased. Even in 1954, participation would doubtless have been greater had the food been *pakka* instead of a mixture of *pakka* and *kacca*.[3] However, the fact that all castes are now

[2] The *madhyam* castes also provide *pakka* food at feasts. But they usually cook it themselves and hence would meet with refusal from other castes to eat with them, even had they the ability to invite them. In theory, a division 5 household could provide a *pakka* meal, cooked by a Gosain, to which *uttam* castes would come if it were served by *uttam* caste helpers and held outside the ward. I have never heard of this happening, but Bhilalas (of division 4) have had such feasts, which were held in open ground and not in their compounds, to which allied castes have come.

[3] I should note that Dumont was aware of this when, in his analysis of Ramkheri's 1954 commensal pattern, he wrote that *pakka* food was 'not used here in its full capacity as food for festivals', that is, in a capacity which would allow commensality between divisions 2 and 3 castes (Dumont 1970:88). Because of this, he noted that *pakka* food at feasts had a 'no more than a gastronomic significance' (ibid.:85). Nearly 40 years later, his prescience has been confirmed.

able to eat the food offered on such occasions as wedding and funerary (*nukta*) feasts does not mean the immediate end of all distinctions of higher and lower. Rather, the context has shifted. It is now the eating line (*pangat*) which has become the chief indicator of rank. The question now is whether two castes can sit together in one *pangat*, or whether they must be in two *pangats*, or else in one *pangat* but with a gap (*ceti*) between them to symbolise their difference. Hence, most of my questions about group commensality in 1983 and 1992 concerned the *pangat* and the *ceti*, rather than the taking of *kacca* and *pakka* food. Moreover, these questions invoke far from theoretical answers. For, over the past decade, there have been several very large feasts, to which people of *all* the village's castes have come. Hence, answers to these questions are much more 'real' than were those to many of my earlier enquiries. Let me give an example which will include the various aspects we are looking at.

A short time before my arrival in 1983, a funerary feast had been held after the death of the senior Rajput headman, who had been one of the richest men of the village as well as personally highly respected, and whose eldest son was a prominent village leader and farmer. Because of this concatenation of prestige, the son resolved to invite people *sakat neota*—that is, his invitation was to apply to every person in a household, rather than to be a *pagri bandh neota* applying only to a single male. And he invited every household in Ramkheri, as well as castemates and kin in other places. The resulting feast was attended by thousands of people, and its size and cost made it certain that its organiser's name would live in the village's annals.

How was the feeding organised since, on this occasion, there was no restriction on the attendance of any caste in the village? The food was *pakka* of course: it was cooked by the Gosain professional with Gosain and Brahman helpers, and it was served by around 75 Rajput and other *uttam* caste waiters. Feeding took place between noon and early evening, in three open locations near the host's house. One was allocated to *uttam* castes, which included the village's non-priestly Brahmans (the priest took raw supplies home to cook), all castes in divisions 2 and 3, and the two households of Mina from division 4. A second was meant for Pinjara and Fakir Muslims, the three remaining castes of division 4, and the Balai Babaji household from division 5. To the third came two (Balai and Chamar) of the three castes of division 5 (the Bhangi collected the leavings and ate them at home). Women and children were served in the same locations.

Because of the numbers involved, guests to the village were called to eat first. After this the villagers were invited, in theory the people of each ward arriving together and eating at the same time. I am not sure whether women and children came with the men under this system, but their eating lines were surely separate.

What was the composition of the *pangat*s resulting from this procedure? The calling by wards would have resulted in a single caste being fed in only a few cases, since most wards contain more than one caste. In any case, it is clear that some people were not ready at that time and came to eat at a later stage. Hence, in two of the locations there was a mixture of castes at any one time—especially at that allocated to the *uttam* castes. Here, there was said to have been a single, unbroken *pangat*, except for the Gari, who told me that there was a *ceti* between him and the others (he measured this as being between 6 and 12 inches). I was also told by some men that a *ceti* was made for the Minas. It was also said that a few men ate there who should have been in the second location, notably one or two Pinjara Muslims. As to the second location, each of the three Hindu castes ate at a separate *pangat* and were in turn separate from the Muslims.

We can now see in more detail the changes that have occurred since 1954. The biggest has been within the *uttam* castes. No longer do the castes of division 3 refuse to eat at feasts but take supplies home. There has been a positive coming together—led by the example of the two largest castes, the Rajputs and Khatis. The shift started in the early 1970s, the first Khatis to eat at a Rajput feast being from a lineage with educated and progressive members. By the time of a brief visit in 1976, Khatis were said to be generally eating *pakka* food at Rajput feasts (with professional cooks) but to sit in a separate *pangat*, or with at least a *ceti* between themselves and castes of division 2. By 1982 the question of a separate *pangat* was no longer mentioned, but some

Khatis were said to leave a *ceti*. In 1992 the most conservative Khati I spoke to said he was now sitting in a single *pangat* without a *ceti* with vegetarian *uttam* castes, and with members of meat-eating castes 'if there are no more than one or two'. I believe that the great majority of younger Khatis no longer have such scruples and that they and all the *uttam* castes sit without a *ceti* between them.

The case of the Gari, the most marginal of the castes of division 2, further illustrates the change. In 1954 he was denied access to the allied caste *pangat*. In 1983 he sat in the *pangat*, but with a *ceti*. And in 1992, the cook at the largest of recent feasts, at which the Gari had been present, told me that the *ceti* had disappeared. This change applies even more to the two other non-allied castes of division 2, the Teli (now called Rathore) and the Ahir, who are now entirely assimilated, according to all the accounts given to me. Moreover, to the now solidary castes of divisions 2 and 3 are added the Brahmans of division 1. The farmer-Brahmans had sat in the *uttam pangat* for some time, but in 1992 the village priest told me that he (and his womenfolk) now ate in the *uttam pangat* at feasts given by those castes.

We can see that this progression has been aided by several enabling features. One is the subjective notion of the *pangat* and the *ceti*. For there is no publicly accepted minimum distance for either. At one end of the scale, a conservative can say that he has left a *ceti* if he makes a gap of, say, six inches. But his neighbour can ignore this by defining a *ceti* as being, say, a foot wide. Again, what to some may constitute separate *pangat*s may to others be a *ceti* within a *pangat*. In this way, common commensal relations may be said by some to exist, without ruffling conservative feathers: and, little by little, change takes hold. The process is helped by the notion that 'one or two' intruding caste members are acceptable, though not when more numerous and thus seen to be a group. Again, this allows for the attrition of caste separation, since it then slowly becomes customary to allow greater numbers to eat together. A further factor is the sequence of feeding. Large feasts take place over a period of several hours. At the start the space is filled at one time, and the question of *pangat*s is a real one. But later, guests simply sit down where there is a place when they arrive, in no particular order. Again, some of the guests are youths, representing their households since their seniors are busy: such people may well have no strong views about commensal restrictions. In this way, the actual situation becomes fluid for all but the main distinctions—in a Khati feast I witnessed in 1992, only a division 5 man (a Chamar) was seated separately at a distance (but he was served at the same time as everyone else, which would not have happened in 1954).

We can also see that the boundaries of the *uttam* caste category continue to expand. For instance, the Mina had been included with *uttam* castes in the feast described above. Note that there were only two Mina men in the village, a well-regarded ex-army man and his father: they could thus come under the 'one-or-two' rule at this stage. Similarly, the single Balai Babaji man, a teacher and ritualist, could be included with division 4 rather than 5. But Bhilalas were not included in the *uttam* space in 1983, being a large group. However, by 1992 some Rajputs said that they would sit in the same *pangat* as them, as well as with the Minas; even the Nath was mentioned. A Nath respondent, speaking of a Rajput feast in the late 1980s, said that people had come to eat as it suited them, and that he had simply sat down where there was a space and that there had been no question of his sitting at a separate *pangat*. But other respondents said that though there had not been separate *pangat*s, people had made *ceti*s when it suited them. A situation is thus perceived in different ways by different people, and hence the margins of the *uttam* category are fluid. But there is an undoubted reaching down, so that by now only the division 5 castes, as well as the Doli (who told me himself that he ate with nobody) are unequivocally in the *madhyam* category. These castes continue to eat separately from each other. At a recent feast, for instance, the Gosain cook told me that the Chamar, Bargunda, and Malwi and Gujarati Balai guests had eaten at separate *pangat*s (though some Balais denied this for their subcastes). At this level, things have changed little if at all.

The further shape of things to come, in which higher and lower group commensal categories will disappear entirely, may already be discerned. A Rathore and a Khati—both senior schoolmasters—had held wedding feasts in Dewas rather than in the village. Feeding had taken the form of a buffet (the English word is used). This of course involved no *pangat* at all. People were served food as individuals, stood where they wished, and associated with whom they pleased. Persons of all castes were fed in this way. The physical form of the buffet may not reach the village for a while longer, if at all, but the idea behind it may influence further change.

A further concomitant has been the changing behaviour of women. I say 'concomitant' rather than 'cause' because women, though not I think initiating change, may well have helped it along. In 1954 women were much more conservative than their menfolk (ibid.:51). The women I asked said that they still do not go to restaurants or teashops in Dewas or the village, though they now have the example of the women teachers and health worker, who order tea from time to time. But their behaviour at feasts now follows closely that of their menfolk. Thus, Khati and Brahman women sit in the same *pangat* as Rajputs and most other castes of divisions 2 and 3, to eat food from professional cooks. Only a few women are conservative, notably the Ahirs. As to sitting with the Gari or the Mina and Bhilala, the older women I asked said they would certainly leave a *ceti* if not sit in a separate *pangat*, but some younger women denied this. This trend is significant for the general interaction among the village women, and it could well eventually influence behaviour in the home, and thus commensality at the level of the individual household.

When we turn from contexts of group behaviour to individual-based commensality we are dealing with two kinds of situation. One consists of eating together in people's homes: and the other concerns public places such as restaurants.

I had assumed that a pattern of *kacca* food eating would appear from my asking about invitations given by friends to eat at each other's houses. However, it became clear that a sharp distinction between public/*pakka* and private/*kacca* cannot be made. For all but the most impromptu of personal invitations will involve *pakka* food being served as a matter of hospitality. Hence, the answer to a question 'can you eat *kacca* food from the kitchen of caste A/B/C/...?' is a largely notional one. Moreover, there will be a wide range of answers, depending on how conservative the respondent is. For instance, one middle-aged Khati told me that he would eat *kacca* food at the house of a Rajput personal friend, and had in fact done so; but another older Khati said he would not eat *kacca* food at any Rajput house, and would eat *pakka* food only if it were offered at the host's field well (the implication being that food offered in the house could be impure through being cooked on or near a hearth used for non-vegetarian meals). Again, several respondents said that they would not eat *kacca* food in any other caste's house because the water for cooking might have been rendered impure by children dipping a glass several times into the water pot, turning the water into 'leavings' (*jhutha*)—this did not of course apply to the oil used in cooking *pakka* food for guests.[4]

At the individual level, then, there has been little relaxation of restrictions, and this mainly between the castes of division 2 and to a lesser extent division 3. Because individuals in the latter division have started to eat meat and drink liquor (how many being a matter of gossip and conjecture) the reason for their distinctiveness has diminished. In particular, this was alleged for the Khatis, among whom are many 'advanced' men. It may well be that this will facilitate growing Khati-Rajput commensal links at the private level of *kacca* food, which will lead the way to further general relaxation, as happened at the level of group commensality. But this trend has a long way to go. At present any eating of more than an *ad hoc* kind between friends is likely to involve *pakka* food. But there is the possibility of individual choice, and it is in this sense that I speak of the double standard—between private and public behaviour—as having now entered the village, rather than being a contrast between village and town.

The taking of food and drink in public places had started at the time of my stay in 1954. I noted that many men took tea and *pakka* snacks in Dewas when they went there for market, etc., but that very few ate *kacca* meals there. Much has changed since then. Partly it is because villagers go to town very much more than they did. Some 130 men have

---

[4] This is a form of that general suspicion of the domestic and private habits of other castes which lies at the basis of arguments in favour of caste endogamy, as I shall note below.

daily work in Dewas, for a start, and others are constantly in and out. Hence, the taking of *kacca* meals in town is not remarkable. Some men may not go to meat-serving restaurants and a few may never have had a meal, but these are individual choices, and eating in town need no longer be concealed. Moreover, the village itself now provides such choices.

There are three teashops in the village, at the junction of the approach road and the national highway. They are places where people wait for a bus, come to read the newspapers, or play cards. In fact, they provide the same contexts for casual gatherings as did the artisan workplaces in 1954 (see ibid.:Plate IIA). One is run by a Nai, and two by Pinjara Muslims. To some extent they attract different clienteles, the Nai's the older men and *uttam* castes, the Pinjaras' the younger commuters and *madhyam* castes. But it would be wrong to press this distinction too far. For I have seen the Bhangi take tea at the Nai teashop, for instance, and *uttam* men may patronise the Pinjaras. I asked one such client, a Khati, whether he had any problem in taking tea from Pinjaras. He told me that he would not do so at a Pinjara's house, for the glasses might not have been properly washed. But at the teashop, glasses are washed in front of everyone (this, presumably, is the reason that the Bhangi can use the teashop, for I did not see him use a special glass). The teashops, then, are part of the public domain, as are similar establishments in Dewas, and as are the four roadside restaurants (*dhaba*) that now exist to take advantage of the heavy lorry traffic on the national highway. These establishments have a place to eat open at all hours, cots for the drivers to sleep on, and a tyre repair shop. The first *dhaba* was started in 1980 by a Sikh and there are another Sikh and two Pinjara *dhabas* now trading. Not only the clientele but also the staff are of various castes, cooks and dishwashers including both *uttam* and *madhyam* castes such as Chamars and Balais. Meat is not served, but liquor is said to be available in one or more of them. Most villagers said that they did not eat there—this is not surprising, since a person usually eats only when travelling. But I have seen men taking meals at the Sikh *dhabas*, as well as tea. On the whole, the *dhabas* are not places for casual village gatherings, but they add a significant element of 'casteless' activity within the village's confines.

In 1954, I reported that vegetarianism was gaining strength, as the favoured value of Gandhiism and the new government (ibid.:45). In 1992, by contrast, meat-eating was on the rise. Several young men of traditionally vegetarian castes whom I questioned admitted to eating meat from time to time.[5] By contrast, *uttam* caste women, with a few well-known exceptions, do not eat meat, and the presence of a meat-eating husband presents problems to them. The cooking of meat is of course done in separate vessels, and in some cases outside the house. I asked what a wife would do if her husband made himself impure by starting to eat meat. The answer was that it depended on her influence. She might try to make him give up; but in the final analysis there was nothing that she could do—and she would get beaten if she tried to oppose him too strongly. Thus change has come into the heart of the household's dietary habits.

Similarly, some men from previously teetotal castes now drink country liquor. This had in 1954 been provided by members of the Kanjar caste, who lived nearby. But in 1992 these had taken up other work, and liquor was now supplied by some Chamar households, to which clients might go to fetch their drink. Both meat-eating and drinking mix up the values and contacts of castes formerly distinct, and start to provide a more uniform approach to diet which might eventually further weaken commensal distinction.

I have been dealing with food as the commensal medium. But it will be recalled that smoking and drinking water were also subject to restrictions based on caste rank. In 1992 only a handful of men smoked the small clay pipe (*cillum*) which in 1954 was handed round those castes able to eat *pakka* food together. For these, the same rules appeared to hold good, and have thus changed with the extension of *pakka* commensality, but the vast majority of men smoked cigarettes on

---

[5] I did not further investigate this trend, and cannot say to what extent there is more to it than personal taste—for instance, that it is a statement of a person's modernist aspiration. In at least some cases, those working in Dewas had tried meat at restaurants there and developed a liking for it. Such men may have to hide this habit if they live with their parents, but if they are householders can bring it to the village.

an individual basis. As to water, I did not enquire into the present pattern. But I noted the change in the provision of drinking water for the villagers. In 1954, there were four drinking-water wells in the village. The main one catered to all castes in divisions 1-4, and the others to each of the three division 5 castes separately. In 1992, the main well is still in use, but water is not normally drawn from it but taken from a tank to its side which is supplied by a pipe from a more copious tube-well at some distance. Besides this, there are five handpumps in different wards of the village, and two others serving the new settlement near the national highway.

In normal times, the Chamars have the exclusive use of a handpump in their ward and Balais tend to use a nearby well or multicaste handpump. But when there is a shortage of water, both castes will come to the main tank. Here there are four taps and a platform on which women can wait their turn. There have been altercations in the past, when *uttam* women have made the Chamars stand apart until they have finished. As one woman put it: 'There's no problem about the water, but we don't like to see them there'. Nevertheless Chamars do at such times use the common water supply, and in the new settlement one handpump is normally used by the Bhangi family without hindrance from other castes. Of course, the system of taps or pumps makes such a change easy: the lower caste woman no longer has to touch with her vessel the water from which others will later draw (although in the past this if necessary was condoned because undrawn water was regarded as a natural manifestation and thus inherently pure). Hence this situation also shows a loosening, if not an entire ending, of caste distinction.

Caste and occupation

I come now to caste differences as expressed in other spheres of activity, and start with the link between caste and occupation. In 1954, almost all the members of castes providing artisan services to the village (Smith, Carpenter, Potter, Barber, Drummer and Tanner) followed their traditional occupation either wholly or partially. Members of castes performing ritual duties in return for alms were evenly divided between those continuing and those who had taken up other work. For the rest, castes traditionally agriculturalists (Farmers, Gardeners, etc.) continued in this work and were joined by other castes, some of whose traditional occupations had ceased (for instance weaving and oil-pressing), since farming was a caste-free occupation. Only 12 men commuted to work outside the village, and of these only two worked in factories in Dewas. It can thus be seen that over half the village's men were engaged in their caste-traditional work.[6]

The position in 1992 is rather different. Of the artisans, only the Carpenters have continued their trade to a significant extent—of the sixteen adult males, four are full-time carpenters in the village and three more work in Dewas; the rest are tailors, a mason, a mechanic, etc. None of the Blacksmiths practises his trade in the village. The Tanners no longer tan hides and make shoes, their only remaining work being the gathering of hides for sale in Dewas. Only one Potter knows how to make pots, the rest either make bricks (an ancillary traditional work) or do other work. There is only one full-time barber, two more of the thirteen adult Barbers working part-time. And the Drummer says he works only if he has no daily labour, since the latter pays him more than the usual honorarium for drumming. Thus, a minority of artisan males follow their traditional callings. For alms-takers the situation is similar. The village priest, a Brahman, and some of the Naths and to a lesser extent the Bairagi priest[7] continue their ministrations, but most men are in other work. Again, only three families of Pinjaras are cotton carders and mattress makers. The Goatherds now farm for a living, the village's goat herd being led by a Pinjara and many other castes having a few animals.[8] Of the nine Tailors, only two are practising, their sons having taken up other work when this was better paid than tailoring—a

[6] The proportion would be higher if the Rajputs, Minas and Bhilalas had been enumerated as agriculturalists.

[7] The shrine which was formerly the responsibility of the Gosain is now in the charge of a saddhu who came to the village some years ago.

[8] The care of goats has even spread to *uttam* castes. Both a Rajput and an Ahir told me that they kept one animal, the latter saying that it was for its milk, and the former so that he could offer a meat curry to any guest at short notice. But this is not counted as herding, which is thought to be low-status work. Perhaps it can be said to fall under the 'one-or-two' rule to which I referred earlier!

decision that some now regret.

Change has involved the agricultural castes too. For one thing, many of them have become commuters to Dewas—there were 106 commuters of all castes in 1983 and 124 (19 per cent. of adult males) in 1992. These were men who returned to the village every night. In addition, 29 men were located elsewhere (in the army or police, for instance, or as schoolmasters), at least some of whom could be expected to retire in the village. The range of commuter occupations is wide—work in a variety of firms (mainly textile and engineering), in government concerns such as the State Electricity Board, and as teachers, bus conductors, security guards, etc. Men from 18 castes are involved, in some cases two-thirds of the males, in the larger castes a smaller though significant proportion (e.g., Farmers 17 per cent., Rajputs 16 per cent., Balais 23 per cent.).

Besides urban work, several new occupations have opened up in the village itself. For instance, men are well-borers and repairers of pumps, cycles, televisions and radios; they act as agents for cattle feed cakes and seeds; they operate three larger and two smaller grain mills; they own two five-ton trucks used extensively by the villagers for transporting their crops and other articles, and two heavy-goods lorries which ply long distances in Madhya Pradesh and beyond; they are the proprietors, and the cooks and servants, in roadside restaurants—the list is a long one. Some men do this work part-time together with farming or commuting, but others have taken it up as full-time work. There is, in fact, an increasingly important new category of service work in the village, perhaps stimulated by pressure of population on existing agricultural and commuting opportunities, as well as by the prospect of rewards. None of these jobs is caste-restricted, although they tend to be done by the *uttam* castes, who are more likely to have the education and capital required, and also by the Pinjaras who have for long been traders and entrepreneurs.

All this has meant a general disengagement of occupation from its association with a particular caste, and with any ranking which might stem from this. In 1954, some occupations were thought to carry their impurity to the caste performing them—and to the extent that these still exist, there is a link which affects the caste's status. That the Chamars still skin dead cattle and sell the hides must affect thinking about them as a whole, although this is a small part of their normal work, which now mainly concerns the making of leaf plates and general labour. Again, the occasional scavenging by the Bhangi marks him, although he is now a labourer for most of the time, by contrast to his predecessors who raised pigs and considered manual work to be inappropriate for them. And the work of the Drummer, involving as it does the home-cured goatskin on his drum, also affects his standing. It is also the case that the proverb 'highest agriculture, middle trade, next service, most worthless begging' is still quoted (ibid.:75). But its force is vitiated by the fact that a basis for the desirability of agriculture, its independence, is no longer unique to it—lorry owners, for instance, have the same power of independent decision. Also, the aim of many young men is now to go into 'service', usually in government, where the work is thought to be easier and more rewarding.

Hence, the rank of occupations is less clear-cut, and so is the correspondence of caste membership to an occupation. Nevertheless, just as in 1954, I believe that an association is still made which in some way links castes with their traditional occupations, even though they do not follow them, and that this identifies them in very general terms with the rank which was traditionally given to the latter.[9] It would explain, too, why some castes have changed their identifying names—Teli (oil presser) is now Rathore, Nai (barber) is Sen, Darzi (tailor) is Mehta; and conversely why, when a man was criticising a Rathore to me, he used the traditional caste name to disparage him. There is a feeling too, that, say, Farmers farm better than castes who do not have farming in their traditions. But this feeling is now much weaker because men do such a variety of work, and the caste name now tends to denote a more general separateness rather than rank, and thus reinforces the endogamy which still rules as a basis for caste organisation.

---

[9] That this is an extremely tenacious feature is shown by its survival in overseas Indian communities after half a century, during which occupational specialisation had disappeared and the association of caste with an actual occupation did not exist (Mayer 1973:161).

Caste, wealth and power

After what I have already written, it will come as no surprise that
inequalities of wealth and power within the village are less identified
with caste than they were in 1954. At that time, there was little wealth
unconnected with land ownership. The few traders were modest and
there were no large moneylenders (ibid.:85). Only the six village
accountants derived significant income from work outside the village.
Moreover, there were no very rich and large landlords. However, it was
true that the Rajputs were by far the main owners, having 38 per cent.
of the village land and the largest per capita holdings. Only the Khati
caste approached this figure with 26 per cent. Hence Rajputs were
better off as a whole though there were a few landless households
within the caste. In the last decades, land has moved out of Rajput
hands, and many of the buyers have been Khatis, who now own 36 per
cent. of village land to the Rajputs' 32 per cent.; and though the latter
still have appreciably more land per capita, the difference has
diminished from more than double to less than half as much again. No
other caste has even 10 per cent. of the total area, and their per capita
holdings are also much smaller.

But it is now much less easy to correlate income with the extent of
land ownership. In 1954 there was a pretty restricted repertoire of crops,
and most farmers grew a similar combination of rain-fed crops, and of
irrigated crops if they possessed one of the relatively few wells. At
present, the major crops are still generally grown, but the possible range
of other crops has greatly increased, and methods of farming are also
open to choice. Some men, for instance, simply plant sorghum in the
traditional manner; but others inter-plant it with soya. And the
cultivation of crops like garlic, potatoes and onions give a higher
(though riskier) return than do traditional crops. Some farmers are
becoming adept in finding commercial niches to fill—sending cori-
ander several hundred miles to Ahmedabad, or their potatoes to
Bombay rather than to Indore or Bhopal when the higher price more
than covers the extra cost of transport. This sort of enterprise is not
particularly caste-specific, though it is to be found among the *uttam*
castes and the Pinjaras, rather than the *madhyam* castes who do not

have the know-how or the necessary level of production. Hence, there is a number of farmers with good incomes from a number of castes, and the picture is more diffuse than in 1954.

In addition, it is no longer as accurate to correlate wealth with land because of the new employments I have mentioned. Not all commuters to factories are well paid, and many work on a temporary basis in any case. But there is a significant number of men making a decent living from their urban work, or from non-agricultural work in the village, perhaps adding to this the income from farming. And here there is no pre-eminent caste correlation, although it would be true to say, again, that the major benefits flow to the *uttam* castes. A bank now exists in the village, and its manager estimated that some 50 households could be said to be well off. Of these, about 30 had savings deposits of more than Rs. 20,000. Again, he said that there was no particular emphasis on any caste: among the largest account holders he identified two Khatis, two Pinjaras, one Rathore and one Rajput. Of course, wealth is held in other forms: but, even allowing for the notorious difficulty of assessing people's financial position, it does seem as if we can see wealth as spread more widely castewise than it was in 1954. But this, as I have suggested, applies mainly to the *uttam* castes, and it could be asked whether the gap between them and the *madhyam* castes has grown wider, making categories of rich and poor castes which parallel the tendency towards a two-category commensal picture.

It is difficult to answer this question without data from comprehensive surveys of household incomes and per capita wealth in 1954 and 1992. Lacking these, I can do no more than cite some indices which could imply an answer, as well as give my admittedly impressionistic views of the pattern in 1992. With respect to my earlier points about land ownership and outside work, I ask: has the proportion of land held by *madhyam* castes decreased, and is their share of outside work proportionate to their population?

The percentage of village land held by *madhyam* castes has varied little—from 7 per cent. in 1954/5 to 7.6 per cent. in 1988/9 (Bronger 1991:300). My 1992 figures for caste size show that their per capita landholding has decreased from 0.22 to 0.14 hectares (ha): but then, so has the per capita area held by the major landowning castes (Rajputs from 2.76 ha to 1.20 ha, and Khatis from 1.24 ha.to 0.84 ha). This is a function of the village's population more than doubling between 1954 and 1992. If the relative size and extent of holdings seem not to have greatly changed, neither has the distribution of holdings. A handful of households in each of the large *madhyam* castes has significant holdings; the rest have little or no land at all. Some of those with land have benefited from irrigation. For instance, Bhilala and Chamar farmers irrigate roughly half of their holdings, the Balais only some 15 per cent. on the other hand. But the areas are small, and even if almost all the land is irrigated, it does not mean that the farmer is wealthy. For instance, almost all Doli-owned land is irrigated, but since it is only three hectares and must support two large families, their standard of living is low. The conclusion must be from this that the gap has not increased in statistical terms, that it was always large, and that it prevents the *madhyam* castes from acquiring reserves from which they might start other ventures.

As regards non-agricultural work, the *madhyam* castes together have the same percentage of men who commute (19.5 per cent.) as the village as a whole (19.2 per cent.). Of the 32 men, ten work in factories, five for the road gangs of the Public Works Department, and ten for the State Electricity Board. Chamars have fewer workers proportionate to caste size than the other castes. They seem to be especially affected by the fact that the wages of an unskilled worker may be too low to justify the cost of the fare to work.

In real terms, the *madhyam* castes do not appear to be worse off than they were. Many landless families live in poverty with few or no reserves for emergencies, but this is not new. A few have managed to better themselves, including the three or four who have become farmers on a par with the lesser *uttam* farmers, and a few have outside jobs which also bring them into the middle rank. It would also be true to say that the gap between the *madhyam* castes and the richest villagers may well have widened. But so, too, will it have widened between richer and poorer within the *uttam* category. For there are a few *uttam* house-holders who have especially benefited from the new economic opportunities. As farmers, they have prospered under government policies of subsidising inputs and of floor prices for crops as well as the absence of agricultural income tax, and to this they have added the income(s) from professional jobs in government service and/or in industry or commerce. Such households now boast colour television, fans (and by now an air cooler), perhaps a tractor, a motor cycle and/or a jeep, and modern furniture, clothes and so forth. In this, they are starting to resemble the 'ruppy' of more advanced regions such as Haryana and Maharashtra.[10] And they may well generate new inequalities of wealth, lifestyle and linked economic and political influence.

When I turn to the question of power and influence within the village, I see much the same picture, of a diversification from the earlier position. Before independence, leadership of the village was in the hands of three Rajput headmen. It was their duty to maintain order, collect the land revenue, and in general act as a link between populace and government. From this authority flowed informal duties: to organise and lead the major calendrical festivals, to arbitrate in disputes, etc. Of course, the headmen took notice of influential men of other castes, and of course some headmen were less effective than others. But their possession of the position of major authority in the village gave them a weight which overflowed to other Rajputs in the village.

By 1954 this picture was changing because of the introduction of an elected Village Committee (VC), whose members and especially chairman were starting to act as another centre of power. This trend has continued over the years. The headmanship has been reduced in importance, with fewer functions, both formally and in village matters, until it is now a post of hardly more than historical and symbolic content, giving neither great power nor economic benefit (instead of being given land, as formerly, headmen are now paid a small

---

[10] I first saw the term 'ruppy' in an article examining the emergence of rural, upwardly mobile, young and newly-rich men (Kulkarni 1991). These are said to be mainly from middle-ranking castes rather than from the traditional landowners of the upper castes. They are entrepreneurial proprietors, developing new crops and village-based products, as well as spreading into the control of rural institutions.

commission on the revenue they collect). By contrast, the VC chairman has continued to be a person of importance, and elections to the post, as well as to VC membership, have attracted numbers of candidates and resulted in some fiercely fought elections. Moreover, other positions of importance have emerged, such as the chairmanships of the societies concerned with milk and soya marketing.

In elections to all these bodies caste has been an element affecting the pattern of voting. But just as it is only one factor among others at the national and regional political levels, so it is not the exclusive factor in the village's politics. There is no space to analyse the complex and changing alignments that have characterised elections in the village. Support may be sought on the basis of a candidate's record—his success in bringing benefits, or his alleged corruption and inefficiency in implementing programmes. Again, one election was at least partly fought on the basis of residence, since one candidate was a newcomer who was held to be presumptuous in seeking the chairmanship. Suffice it to say that elections have been fought on many issues. But, because these competitions are small scale, they often have at their base interpersonal friendships and enmities, as well as social factors stemming from quite different contexts and histories. Support is affected, for instance, by factional alignments in a caste—each of the three largest castes has a long-lasting split of this kind, which has a social rather than a political origin. Hence, while men may support each other because of their common caste, and oppose someone on this basis, it has been rare to see all Rajputs, say, supporting one of their number, and possible on occasion to see two Rajputs competing against one another. It would thus be an oversimplication to speak of a 'caste vote'.

Nevertheless, the main underlying trend in village politics does have reference to caste. It is the gradual change of the village from one dominated by Rajputs, both politically and economically, to one in which prominence is more widely spread, and in particular to one in which the category of the younger and politically interested villager crosses caste boundaries. Though Rajputs have been VC chairmen for 27 of the last 35 years, they have been challenged several times by

Khatis, with and without success; and at present, candidates come from a wider field. The VC was in 1992 suspended, along with others in the State. But the candidates for a cancelled election in 1991 were a Rajput and an Ahir, who then withdrew for a Pinjara compromise candidate. And men of Khati, Rathore and other *uttam* castes are also active politicians.

A further complicating feature is the introduction of national party alignments.[11] The village had a reputation of voting for Congress. But in the last State election it overwhelmingly supported the BJP, a change not unconnected with the fact that the BJP candidate was the Yuvraj of Dewas Senior, whose family had had close ties with the village (Mayer 1960:18) and who was thus expected to give it favoured treatment. Though there have always been some people who did not support Congress, party difference is now more explicit, and it makes for a further feature cross-cutting caste when it becomes linked to support given to village leaders. In short, the correlation of caste and political power is not as close as it was.

The internal dimension of caste: morphological and normative

Although gradations of caste rank no longer exist to such an extent in commensal situations, and although the political and economic spheres no longer show such a clear correspondence with caste differences, it is clear that castes continue to exist, and that one's caste membership is as unambiguous as it has always been. What makes it such? Morphologically, it is the continuing internal composition of the caste.

In my analysis of the 1954 situation, I distinguished the external from the internal dimension of caste. I saw the former mainly in the relations between castes in the village, and the latter in the relations of kinship and marriage which linked the households of a village with those of similar caste (or usually subcaste) in the other villages into which there had been marriages. The people in those villages formed a kindred with relation to any individual in Ramkheri, as well as a total

---

[11] This was given formal recognition for the first time in the 1991 election to the VC, when candidates were required to state their party allegiance on their nomination forms. I believe the provision has now been withdrawn.

kindred for all the subcaste members in the village. I then distinguished between the kindred of actual co-operation in the obligations taken on through marriage, and the kindred of recognition which was, at the outer limit, the total population within which marriages could be made with the certainty that they were taking place with reliably attributed spouses and hence unequivocally within the subcaste (ibid.:161, 212).

If there is one thing which has not changed over the years, it is this notion of the endogamous caste/subcaste unit. Respondents in 1992 found it difficult to grasp that there was no such unit in my own country—they simply could not understand how marriages could then be made. And when I asked them why, if eating together had arrived without objection, there should not be marriage together, they did not see this as even a theoretical possibility. To intermarry would be to dissolve the castes and then where would people be—this was the sort of reaction I encountered. It was similar to what I had noted in 1954, when I was told that if restrictions on commensality were to be abolished there would be no ban on intermarriage and then where would caste be. Of course, people may know about what for them are sometimes scandalous inter-caste marriages in Dewas town. But these are taken to be warnings of what should be prevented, or are seen as the sport of the elite.

Hence, the building blocks of the system are still in place, and are still seen as being basic to society itself. It is possible that there is now a less-embracing pattern of social control within these blocks. I was told in 1992 that there were no longer the inter-village circle councils (*pankheda*) which, though sometimes somewhat shadowy bodies, at least stood in 1954 for the belief that the local subcaste population was an entity which could enforce acceptable behaviour. However, it is still the case that breaches of rules, and disputes, can be brought before kindred councils at wedding or funerary feasts, or before village gatherings—one such instance had occurred in the Khati caste a few years previously, for instance. Hence, there is still a control mechanism, though it was said that people were now more inclined to bring disputes to the law courts. At the level of the province or region, caste temples and their managing committees continued, mainly in the sacred city of

Ujjain. In some cases decisions had been taken there about general matters—the limiting of wedding costs for example. In sum, a defining context for the local subcaste is still in place, with the twin pillars of endogamy to maintain boundaries, and councils (however informal) to maintain behaviour.

I have so far considered the morphological aspect of caste, what Béteille calls the 'social arrangement' (1992:13). This he distinguishes from its normative aspect, the beliefs and values underlying this arrangement. His view, based on research among urban professional people, is that whereas castes may exist morphologically, they are increasingly without normative backing and any moral commitment to them among their members. This he contrasts with the high positive value given to the family as an institution. What do my village data suggest?

The strength of normative values is hard to assess, and harder to measure over time. Even in 1954 it was unfashionable publicly to defend distinctions based on caste—hence the saying that the 'new wind' had swept almost all of them away. But how far were they also believed to be morally reprehensible? The same thing is said today: but with how much more moral justification? The loosening of caste restrictions and ranking at the morphological level, especially in commensal relations among the *uttam* castes, can support a view that underlying values have also changed. More generally, there has been a palpable shift in the daily behaviour of high and low castes. For instance, the Bhangi, who was in 1954 kept apart under all circumstances and who was literally untouchable, now makes up part of the group at teashops and in the village square; he tends to be on the periphery, but this may well be as much because he is poor and uneducated as because of his caste. His house, too, is no longer isolated but stands in an unbroken line with those of other castes. Interaction with other castes of division 5 has greatly eased too, as they will agree; in public, no overt distinction is made, and it is only the question of entering another's house that involves restrictions at least for the more conservative.

If one thinks that people cannot indefinitely behave in ways which contradict the values they hold, one might conclude that the values making for rank restrictions between castes have weakened, and that the 'new wind' continues to blow in a direction which is morally accepted by the villagers. The alternative use of the neutral and morally inoffensive word *samaj* (association) in place of the more loaded term *jat* (species) when referring to caste may be an indication that caste distinction and discrimination are seen as values which should not be publicly supported. The word used for discrimination (*bhedbhav*) suggests this view of caste, for it is a pejorative term referring also generally to situations, such as factional differences, where divisions exist which are thought to be bad.

Why, then, are castes still separated by endogamy?[12] Villagers often justify the prohibition of inter-caste marriage by saying that the *khan-pin* or the *rahan-sahan* of castes is different and therefore that marriage, the most intimate and comprehensive of relations, is barred between them. Now *khan-pin* literally means food and drink, and one might wonder whether it represents a very strongly held value since there has been so much change at the commensal level. But remember: little change has so far occurred in the taking of *kacca* food at the individual level. Now, it is *kacca* food that is the staple diet in all households, the cooking of which would be the duty of a new bride of different caste. People may therefore be saying that the old value of caste purity, conveyed by *kacca* food, still exists for them.

The significance of the changes in public commensality must be considered in this light. Specifically, one must ask whether the extension of commensality through the exclusive use of *pakka* food was made to extend equality between castes or whether it was for other reasons. I think that the move to *pakka* food came because this included more prestigious dishes—*puri* being seen as a more modern and *batti* as a more rustic dish—and because increasingly prosperous circumstances meant that many villagers could now afford the necessary materials and professional cooks (and others had then to follow the trend). It was, in this view, a sumptuary change of the same kind as the

---

[12] Fictive kinship still crosses caste boundaries (Mayer 1960:139). But this accepts, by implication, the caste separation which it is designed to mitigate.

change of the staple *kacca* food from sorghum to wheat chapattis. Hence, I think the reason had little to do with caste. But the consequence has been socially significant, for the provision of *pakka* food has enabled people to conform to an ideology of equality (especially if the niceties of the *pangat* and *ceti* are ignored), whilst the backstage element, of *kacca* food usage, can continue much as before. People therefore say, as they did in 1954, 'there is no more caste' (conveniently forgetting division 5), and stress the change that has undeniably occurred; but at the same time they adhere to largely traditional behaviour where it concerns them most.

To return to the use of *khan-pin* to justify endogamy, I think that the phrase has a connotation wider than food alone, and that it means the general domestic habits of a caste. I recall being told several times that men do not marry girls of other subcastes within the caste because, when they came to cook in their conjugal households, they 'would put too much salt in the rice'. This is not a purely culinary statement: it denotes custom of all kinds. And in this it approaches the meaning of the other phrase, *rahan-sahan*, which is 'way of life'—the double, rhyming words in each phrase denote a certain diffuseness, a generality which is exactly suited to the value being expressed.

People could, no doubt, specify which aspects of the different way of life they would object to. Some might be minor, though highly symbolic, like the salt in the rice; others would be about formal differences of custom. For instance, each clan worships a tutelary goddess on a day in the Nine Nights festival, but the day on which this is done varies between castes (Mayer 1960:186). Again, castes perform funerary rituals and hold the funerary feast on different elapsed days after the decease, as well as with a different order, and sometimes location, of events. Such differences would produce, in an intermarriage, a feeling in one of the spouses and their kin that the rituals had been incorrectly performed. Beyond this there exist general feelings of difference, and even of suspicion, about the intimate household behaviour of other castes, as the fears about impure water, cited above, indicate.[13]

---

[13] It is in such contexts that one might follow Bouglé (1971:9) and speak of

Note that I have not used the word 'family' here. Of course, it is pairs of families which would be directly involved in any such intermarriage. But the values preventing it are those of the subcaste's internal definition, or rather the usage of its local refraction, the kindred of recognition. Here, then, the family and the local subcaste kindred meet. At the village level, subcaste is also kinship—in large subcastes through the linking of individual families and households. That this linking has a positive moral content is indicated by the efforts which people make to reconcile families or lineages estranged through disputes. If loyalty to the immediate family were enough, such splits would surely not be condemned as they are. But family cannot be disengaged from caste where its constituent values are involved; not the caste of hierarchy so much as the caste of separate existence, whose continued presence provides a resource for politicians and others concerned in the recruitment of support.

It is here that my data meet Béteille's, because he is also speaking of families generally linked through marriages within the caste. It is true that he does not emphasise the implications of this. Caste endogamy is mentioned only once, in the second of his two articles on the subject, where he states: 'so long as the family arranges the marriage, the practice of caste endogamy will continue' (1992:17), though he qualifies this by saying that some families do arrange inter-caste marriages. His own material shows that professional people are above all interested in the advancement of their children, and the transmission to them of their social and economic advantages. This being so, one would expect them to marry their children into similarly benefited families of whatever caste, especially since they have abandoned any moral claims that caste may have upon them and only 'use caste instrumentally' (ibid.:18). This has presumably started to happen in the few inter-caste marriages. But to the extent that family arrangement of marriage generally entails caste endogamy (and this is how I read the sentence cited above) one may ask: all things being equal, why is marriage within the caste held by these families to be better than across caste? Might it be because of the

---

a relation of repulsion, although in general I believe that the word 'separation' is more appropriate.

common *rahan-sahan*, which will make life easier for the children and override advantages of a more material sort? And is not an implication of this that intra-marrying caste populations continue to exist, even among professionals, because they have normative support since they are constituted by valued marriages?

I would suggest a reformulation of Béteille's proposition, at least if it be enlarged to include the kind of people about whom I have written. It is not so much that these people are strongly committed to family but no longer to caste as a basis of loyalty and positive behaviour; rather, it is the morphological as well as normative parameters of caste that have shifted. The dominant morphology of caste is no longer primarily that of ranking, rather it is of separation; and the normative basis is less that of purity than it is of difference within which lies familial solidarity. Of course, this is a very broad-brush statement, which contains the three elements that I have identified in this paper. (1) There has been a change in ideology as far as 'overt' relations are concerned. This is shown in greater public commensality and a general loosening of inter-caste interaction and of the significance of caste in the economic and political fields. (2) There has been a continuity of 'covert' relations based on *kacca* food restrictions, which are in part a question of purity and inequality and in part of cultural separation. The dual standards of (1) and (2) now exist not between town and village boundaries but between public and private within the village. (3) Insofar as this duality is eroded by a liberalisation of *kacca* food usage, we will be left with the maintenance of caste identity through endogamy defined more in general cultural than in purity terms.

In so far as separation rather than rank is becoming the main organising feature, Ramkheri follows the trend identified in other analyses.[14] This is that caste has moved from being a system of inter-dependent parts to one in which castes are independently in competition

---

[14] For instance, we read of the move from organic to segmentary organisation (Bailey 1963:123), from vertical to horizontal solidarity (Srinivas 1966:114), from 'a structure to the juxtaposition of substances' (Dumont 1970:227), or of such titles as *Caste in contemporary India: beyond organic solidarity* (Kolenda 1978).

with one another. Inequality thus exists less in an explicit hierarchy made manifest in such contexts as commensal relations, than in a more generalised pattern of contexts in which caste is kinship-led. And, in so far as new inequalities may emerge through the neo-rich 'ruppy', it is worth noting what Kulkarni (1991:7) has written of regions where this trend is more developed. There, such people, however marked by economic prosperity and contacts with the outside world, have not 'questioned traditional values about caste, marriage and status of women....Intercaste marriages are still taboo and marriage itself is more a bond between families than between individuals'.

Caste in Ramkheri is still recognisable to someone who knew it in 1954, for change has occurred through a realignment of those ideas about rank and equality to which I have already referred. Their proportions have changed, with the ideas of hierarchical rank less ostensibly expressed, and with a spreading sphere of equality. But just as in 1954, it is difficult to assess how great has been the change. I have suggested, for instance, that the shying away from the use of the word *jat* implies a change in the value given to inequality: but one might also suggest that other words used in its place are part of a code which is generally understood, through which unequal relations continue to be expressed although in more neutral ways. As in 1954, the problem with assessing the strength of caste lies in deciding the weight to give to the 'ingredients' involved. But, whatever one's judgment, it seems clear that changes in village society, and the bases for inequality, will continue to include caste as a component for some time to come.

References

Bailey, F.G. 1963. 'Closed social stratification in India.' *European Journal of Sociology* 4:107-24.

Béteille, A. 1991. 'The reproduction of inequality.' *Contributions to Indian Sociology* (n.s.) 25:3-28.

———. Caste and family.' *Anthropology Today* 8, 1:13-18.

Bouglé, C. (trans. D.F. Pocock). 1971. *Essays on the caste system.* Cambridge: Cambridge University Press.

Bronger, D. 1991. 'Ramkheri 1955-Jamgod 1990.' *Erdkunde* 45:291-307.

Dumont, L. 1970. *Homo hierarchicus: the caste system and its implications.* London: Weidenfeld and Nicolson.

Kolenda, P. M. 1978. *Caste in contemporary India.* Menlo Park: Benjamin-Cummings.

Kulkarni, S. 1991. 'Rise of the ruppy.' *Sunday Observer*, 17-23 November:7.

Mayer, A.C. 1960. *Caste and kinship in central India: a village and its region.* London: Routledge and Kegan Paul.

———. 1973. *Peasants in the Pacific.* London: Routledge and Kegan Paul.

Srinivas, M.N. 1966. *Social change in modern India.* Berkeley: University of California Press.

Chapter 3

AT THE THRESHOLD OF UNTOUCHABILITY:
PALLARS AND VALAIYARS IN A TAMIL VILLAGE

Robert Deliège

The village of Alangkulam is located about four kilometres away from
Manamadurai, a small town in Pasumpom Muthurama Linga Thevar
(formerly Ramnad) District, Tamilnadu. Sociologically, the village is
fairly atypical since the vast majority of its population belongs to two
castes only: the 'untouchable' Pallars and the 'non-untouchable'
Valaiyars. This is striking since in the Tamil caste hierarchy, the Pallars
are generally considered the highest among the 'untouchables' whereas
the Valaiyars are undoubtedly among the lowest of the non-untouchable
castes. In other words, Alangkulam is a privileged area in which to
study what happens on the verges of the so-called 'pollution line'. The
question then arises as to why Pallars are considered untouchables
whereas Valaiyars are not? Is there an absolute criterion which explains
this difference or is it fairly arbitrary? It is however beyond the scope of
this article to analyse the historical conditions which led to the official
classification of certain castes as 'scheduled' whereas other ones were
not. A history of untouchability and untouchables has yet to be written.
We shall thus content ourselves with analysing the present situation as
observed in Alangkulam and I shall focus on the relations and differences between the two castes.

Untouchables as a category

The use of the concept of untouchability by anthropologists is fairly
loose. First of all, we speak indistinctively of 'Untouchables', 'Scheduled Castes' and 'Harijans'. In most cases, we are reasonably justified
in confusing administrative categories ('Scheduled Castes') with
sociological ones ('Untouchables'). Consider, for example, the case of
the Sakkiliyars. These shoemakers of Tamilnadu are a very low caste
indeed and by any criteria, it is clear that they are 'untouchable'. Their

classification as a 'Scheduled Caste' by the Indian government was surely uncontroversial. But untouchables do not form a homogeneous category. As is well-known, they are themselves divided into a multitude of castes which are more or less hierarchised and, in any case, strongly differentiated. Thus, for example, the very lowest castes resemble the various gypsy groups which live outside society; in Tamilnadu, this is the case of the Kuravars. At the other end, the highest castes do not perfectly fit a strict definition of untouchability; this is clearly the case with the Pallars who are mainly agricultural labourers and whose association with ritual pollution is rather unclear. In an important study on Coimbatore district, den Ouden (1975) has well illustrated the heterogeneity of the different untouchable castes and the higher status of the Pallars, who have a much closer relationship with the dominant Kavuntars than the other untouchable castes or even the Valaiyars themselves.

This heterogeneity of untouchable castes is further illustrated by the absence of a traditional vernacular concept to denote them as a single group. The term *chandala,* used in the Sanskrit literature, has probably never been used by ordinary people and, in any case, we do not know to which specific castes it applied, more especially because the sacred literature contains several other terms to designate people even lower than the *chandala*s. Terms such as *tindajati* in Tamil and *achut* in Hindi probably only became widespread during the colonial period. This is also so for some caste names such as Ad-Dharms, Adi-Andhras or Adi-Dravidas, which became popular in the early twentieth century to legitimise social protest by 'assuming that the Aryan conquest, not inherent pollution, reduced the Untouchable to a low status' (Zelliot 1992:57, 200). What is even clearer, however, is that all the words commonly used today to denote these lowest sections of the Indian population, such as 'Untouchables', 'Harijans', 'Scheduled Castes' and 'Dalits', are recent coinages.

Moreover, the concept of untouchability is a relative one. In a way, one can say that, within Indian society, everyone is to some extent or, in some circumstances, untouchable. This is the case for a mourning Brahman or, as is now well known, for Brahman funeral priests. In theory, however, there are some social categories which are made permanently impure (and therefore untouchable) by reason of their professional or ritual association with organic pollution, demons and death. Yet, this criterion of ritual pollution is insufficient to decide which caste is or is not untouchable. Barbers and washermen, for example, fulfil polluting tasks and perform all sorts of rituals associated with death, and yet their status is never as low as that of some castes which are traditionally held to be untouchable. Ritual pollution is thus not a sufficient criterion to decide whether a group is untouchable or not, for it must *also* be economically weak (in comparison to others) and socially deprived (Béteille 1969:6).

Although, in the pre-colonial period, there was probably no single term to embrace all the castes now labelled as untouchable, we have other evidence which tends to show that a part of the population was considered as different. In Tamilnadu, for instance, the sharp contrasts among the *agraharam* (Brahman settlement), the *ur* (village) and the *cheri* (untouchable hamlet) strongly point to such a difference: in no case were the lowest castes allowed to settle in the *ur* itself. According to Béteille, this spatial arrangement reflects sociologically significant divisions among the Brahman, non-Brahman and Adi-Dravida caste categories (1965:25). Similarly, the farm labourers of Tamilnadu fell into two categories: on the one hand, the *panniyal*s belonged to the Harijan castes whereas the *velaikarar*s were drawn from the non-Brahman castes. Their wages and duties were different: the latter had more supervising functions and received better emoluments (Gough, 1989:298, 430). The artisan castes made similar distinctions; thus the barbers of Kangra distinguish between clean castes (*andarke*) and untouchables (*bakarke*) (Parry 1979:73). Interactional relations also tended to distinguish between the very low castes and the rest of the population: in Kangra, all the so-called 'clean castes' accept water and *roti* (bread) at each other's houses, and may be invited to eat in each other's kitchens (ibid.:96). In other words, whereas there is some degree of separation among all castes, and the untouchable castes themselves do not form a homogeneous whole, the gap which divides the latter from the rest of the population tends to be wider and more sociologically significant.

Yet, the fact that there was traditionally a section of the population which was considered as untouchable does not mean that the border-line between it and the rest of the population was clear-cut and well-defined. *Mutatis mutandis*, we could say that although in many societies, 'old age' is a significant category with specific social, medi-cal and economic problems, it is not easy to determine when one becomes 'old'. Similarly, we can now say that some sections of the Indian population were traditionally considered as different; owing to their ritual impurity, mostly deriving from their traditional occupation and their association with death and organic waste, to their exclusion from any significant rights of possession in land, and finally to the various types of social discrimination and disability imposed upon them. This combination of criteria was extremely potent in many cases, as with the Sakkiliyars, but the uncleanness of some other castes was less marked; thus, for example, the ritual impurity of the Pallars was to some extent debatable, while the Valaiyars were allowed some rights in land.

The uncleanness of some castes was thus probably open to debate, but today the protective laws concerning untouchability have con-siderably contributed to simplifying the sociological ambiguity by transforming a relatively open category into an absolute and closed one. Nowadays, untouchables are those groups which are recognised as 'Scheduled Castes' by the government. This classification, I believe, has had important consequences for the people concerned. It has, first of all, created a clear dividing line between untouchables and non-untouchables. All the groups which are 'scheduled' now share some interests and are perceived as different by other sections of the Indian population. Thus, at a stroke, the untouchables have now been stig-matised as separate from the rest of the population.

Hence today, when we say that Pallars are untouchable while Valaiyars are not, we mean that the former are recognised as 'Scheduled Castes', while the latter are not. The government no doubt had some economic and social reasons for making this separation, but it is equally certain that the two castes were socially and economically very close and it is, therefore, interesting to see what differences between them really exist in day-to-day life. We shall also focus on the changes which village society has undergone in recent decades and see to what extent the gap between untouchables and non-untouchables has been reduced.

The village

At the time of fieldwork, which was undertaken during the six months January-June 1989, the Alangkulam population of 257 people living in two hamlets was divided into four castes.[1] Valaiyars and Pallars constituted the bulk of the population with 131 (51 per cent) and 108 (42 per cent) people respectively, while there were also nine people in two families of Vannars (washermen), and one family of Agamudaiyars (also nine people).

The villagers are unaware of these figures and generally assume that both communities are equally represented in the village. Some even think that the Pallars constitute the majority, since they are generally considered to be the first settlers in the place. Actually, it seems that this is correct and that the Pallars were the first inhabitants of the village. The tradition has it that the ancestors of the Pallars lived in a village called Rajageembiram. As land was scarce there, five brothers decided to leave and come to this new place, which they purified with sacred water brought from the temple of Alagarkoil (near Madurai). Soon afterwards, they went to Alagarkoil to offer two goats to Alagar (Vishnu). On the way, the goats disappeared and they could find only one; they prayed to Alagar and told him that if they did not find the goat, they would never pray to him again. On reaching the temple, they discovered the missing goat waiting for them there. They praised the god and named the village Alagarkulam which was eventually trans-formed into Alangkulam. Now it is the duty of each family to go to Alagarkoil once a year to offer a goat or cock to Alagar.[2] My inform-

[1] Fieldwork was financially supported by the Fonds National de la Recherche Scientifique.
[2] I objected several times that Alagar was surely considered, by temple priests at least, as a vegetarian deity, but my informants all insisted that the goats and cocks were offered to him. The animal is sacrificed outside the

ants claim that this story is historical but it has a curious resemblance to some versions of the untouchable myths of origin which also have five brothers as heroes (Deliège 1993b). The Valaiyars settled in Alang-kulam later. They all came from Kalkuruchi, the neighbouring village, which is also the panchayat headquarters and dominated by Valaiyars.

All Valaiyars in Alangkulam are still related to a family in Kalkuruchi whereas most Pallars seem to be descended from a common ancestor. The pattern and circumstances of their settlement in the village are unclear. What is plain, however, is that neither of the two castes can claim any exclusive right to the land. The village clearly 'belongs' to both castes. Recently, a large plot of communal land (*ur purambokku*) was allotted to the village as a housing plot (*nattam purambokku*); this new colony was named Thideernagar ('mushroomed settlement') and divided between members of both communities. Predominantly it is young people who have come to settle in this hamlet which is about 500 metres away from the rest of the village. Several among them took advantage of the land there to establish a brick factory.

In neither of the two hamlets is there a clear pattern of settlement according to caste. Both castes are mixed up and live in common streets. There is thus no *cheri* or untouchable colony here. In the main settlement there is a common handpump which is used by all castes, including the Agamudaiyar family. It is impossible to recognise the Pallars apart from the Valaiyars; nothing in their houses, clothes, speech or behaviour could betray their caste. Even the cultural features which sometimes distinguish low castes from higher ones are absent here. On the contrary, some Pallars are better-off than the Valaiyars and live accordingly; they, for instance, dress in dhotis and white shirts, whereas most Valaiyars wear coloured lungis. More surprisingly

---

temple and the meat is shared by the party. The practice of collective pilgrimage to Alagarkoil is found among all non-Brahman castes of the region who also sacrifice some animals there. Fuller (1992:95) comments that the animals are sacrificed in an outer gateway of the temple in front of the never-opened door of Karuppan, a subordinate guardian of the main deity. I must add, however, that my informants are convinced that the animal is sacrificed to Alagar.

perhaps, the Valaiyars do not claim much superiority over the Pallars. When interviewed by an anthropologist, they might say that the Valaiyars are traditionally superior to the Pallars (which is correct) but in actual social practice this superiority amounts to very little, as we shall see. Besides, some of them point out that nowadays things have changed and that Pallars have risen economically. The structural distance between the two castes is thus very small indeed. This proximity is to some extent acknowledged by people from higher castes who stress the very low rank of the Valaiyars and point to the fact that only such a very low caste would ever agree to share a settlement with Pallars. Nevertheless, the higher castes, as we shall see, never consider the Valaiyars as untouchable.

While both castes are structurally very close, it does not mean that they mix freely and that caste is not significant for them. Even if there is only a slight hierarchical difference between the two castes, they remain quite separate and several disputes continue to follow caste lines. There is certainly, as we shall see below, a form of 'substantialisation' of caste which characterises the social structure of Alangkulam.

There are no remarkable buildings in Alangkulam. The Aiyanar temple, slightly outside the settlement, is now abandoned. Further away, on the banks of the reservoir, there is a temple devoted to the fierce god Muniyandi. Kandaswami, the head of the Agamudaiyar family, acts as priest of this temple. He occasionally gives a *puja* to this god who is considered to be the chief deity of the village, or at least the most 'powerful' one.

The Valaiyars

As already pointed out, the social position of Valaiyars is generally considered as low. They belong to the category of castes, such as Nadars, Izhavas or Kolis, which are 'semi-untouchable'. Many of those castes were able to take advantage of modern opportunities to improve their socio-economic conditions, but not the Valaiyars who, on the whole, have remained poor and powerless. Like many of those castes, however, the Valaiyars' social position displays some important regional variations, which are expressed in their very caste names since they are also known as Mooppanars, Muthurajas, Muthuraiyars and Ambalakkarars. The Valaiyars of Alangkulam are not sure what to call themselves. They all agree that the very name Valaiyar is demeaning, and they tend to reject it accordingly; they have started using the name Mooppanar but this is not yet very widespread. Many people call themselves Ambalakkarars. In some related and more self-conscious villages, people say they would start a fight if called Valaiyars.

The explanations of the Valaiyars of Alangkulam about their origin and traditions perfectly match those of Thurston. Their name is said to derive from the word *valai*, which means 'net', and is connected to the traditional occupation of the caste which is said to be hunting. In fact, Valaiyars specialised in hunting small game with their various snares; according to Thurston (1909, 7:272-4), people say that their low status mainly derives from their catching and eating rats and frogs. Some of my informants tried to conceal this by claiming mainly to catch rabbits, an unlikely claim given the latters' scarcity in the area. Others assured me that only one section of Valaiyars, the Putchi Katti Valaiyars, hunt and eat turtles, insects and snakes, and are therefore held to be inferior.

As Alangkulam Valaiyars themselves do, Thurston connects them to Mooppanars, Ambalakkarars or Muthuraiyars. He points out that the sections in Madurai tend to rank lower than those in the eastern districts, but he nevertheless qualifies them as a 'low and debased class', and notes that they live in separate settlements outside the villages.

It is interesting to note that the Valaiyars' myth of origin closely resembles untouchable myths.

Lord Ishwaran was giving his blessing (*asirvatam*) to all people and distributed sacred ashes (*tiruniru*). The Konars came up with a big pot and thus a lot of ashes fell into the pot. They were very blessed and that is why today many people among them are well off. Other people came with their hands and they were also blessed; today they are also well off. The Valaiyars were fool enough to come with a *valai* (net) and thus when Ishwaran gave the ashes most of it fell on the ground. Only a few particles remained on the knots of the *valai* and the Valaiyars were little blessed.

This myth, which I collected in Alangkulam, is also reported from

Paraiyar informants by Djurdfeldt and Lindberg (1975:222-3). It expresses the foolishness of the low castes who are unable to 'come up' (see Deliège 1993b on the untouchables' myths). This impossibility is further reinforced by the Valaiyars' gift of cursing: the Valaiyars of Alangkulam claim that their subcaste, the Ambalakkarars, is the highest of all because it received from God the power to curse people effect-ively. If, for instance, they say to someone: 'You will not come back', a few days later, the person is dead. One man in the village is particularly known for his cursing power (*rakku*); it is said that one day, as he watched a group of storks flying in the sky, he just said: 'So you are flying together', and instantly all the birds died and fell to the ground. However, this power is mainly used during the collective hunting parties of the Valaiyars. If a man forbids them to hunt on his fields, he will be cursed; so generally, people do not like to prevent them from hunting wherever they go. People say that in the past, they would hunt every day, but the animals were disappearing, so a king named Pari asked them to hunt on a particular day. Once a year therefore, on *Parivettai* ('the day of king Pari'), they organise a collective hunt. All families must send one representative to that hunt and those who prevent them from hunting on that day will be cursed. Because of this power, however, the Valaiyars are not able to come up in society and remain backward.

In summary, we can see that the Valaiyars' self-representation is fairly typical of a low caste: their very caste name is considered dis-graceful, but they do not know exactly what to call themselves. Their myth expresses their foolishness and they are given powers which seem to correspond to the religious powers of the weak as against the jural-political power of the strong (Turner 1974:234). Their lowness is rit-ually explained by the fact that they hunt—and thus eat—small game, mainly animals which are considered as inferior or even disgusting, such as rats and turtles (*amai*), the latter being particularly inauspicious.

This structural inferiority is also marked economically since hunting is not the only occupation of the Valaiyars and no Valaiyar relies solely on hunting for a living. In Alangkulam, hunting, though still practised, is actually a very subsidiary occupation, something like a traditional

pastime. The Valaiyars are poor and, like the Pallars, the vast majority
of them work as porters or agricultural labourers, or fulfil all sorts of
menial services. A good number of Valaiyars own some land, but, as
land is so unproductive in this dry area, it is generally insufficient to
sustain a family and they continue to work for daily wages.

Their low status and economic weakness were insufficient for the
Valaiyars to be classified as 'Scheduled Castes'. There are several factors in Alangkulam which might explain and justify this official decision. First of all, it must be noted that the neighbouring village of
Kalkuruchi is 'dominated' by Valaiyars who constitute the majority of
the population there, cultivate the land and hold the post of panchayat
president. This does not appear to be exceptional in the region. Some
Valaiyar families of Kalkuruchi seem better-off than those of
Alangkulam. It thus seems that, unlike untouchables, the Valaiyars can
'dominate' a village, that is, they constitute its main landowning caste
around which ritual and political life is organised (Srinivas 1971:10)
and they traditionally do not perform the *adimai tolil*, or 'slave work',
which is compulsory for the castes below them. The villagers themselves confirm this hypothesis and stress that in the past Pallars had to
undertake 'slave work' and were thus inferior to Valaiyars. In Pudu-
kottai, the Valaiyars were sometimes referred to as *adimai*, 'slaves', but
they could also cultivate the land as tenants and, as Dirks notes, they
'never became as fully dominated as the Pallars and the Paraiyars'
(1987:270-1). In this region, the Valaiyars 'often lived in their own
villages', and their residential area was called *ur* and not *cheri*. In other
words, it seems clear that the Valaiyars traditionally enjoyed some
rights in the land, so that their social status was distinguished from that
of the castes below them.

A second important point, probably a corollary of the first, is that
the service castes seem to agree to work for the Valaiyars, while they
refuse to do so for the lower castes. Thus, for example, the Vannan
washermen of Alangkulam agree to wash the clothes of Valaiyars on a
traditional basis, but refuse to do so for the Pallars. The economic
position of the washermen families in the village is precarious. Yet they
wash only the clothes of Valaiyars and could not imagine washing

those of the Pallars, let alone participating in the latter's funerary ceremonies. The Vannans thus make a sharp distinction between these two
castes and claim to wash the clothes of 'high castes' only. The Vannans
insist that it is unthinkable for them to wash the Pallars' clothes, that
they have never done so and that their caste fellows as well as the
Valaiyars would object if they did. It must be noted, however, that there
is a serious exception to this rule since the washermen's work falls into
two categories. In the first place, they wash clothes and perform ritual
duties for the Valaiyars of Alangkulam on a traditional basis; they must
be paid between three and six measures of paddy per household,
according to the size of the family or, if the family is landless, they
receive 50 paise per washed item. Given the economic situation of the
village, however, this work is not sufficient to make a living and the
Vannans also wash clothes for some people in Manamadurai. There, the
prices are higher and they receive at least one rupee per washed item.
The Vannans stress that in Manamadurai, they do not care about the
caste of their clients, and wash the clothes of untouchables or anyone
else who pays them.

As stated above, most people of the region whom I interviewed on
this matter stressed the very low status of the Valaiyars. Yet at the same
time, the latter are not considered untouchable. The Vannans are not the
only caste to acknowledge this; members of one Valaiyar family of
Alangkulam, presently living in the hamlet of Thideernagar, work as
cooks at weddings and other ceremonies. They are employed by people
of all castes (though probably not Brahmans, but I was unable to check
this), including respectable peasant and urban communities. It would be
unthinkable for Scheduled Castes to do such work, for they would
surely have no clients.

The Valaiyars thus hold a quite ambiguous position: most people
stress their lowness and yet they are served by some castes and even
accepted as cooks. Den Ouden recognised the same ambiguity in
Coimbatore District where the Valaiyars were formerly classified as a
'criminal caste'. He points out that the high-caste Vellala Kavuntars
rank the Valaiyars as lower than the Pallars and discriminate against
them accordingly. But the interesting point is that here too the Vannan

washermen agree to serve the Valaiyars and therefore consider them as higher than themselves (1975:55). Furthermore, in Irupatur village, the Valaiyars, unlike the Pallars and Paraiyars, do not live in separate hamlets (*cheri*) (ibid.:66-7).

Let me now briefly describe the internal organisation of the Valaiyars, who are divided into several subcastes. The Valaiyars of Alangkulam say that they belong to the Ambalakkarar subcaste, which they claim is the highest. They recognise, however, that there are no real differences between subcastes except for the Naickers, who can be seen begging with a decorated bull and are said to rank lowest; the Putchi Katti Valaiyars are also said to be inferior because of their food habits. The subcastes tend to be endogamous but nowadays men may try to marry women from different subcastes. Yet it is clear that the Valaiyars of Alangkulam have married within a few villages only and have not taken wives from certain neighbouring villages. It must be said that, compared to some Valaiyars from other villages whom I met, the people of Alangkulam were rarely militant and were uninvolved in their caste association. They had vaguely heard about the latter but did not feel much concerned by it.

The Pallars

The Pallars are one of the largest Scheduled Castes in Tamilnadu. Among these castes, they also enjoy a relatively high status, partly because the source of their ritual impurity is unclear. They are not associated with a specific degrading ritual task and mainly work as agricultural labourers. Being quite populous, they were able, in recent decades, to take advantage of their strength in numbers to assert their rights, fight for them and somewhat improve their condition. Apart from a few well-known studies (for example, Carstairs 1957), the *ethos* of different castes is relatively neglected by anthropologists; yet we all know that the values and behaviour of some castes sharply differ from those of others. The case of the Kallars of Tamilnadu is a clear example of a fierce and warlike caste which inspires awe in other communities. I believe that among the untouchables, the Pallars also have a caste tradition which makes them different from other castes. Compared to the Paraiyars whom I studied earlier, they are more aggressive, more socially and politically conscious, more militant and better organised. This difference is also mythologically expressed since the Paraiyars claim a Brahman ancestry (Deliège 1989), while the Pallars are closer to the Kallar model and recent myths associate them with a more martial tradition (Mosse 1985:356). Militant Pallars have started to claim descent from the god Indra.

The Pallars are thus generally considered as higher than other untouchable castes from whom they maintain a certain social distance. Whereas the Paraiyars typically prefer to call themselves Harijans, the Pallars tend to refer to themselves by their caste name, so that they are not amalgamated with lower castes. Besides, the very name 'Pallar' is not as shameful as other untouchable caste names and it is not itself associated with any defiling occupation. Thurston rightly defines Pallars as 'a class of agricultural labourers' (1909, 5:472). Their name is sometimes said to derive from *pallam*, 'pit', because it is said that the Pallars dig the burial pit when someone dies in the village. In Alangkulam, some Pallars referred to this practice to explain the origin of their names and indeed they do dig the pits when a death occurs in the village, but they do not consider this work demeaning and they freely accept it, particularly since they are paid ten rupees each time. Digging pits does not bring Pallars into contact with human corpses, and they would also never remove dead cattle from the village. Theoretically, it could even be argued that, on purely ritual grounds, the Pallars are superior to the Valaiyars, who do kill and eat inferior types of animals. But the crucial point here is that, in the past, the Pallars had to perform 'slave work' (*adimai tolil*) for the community, and had no right to own land. On the whole, therefore, they were clearly regarded as socially inferior to the Valaiyars. This inferiority was spatially marked by their residential exclusion from the village centre, and by their attachment to villages dominated by other castes (Dirks 1987:273).

As the Pallar caste is very large, it is divided into many sections. In the Ramnad region, the most famous division is between Amma Pallars and Atta Pallars, differentiated according to the way they address their mothers (*amma* or *atta*). Both sections are normally endogamous. The Pallars of Alangkulam are Amma Pallars but there are Atta Pallars in some villages of the area. The two sections are not ranked and stress is placed on the basic equality of all Pallars. Matrilineages (*kilai*) such as those I encountered among the Pallars of Pani Pulan Vayal near Devakottai (Deliège 1988a:203), are totally unknown in Alangkulam.

The relations between Valaiyars and Pallars

Although the two castes are structurally very close, the Valaiyars are generally held to be superior to the Pallars. The Pallars' relative inferiority is acknowledged, and probably reinforced, by the fact that they are recognised as a Scheduled Caste, whereas the Valaiyars are just one of the very numerous Backward Classes. To enjoy the advantages the government provided for this latter social category, Valaiyars have to compete with much more powerful and more socially advanced communities. While they are satisfied to be socially classified as a 'high caste', they resent the fact that the Pallars, who are not worse off than themselves, are classified as a Scheduled Caste. This is a typical dilemma for those inferior castes who are very low but not untouchable (Parry 1970).

Within the village, it is striking that the superiority of the Valaiyars, as acknowledged by the Vannans, is hardly reproduced by the Valaiyars themselves. The latter stress, rather, the equality between them and the Pallars. Most people say that in the past the Valaiyars were a 'high caste' (*sic*) because they did not perform *adimai tolil*, but they add that nowadays the Pallars have 'come up' and are better-off than the Valaiyars. This last assertion is certainly an exaggeration but it is worth noting that it was constantly repeated by the Valaiyars who stress the Pallars' economic superiority, partly because there are, among Pallars in Alangkulam, a few people who hold a relatively better position. Two of them are factory workers in a textile mill; they are young, intelligent, and enjoy some influence over the rest of the villagers. On the whole, the Pallars are by no means economically inferior to the Valaiyars, as we shall see below. The Valaiyars surely know that they are ritually superior; they know that the Vannans agree to serve only them. Yet it becomes increasingly clear to them that this relative superiority has become irrelevant and, in any case, it is not (now) a real issue for them. Their insistence upon the equality of both castes and the alleged material wealth of the Pallars perhaps reflects their current material preoccupations.

This stress on the equality of the two castes within the village is, moreover, supported by the facts. The problem of ritual hierarchy in general, however, is not an issue which excites the people of Alangkulam with any passion. They rather consider it as irrelevant and are more concerned with 'bread and butter' matters. That is why the handpump in the village is used indiscriminately by both castes. People go into each other's houses and there are no commensal taboos or food restrictions between them. Kandaswami, the head of the Agamudaiyar family, says that he does not take food from the other castes because he is the *pusari* of the Muniyandi temple, but his married sons are close friends with some Pallars, go to their houses and eat there. His family also takes water from the village handpump.

The Valaiyars have little opportunity to express their alleged former superiority, and, as seen above, they do not really bother about it. The striking feature of inter-caste relationships within the village is that there is no organic link between the different communities, which do not depend upon each other, on either economic or ritual grounds. More importantly, both communities are co-resident in the village but do not interfere in each other's lives. There is a sort of village committee which is composed of members of both castes, but I have not seen it functioning and its activities must be very limited. The committee is in charge of collecting funds for religious festivals but in recent years no such event has been organised. The Aiyanar temple lies in a pitiful state of deterioration, and I have attended a seance at the Muniyandi temple when the deity possessing its priest complained that the poverty of the village was caused by the people's failure to organise a festival in his honour; the rather frightening Muni also confessed that he was responsible for the deaths of many babies. Both he and Aiyanar are said to look after the 'village', that is, both its communities. The temples are outside the village boundaries which the gods are said to protect, although Aiyanar is said to look after cultivation and to protect the banks of the reservoir as well. The solidarity of the village is also expressed when a villager dies; then all the others should take one day off, express their sympathies to the family of the deceased by offering a garland, and, in most cases, accompany the corpse to the burial ground. The village committee also has to organise the sale of the communal firewood, but this had not been done for a few years owing to a dispute. The committee also decides when someone is allowed to use the waters of the reservoir for irrigation.

There is no official headman in the village. The Valaiyars have nobody who seems to be granted any sort of precedence. This is because they have close links with Kalkuruchi where there are some people who head the community, like the panchayat president and some other well-off farmers. On the other hand, a few Pallars have risen to a certain status within the community of Alangkulam. They are not official leaders but are nevertheless influential and involved in most village matters.

For the most part, the practice of untouchability is absent in Alangkulam. The only traces of it which I could find were in the way people address each other or refer to members of the other caste. When speaking of a Valaiyar, a Pallar would use a respectful, deferential verbal form: for instance, he would say 'Ganesan Ayya' when speaking of a Valaiyar named Ganesan, even if the latter were younger than the speaker. Interestingly enough, a Pallar employing a Valaiyar worker on his brick factory would not give straightforward orders to him and would certainly not use the form *poda*, *wada* ('go, come') as he would with other lower-caste workers. Some Pallars even referred to the Valaiyars as 'high-caste people'. Conversely, the Valaiyars never called the Pallars 'low-caste' or 'Harijan', but merely referred to 'the others' (*avanga*).

The terms of address, the practice of digging pits, and the refusal of Vannans to serve the Pallars clearly point to the theoretical superiority of the Valaiyars over the Pallars. We might think that this superiority is a survival of the past for in today's daily social life both castes live in a relationship of relative equality. There are no food or commensal

taboos between them, some people of both castes address each other by
kinship terms, people go to each other's houses, they work in the same
agricultural teams, and so on and so forth. In other words, the relative
ritual superiority which the Valaiyars might have enjoyed in the past is
nowadays reduced to very little and the rank differences between the
two castes have been severely attenuated by the economic progress of
the Pallars and their socio-political awareness. When interviewed on
the subject, people of both castes consistently confirmed such a view:
they asserted that the former superiority of the Valaiyars has now
vanished and that today there is a complete equality between the castes.

Substantialisation

However, this basic equality does not mean that the relevance of caste
has been eroded. Alangkulam might be taken as a good illustration of
the process of 'substantialisation', a concept formulated by Dumont to
define what he called an 'essential phenomenon'. Unlike 'Sanskritisation', however, the concept of 'substantialisation' has been somewhat neglected by contemporary anthropologists, and yet I think it can
help us to understand some of the transformations which Indian society
is currently undergoing. According to Dumont, the substantialisation of
caste is 'the transition from a fluid, structural universe in which the
emphasis is on interdependence...to a universe of impenetrable blocks,
self-sufficient, essentially identical and in competition with one
another' (1972:269). This process is changing the nature of caste but it
has not undermined its importance in contemporary society. One could
even argue that caste has now become even more significant since the
traditional 'vertical', inter-caste solidarity is being replaced by a
'horizontal' one in which different castes enter into competition for
jobs and various social advantages (Rudolph and Rudolph 1967). The
declining relevance of ritual pollution has thus not diminished the
importance of caste. A process of substantialisation was observed in
Ramkheri by Mayer (ch.2 in this volume), who notes the shift from a
universe of interdependence and purity to one of separation and
'cultural difference'. There has never been interdependence among the
castes in Alangkulam, but the situation there clearly resembles the

present reality of Ramkheri, since its two castes coexist as rival blocs
between which the issue of untouchability has virtually disappeared.

It seems that until recently, relationships among Valaiyars and
Pallars were quite friendly and close. People lived in the village without
discrimination and visited each other's houses, and some friendships
also developed across the caste divide. Elections in 1988, however,
revealed differences between the two castes and spoilt this friendly
atmosphere. The election of the panchayat president of Kalkuruchi was
the first event to indicate a political difference between the castes. A
Pallar from Alangkulam, O. Alagar, stood as a candidate against the
Valaiyar candidate of Kalkuruchi. O. Alagar is one of the active Pallars
who has emerged as an important figure in his community. He is of
course literate (and has a Secondary School Leaving Certificate) and he
works in a spinning mill as a factory worker. He is thus comparatively
better-off than other people in the village and he enjoys a fairly high
status within the community. Like most other Pallars, he is a Congress-
I supporter, and he is also a member of the party. In the panchayat
elections, he was defeated by the Valaiyar candidate, Devimurugan,
who also belongs to Congress-I. The election results followed caste
lines: Pallars of Alangkulam and Kalkuruchi voted for O. Alagar,
whereas Valaiyars and other high castes voted for Devimurugan. The
unfortunate Pallar candidate does not seem to be bitter about his defeat,
but the elections have clearly revealed a split between the communities.

There is also a land dispute which opposes the villagers of
Alangkulam to another Valaiyar of Kalkuruchi. This man, named
Manikalai, has sold, as a housing site, a plot of land which the villagers
claim as theirs. Here again it is O. Alagar who has taken the lead and
filed a case against the Valaiyar. Typically, the Valaiyars of
Alangkulam did not get involved in the problem since Manikalai is
related to some of them. Village interests are here being clearly
sacrificed to caste loyalty. Besides, it seems that the Pallars are more
interested in the village as such than the Valaiyars who still mostly look
towards the more prosperous Valaiyar community of Kalkuruchi.

The elections to the Tamilnadu Legislative Assembly further
contributed to tension between the two castes. An incident led to a

violent dispute between the Valaiyars and the Pallars. The latter had received some money from the Congress-I party to ensure the vote of the whole community. The exact sum involved is unclear; the Pallars claimed it was no more than Rs.50 or Rs.100 to be spent on snacks and tea for party activists, whereas the Valaiyars said that a sum as large as Rs.1,000 should have been equally distributed among all families in Alangkulam. It is of course quite impossible to check which version is closer to the truth; in any case it was not the distribution of this money which led to the quarrel. One young Pallar, called Valaichami and related to O. Alagar, was chosen as poll witness at the ballot box in Kalkuruchi when another young Pallar, named Krishnan, presented himself with Valaiyar supporters of the Jayalalitha faction of the AIADMK; Krishnan, who is under 21 and thus not allowed to vote, claimed to be a Valaiyar of Alalangkulam who had recently died. Valaichami tried to oppose the manoeuvre but he was immediately assaulted by members of the other party. He had just enough time to jump on his bicycle and rush to Alangkulam. On hearing this story, the infuriated Pallars moved towards Kalkuruchi armed with sticks, knives and other weapons. When they reached the spot, they found the Valaiyars were completely drunk. Krishnan was the first to be assaulted. He was accused of being a traitor to his people and scolded for always moving with Valaiyars. He was also reproached for not supporting Congress-I like the rest of the Pallars. The Valaiyars started shouting 'caste names' at the Pallars, who replied by giving them 'a good beating'. A bus full of policemen was sent to the spot. The deputy district commissioner was called to settle matters, but he could not come as he was on tour. Finally, the panchayat president, a Valaiyar Congress-I supporter, succeeded in negotiating a compromise and both parties agreed to withdraw their complaints.

The Valaiyars of Alangkulam were not politically united; a few were Jayalalitha supporters, whereas the members of the coolies' association followed the directives of their Communist trade unions and voted for the DMK candidate. Yet, because most people are related by blood, the quarrel affected all of them to some extent. The atmosphere of the village had thus clearly deteriorated, especially between families of the people who were directly involved. This does not mean that life has become unbearable and that the two communities are at war. Quite a few people remain relatively uninvolved and there is still friendship between some people of different castes. Yet there is tension too and some people, especially the leaders of each side, tend to avoid each other. The whole incident shows that people expect some measure of caste loyalty. It also reveals the relative equality of the two castes, and that the Pallars do not hesitate to attack the Valaiyars physically. Finally, it also shows the fragility of inter-caste links and their propensity to cause dispute.

Occupation

In Alangkulam, the situation of the Pallars cannot be taken as typical of Harijans in general since they live there as an almost completely independent caste. They do not (or seldom) rely upon the high castes for employment, water, social advantages, rations, irrigation, housing, loans, and so on. The proximity of a town partly accounts for this particular situation. At the same time, however, the case of Alangkulam is interesting for it shows how the Harijans behave when they are not under the yoke of another caste's domination. Their freedom is restricted by the absence of influential social links, their poverty and their political weakness. These serious difficulties, however, do not prevent them from being quite dynamic and, as we shall see, from closing the economic gap which separates them from the rest of the population. The Valaiyars themselves, as we stressed above, acknowledge the economic dynamism of the Pallars and go so far as to claim that the latter are much better-off than themselves. This claim is undoubtedly an exaggeration but it is nevertheless a clear indication of the Valaiyar perception of the other caste. It also shows how active the Pallars have been in their efforts to improve their lot.

In Alangkulam, there is no trace of the interdependence which characterises the 'traditional' village economy, and as a relatively recent settlement, it has never been characterised by relationships of the 'jajmani' type. Thus each of the two castes is totally independent. It is perhaps too narrow a point of view to assign untouchability to a mere problem of economic dependence as Bailey tends to do (1960:130). Yet it is clear that when the bonds of this dependence are loosened, the plight of untouchability is seriously diminished. We have clearly seen that the Pallars are no longer willing to acknowledge their inferiority and this boldness is obviously facilitated by their economic independence.

Traditionally, the villagers were mainly involved in manual labour and, more specifically, in agricultural labour and coolie work. Thirty years ago or so, nearly all Pallars were involved in those occupations, and this was probably the case of most Valaiyars too. The relatives of the latter in Kalkuruchi are better-off and a good number of them cultivate some land, but this is not the case in Alangkulam where three men hold enough land to be classified as cultivators, and two of them are Pallars. Manual labour is not much valued in India and, on the whole, the labourers share the high castes' contempt for this kind of occupation. They do not wish their children to do such work. The Paraiyars among whom I had previously worked viewed hell as a place where you have to carry stones on your head, and that is precisely what they were doing in this world. Besides, the income from manual labour is hopelessly inadequate and most men have at one time or another striven to improve their lot by searching for a better job. Some have succeeded and today's villagers are involved in a greater variety of occupations.

Both men and women work in the 'unorganised sector' of the economy. Among the low castes, the wages of women represent an important part of the household income and therefore basically all the women work as coolies or agricultural labourers. For some of them, such as the wives of salaried workers, it is a subsidiary and occasional occupation, but most families could not make ends meet without the work of women. Women, however, tend to be confined to unskilled labour and work for daily wages; they clearly dominate this occupational sector.

Table 2 shows the importance of women in the traditional occupations, as well as the diversity of occupations. The first column accounts for nearly half the village workforce, but 73 per cent of the workers here are women. This predominance of women is somewhat

Table 2: *Occupations of Valaiyars and Pallars by sex*

		1	2	3	4	5	6	7	8
Valaiyars	M	8	2	5	10	1	-	8	34
	F	23	-	6	-	-	-	1	30
Pallars	M	8	4	3	5	2	3	8	33
	F	20	-	6	-	-	-	-	26
ALL		59	6	20	15	3	3	17	123

Key: 1. Agricultural labourers, coolies; 2. Brick and tile factory owners;
3. Brick and tile factory labourers; 4. Loaders; 5. Cultivators: 6. Mill workers;
7. Others; 8. Total.

paradoxical since these labouring occupations are traditionally associated with both sexes; yet today only a relatively small number of men are still doing such work. This also indicates an important change within the village economy: the efforts of men to leave these poorly-paid occupations (Deliège 1988b:140). This process is illustrated by the second column which includes two Valaiyars and four Pallars who have started their own brick or tile factories; these small industries can be launched with little capital and therefore constitute a good opportunity for the villagers who are all quite poor. With some luck, hard work and courage, they can thereby become fairly successful (at least by local standards). One Valaiyar family owns a tile factory and another a brick factory which employs both Valaiyar and Pallar workers. Four Pallar families own a brick factory and all of them employ Valaiyar workers. The material situation of a brick-factory owner does not differ dramatically from that of his workers, yet the fact that Valaiyars agree to work on a Pallar kiln also points to some equality between the castes. However, one could argue that the job in itself (that is, making bricks or being a coolie) is more demeaning than the social condition of the employer. The sector employs 20 workers (the majority female) who are mostly paid piece rates (column 3). Fifteen men are employed as loaders either at the new industrial zone of Manamadurai or in the town itself. I have classified them apart from other coolies, because these workers belong to an organisation which has a monopoly over loading and unloading all the lorries entering the industrial zone or the town. The loaders' income is thus higher than those who work for daily wages. Among the loaders, Valaiyars are more numerous than Pallars. One of the latter, however, occupied an important position within the organisation, but he had recently been accused of fraud and met stiff opposition from the rest of the workers, including other Pallars.

There are two 'loaders' associations' (*Sumai Tukkor Sangam*) in Manamadurai; one has a monopoly over loading and unloading lorries in the town, and the other in the industrial complex. These associations are interesting attempts to organise the so-called 'unorganised' sector of the economy. To be a member of one of these associations, a worker has to pay a fee. All the lorries have then to be loaded or unloaded by members of the associations, and the workers thereby enjoy some protection. They are more or less guaranteed some work every day. The association also provides some loans for marriage. At some religious festivals such as Divali, workers are also given some money. Significantly the fifteen villagers who belong to these associations are all males. Whereas most coolies in the unorganised sector are female, once a job gets organised by an association, it becomes an all-male affair. All workers stress the absolute equality between Pallars and Valaiyars within the associations. Indeed, all the members have developed a strong feeling of belonging and are proud of the associations. There is clearly some sort of working-class ethos among the members, the majority of whom also belong to the Communist trade unions. Valaiyar and Pallar members call each other by kinship terms, and, as stressed above, some Pallars occupy important positions within the associations. Yet it also struck me that the bulk of the members were either Pallars and Valaiyars, and other low castes in the region were only rarely represented within the association. The relative equality between Pallars and Valaiyars would not, in all probability, be extended to the lower-status Paraiyars and Sakkiliyars.

Only three families in the village can be classified as cultivators because they hold enough land to make a living, although they too have some members in outside employment. Three Pallars work in textile

mills but only two of them are permanent workers with good wages. As
we have seen above, these two men are considered as important figures
within the village. Their standard of living is not radically different
from the rest of the population but they are clearly better-off. The
seventh column includes a variety of occupations which also testify to
the economic dynamism of the villagers: members of one Valaiyar
family (two households) work as cooks for weddings and other
ceremonies, one Pallar is a contractor-cum-broker and is also comparatively well off, and some men are bullock-cart drivers, masons,
electricians, or plasterers. These occupations are usually less onerous
and culturally more valued than coolie work or agricultural labour; as
they require some skill and/or some capital, they also tend to be
relatively better paid. They characteristically constitute an important
economic avenue for ambitious young men. The income they generate,
however, is fairly limited and people would give them up immediately
if offered a job in the organised sector: for instance, in a factory. The
people of Alangkulam largely confirm Holmström's claim (1976:41)
that the organised sector is like a citadel which everyone wants to enter.
Also evidence of this will to improve one's own situation are those few
people who have migrated: two Valaiyar brothers work as boatdrivers
in Rameswaram, and two other Valaiyar brothers work in Dubai. Some
young Pallar men recently went to Madras and some older Pallars had
migrated to Burma before being sent back to India. It must also be
noted that there are no white-collar workers within the village, only
manual workers. There are also no university graduates, or even college
students among the villagers.

We cannot endorse the Valaiyars' claim that the Pallars are much
better-off than themselves. It is true, however, that some of the better-
off people in the village are Pallars: two cultivators, two factory
workers and one broker, while several young men have recently started
brick factories. It is worth noting that this relative economic progress
has been achieved without any help from the reservations normally
granted to the Scheduled Castes. No Pallar of Alangkulam holds a
government job, none of them has ever applied for a scholarship to a
university, and none of them has benefited from the facilities available

to members of the Scheduled Castes. This is even more remarkable when one considers that the Pallars cannot rely on family connections either, because they have no network of well-to-do or well connected relatives who could help them to launch a business or find a job. They have to rely largely upon their own resources. I also felt that the Pallars tend to be more 'Sanskritised' than the Valaiyars; several Pallar men try to dress well, they are fairly religious, at least some of them seemed to me to drink less than the Valaiyars and they are keen to improve their lot.

Conclusions

The remarks above do not imply that the Harijans of Alangkulam are prosperous and suffer no economic hardship. The fact is that the village remains poor and backward and most houses are built in the traditional way with a thatched roof and mud walls. People lead a very simple life, usually managing to make both ends meet, but they can ill afford many other expenses.

Yet, at the same time, it is equally wrong to represent the untouchables as helpless, backward or lazy, as some Indian middle-class people tend to do. Many Harijans still lead a more traditional life, depending upon high-caste people for most of their needs, and hence the Alangkulam Pallars are not representative of all Harijan groups. But nor are they unusual and they may even be typical of some sections of the Harijans who have made radical progress over the last decades. Lapoint and Lapoint (1985:17), for instance, have shown that the socio-economic progress of the Jatavs near Meerut (Uttar Pradesh) is quite remarkable; among the residents of Garupur village, the Jatavs are inferior only to the Brahmans and are well ahead of the Jats and other castes in the proportion of people who hold a secondary school diploma. A similar dynamism was also found among the Jatavs of Agra (Lynch 1969) and the Koris of Kanpur (Molund 1988). The Harijans are usually tough and hardworking people. They are used to suffering and to living in hard conditions. They know that they have to fight if they want to improve their lot. With a bit of luck, some help and a minimum of capital, they are very well prepared to overcome the many obstacles which they have to face.

It is also remarkable that the most advanced castes among the Harijans are those which traditionally enjoyed a higher status among the untouchable castes, whereas the lowest-status castes seem to have remained the most socially and economically backward as well. At the same time, the analysis of Alangkulam shows that ritual pollution has lost much of its importance in inter-caste relations. The Pallars suffer much from their lack of education, capital and family connections in their attempt to improve their condition, but less from the traditional stigmas attached to them. Typically, people would refer to material conditions to illustrate the plight of the Harijans but nobody ever mentioned pollution or ritual exclusion to me. It was generally held that these belonged to the past and that nowadays, 'there is no discrim- ination'. This is surely an exaggeration, as is the constant emphasis on their fundamental equality from both castes. Yet it is also symptomatic of a change of values. Again, I would not claim that this is true for all Harijans, but certainly the same trend can be observed elsewhere.

The diminishing relevance of ritual pollution has not, however, weakened the importance of caste distinctions. The case of Alangkulam is probably a good illustration of the process of substantialisation, which has, to some extent, reinforced the frontiers between castes by lessening their interdependence. Finally, the case of the Pallars of Alangkulam, like that of the Paraiyars whom I had studied previously, invites us to reflect upon the efficiency of a system of protective discrimination that is meant to support the Harijans. It is very striking that neither village has been deeply affected by it and it is perhaps unfortunate too that the system is largely focused upon government jobs, so that it does not provide much incentive to the many individual initiatives taken by Harijans.

References

Bailey, F.G. 1960. *Tribe, caste and nation.* Manchester: Manchester University Press.

Beck, B.E.F. 1972. *Peasant society in Konku: a study of right and left subcastes in south India.* Vancouver: University of Columbia Press.

Béteille, A. 1965. *Caste, class and power: changing patterns of stratification in a Tanjore village.* Berkeley: University of California Press.

——. 1969. *Castes: old and new. Essays in social structure and social stratification.* Bombay: Asia Publishing House

——. 1992. *The backward classes in contemporary India.* Delhi: Oxford University Press.

Carstairs, G.M. 1957. *The twice-born: a study of a community of high-caste Hindus .* London: Hogarth Press.

Deliège, R. 1988a. *Les Paraiyars du Tamilnadu.* Nettetal: Steylar Verlag.

——. 1988b. 'Job mobility among the brickmakers of south India.' *Eastern Anthropologist* 41:127-44.

——. 1989). 'Les mythes d'origine chez les Paraiyar.' *L'Homme,* 109:107-16.

——. 1992. 'Replication and consensus: untouchability, caste and ideology in India.' *Man* (n.s.), 27:155-73.

——. 1993a. *Le système des castes.* Paris: P.U.F.

——. 1993b. 'The myths of origin of the Indian Untouchables.' *Man* (n.s.) 28:533-49.

Den Ouden, J. 1975. *De Onaanraakbaren van Konkunad: een Onderzoek naar de Positie-verandering van de Scheduled Castes in een Dorp van het District Coimbatore, India.* Wageningen: Mrededelingen Landbouwhogeschool.

——. 1977. *De Onaanraakbaren van Konkunad: De Economische, Politieke en Educatieve Positie der Scheduled Castes (1966-1976)* Wageningen: Vakgroep Agrarische Sociologie van de Niet-Westerse Gebieden.

——. 1979. 'Social stratification as expressed through language: a case study of a south Indian village.' *Contributions to Indian Sociology* (n.s.), 13:33-59.

Dirks, N.B. 1987. *The hollow crown: ethnohistory of an Indian kingdom.* Cambridge: Cambridge University Press.

Djurfeldt, G. and S. Lindberg. 1975. *Behind poverty: the social formation in a Tamil village.* London: Curzon Press.

Dumont, L. 1972. *Homo hierarchicus: the caste system and its implications.* London: Paladin.

Fuller, C.J. 1992. *The camphor flame: popular Hinduism and society in India.* Princeton: Princeton University Press.

Gough, K. 1989. *Rural change in Southeast India: 1950s to 1980s.* Delhi: Oxford University Press.

Holmström, M. 1976. *South Indian factory workers: their life and their world.* Cambridge: Cambridge University Press.

Kapadia, K. 1990. 'Gender, caste and class in rural South India.' Unpublished Ph.D. thesis, University of London.

Lapoint, E. and D. Lapoint. 1985. 'Socio-economic mobility among village Harijans.' *Eastern Anthropologist*, 38:1-18.

Lynch, O.M. 1969. *The politics of untouchability: social mobility and social change in a city of India.* New York: Columbia University Press.

Molund, S. 1988. *First we are people... The Koris of Kanpur between caste and class.* Stockholm: Stockholm Studies in Social Anthropology.

Mosse, D. 1985. 'Caste, Christianity and Hinduism: a study of social organization and religion in rural Ramnad.' Unpublished D.Phil. thesis, University of Oxford.

Parry, J.P. 1970. 'The Koli dilemma.' *Contributions to Indian Sociology* (n.s.) 4:84-104.

———. 1979. *Caste and kinship in Kangra.* London: Routledge and Kegan Paul.

———. 1980. 'Ghosts, greed and sin: the occupational identity of the Benares funeral priests.' *Man* (n.s.) 21:453-73.

Rudolph, L. and S. Rudolph. 1967. *The modernity of tradition: political development in India.* Chicago: University of Chicago Press.

Srinivas, M.N. 1955. 'The social structure of a Mysore village.' In M.N. Srinivas (ed.), *India's villages.* London: Asia Publishing House.

———. 1962. *Caste in modern India and other essays.* Bombay: Asia Publishing House.

———. 1965 (1952). *Religion and society among the Coorgs of South India.* Bombay: Asia Publishing House.

———. 1967. 'The cohesive role of Sanskritization.' In P. Mason (ed.), *India and Ceylon: unity and diversity.* Oxford: Oxford University Press.

———. 1971. *Social change in modern India.* Berkeley: University of California Press.

Thurston, E. 1909. *Castes and tribes of southern India* (7 vols.). Madras: Government Press.

Turner, V. 1974. *Drama, fields, and metaphors: symbolic action in human society.* Ithaca: Cornell University Press.

Zelliot, E. 1992. *From Untouchable to Dalit: essays on Ambedkar movement.* Delhi: Manohar.

Chapter 4

CASTE, GENDER AND LOCALITY IN RURAL RAJASTHAN

Helen Lambert

In sociological and anthropological studies of India, the categories of
'caste' and 'kinship' are the two dimensions of social structure predominantly used to define social identity. Place of residence constitutes
a third dimension. From the perspective of men in the traditional
patrilineal and patrilocal context of northern India kinship and place (of
residence) are not easily distinguishable, since men do not move, and
the former is taken to be primary. As castes are famously endogamous,
kinship is subsumed by caste as the primary social distinction beyond
the agnatic kin group. In the programmatic statement which launched
Contributions to Indian Sociology, Dumont and Pocock took this point
to its logical extreme in arguing that in north India, kinship 'does not
exist in the face of caste' (1970:15). In turn, caste was taken to subsume
place or territory. Following the progressive deconstruction of the idea
of a village as a self-contained totality (Dumont and Pocock 1957;
1970; Dumont 1970b; Srinivas 1987), attention to the defining characteristics of the village as social universe and, more generally, to locality
(place, territory) as a component of social identity have been largely
neglected. Locality-based 'fictive' kinship is assumed to be a rather insignificant convention resulting from the practicalities of common residence whereas 'actual' kinship, being caste-specific, reinforces the
primacy of caste distinction.[1] Thus, from a male perspective, place is
similarly subsumed under caste and the latter taken to be the only
significant component of social identity.

[1] The conventional term 'fictive' kinship will be retained in order to maintain continuity with existing literature on this topic, although it is misleading
inasmuch as all kinship (including 'biological' kinship) is a social and cultural
construction. In this chapter, however, the term 'kinship' is used unmarked to
refer to *all* forms of kinship, while the prefix 'fictive' is utilised to specify those
types of 'artificially'-established kinship relationships which are seen by
informants as distinguishable from those based on consanguinity or affinity.

For women, the important distinction between natal home (*pihar, mait*) and affinal residence (*sasural*) reveals a network of affective ties based on co-residence rather than on caste or kinship. The stress in many anthropological accounts on the putative completeness of a woman's transfer from her natal to her conjugal home upon marriage results from an uncritical acceptance of 'the male ideology of residence' (Sax 1990:508, n.29), despite evidence for the significance and enduring character of her links to her natal home (Jacobson 1977a; Jamous 1992; Sax 1990; 1991; Henderson 1994:15). In this chapter I show that these links are not confined to women's natal kin alone but extend to the natal place as a whole and suggest that, due to a pervasive male bias in the collection and interpretation of ethnographic data on India, inattention to these features has obscured a significant dimension of social identity other than caste *for both men and women*. The varying emphases placed on caste, kinship and locality as grounds for identification with others in different contexts suggest a range of alternative discourses that are available to both men and women and which may be employed strategically. Before introducing some of my own ethnographic data and reviewing the anthropological literature that is relevant to my argument, I offer a small illustration that demonstrates local awareness of women's cross-caste relationships in Rajasthan.

A Rajasthani story (*kahani*) that—in the words of the schoolmaster and American anthropologist's research assistant who recorded it in the region where I did fieldwork—'[shows] how women make bonds with one another' goes as follows (my translation from Hindi/Rajasthani):

After marriage, two women from different castes and different villages came to live in a single village. Fetching water at the well they started talking to each other thus: 'Bhabhiji, in your house do you too grind [flour]?' The other replied 'Yes, it's simply a must (*karna hi parta hai)*'. 'Where did you get your grindstone?' the first [woman] asked. The second replied, 'From Toda [Toda Raisingh, a market town in Tonk District where grindstones are made]'. The first woman then said, 'Oh! Now I realise [lit. That's the answer] that we're sisters, because my grindstone was bought from Toda too!'

While this tale probably seems mildly amusing, much of its humour

derives from implicit allusions to local details that would be immediately recognisable to Rajasthani listeners. In Cohen's reading of a
local yarn on a Scottish island his discussion of symbols and boundaries
highlights the necessity, as well as the problematic status, of analytic
interventions to br:ng out the particular local significance and character
of such stories (1986:5-7, 14-17). Of course a variety of readings are
possible for any text, but the precise salience of this story's humorous
absurdity lies in a shared knowledge of several characteristics of social
identity.

First, the choice of the grindstone as apparently ludicrous mediator
for a kinship tie is far from arbitrary. The grindstone is a core symbol of
women's affinal affiliation and marital role, employed in ritual contexts
that emphasise a married woman's identification with her husband's
household and lineage (cf. Lambert 1994:26-7, 30; see also Raheja
1988:87, 123 for a possible analogue in husking). Grinding flour for the
family's meal is a laborious task that is most appropriately performed
by the wives, not the daughters or sisters, of a household. This
introduces the second and main theme of the story relevant to my
argument: the phenomenon of sisterhood recognition among women
married into the same village. Below I discuss the customs through
which honorary kin relationships may be established between women
of different castes in their conjugal village. The third salient characteristic of the story is the use of a locational referent (to Toda) as the
source of the common link between the women. In Rajasthan, as
throughout India, the first question to be asked a stranger is not 'What
caste are you?', 'What is your name?' or, 'What do you do?', but
'Where are you from?'[2] The purpose of this enquiry is to establish
grounds for any possible connection between the speakers.

The particular humour of the story plays upon assumed familiarity
with these aspects; moreover, although I do not know the immediate

[2] In Rajasthani the question is literally translated as 'Which is your
village?', though its meaning is more appropriately rendered by the Indian
English, 'What is your native place?' The use of the term 'village' in various
Indian languages to denote place of origin reinforces the argument made in this
article concerning the salience of 'native' locality, for which the village is
paradigmatic.

source of the story, one way of reading it is as a specifically masculine evaluation of female-female modes of establishing and valuing these types of relationships, since its humour derives from a caricaturing of these modes. The story's use of an unlikely link as a means for two women to establish sisterhood plays on a much more general phenomenon. In rural Rajasthan, 'fictive' kinship may be established between unrelated married women of different castes in their conjugal villages and is also recognised to exist automatically between women who come from the same natal place. Before describing the local forms and types of these institutions and other ethnographic evidence concerning 'fictive' kinship and the salience of village identity among Rajasthanis, a short account of the ethnographic context of these observations is in order.

A Rajasthani village and its honour

My field research was conducted primarily in Chawandiya, a multi-caste village in Tonk District about one hundred kilometres south-west of Jaipur city, the state capital of Rajasthan. Because my primary concern at the time was ethnomedicine and healing, the village *per se* was not initially a prominent focus of study since much of my attention was focused on local and regional therapeutic practitioners, sites and networks.[3] Chawandiya was formerly a *khalsa* village under direct control of Jaipur State, rather than a part of a subsidiary landlord's *jagir* (the Solanki Rajputs resident in the village are originally migrants from the southern kingdom of Toda Raisingh and were never *jagirdar*s of the village). It is twelve kilometres along a rough track from Diggi, the nearest town which contains a temple of Kalyanji that is a major regional pilgrimage centre. Chawandiya is the panchayat headquarters for a group of seven villages and in 1985 had a population of 1,347 residents living in 189 households within 161 houses. There were 19

[3] A fifteen-month stay in Chawandiya in 1985-6 was preceded, first, by a year of residence in Jaipur interspersed with field trips to various Rajasthani locations and second, a period of stay of roughly two months in a couple of villages some fifteen miles to the north of Chawandiya before the latter became my primary fieldwork site. This research for my doctoral thesis (Lambert 1989) was supported by the Social Science Research Council of the U.K., now the Economic and Social Research Council.

resident castes, of whom the Gujars and Bairwas (Chamars) were easily the most numerous, followed by a 'secondary' bloc comprising Mahajans (Banias), Thakurs (Rajputs), Swamis, Ahirs, Kumhars, Minas (technically a Scheduled Tribe, but locally assimilated as a low but clean caste) and Nais. The other castes, smaller in number, were Brahman, Vishnu Swami, Lakskar, Khati, Daroga, Balai, Regar, Khatik, Bhil and Mehtar, and there were two Sayid (Muslim) households.

Almost every household in the village owned some land. Possession of land and size of landholding are less crucial economically in this arid region than access to water (through proximity to a canal branch or the existence of reliable wells on the land) and soil quality, some areas having too high a salt content to produce good yields. Thus although there were very few completely landless families, there were many more whose land was relatively unproductive. The substantial land-owning castes who also owned good wells and had well-situated landholdings were the Rajputs, Brahmans and Banias, as well as some Ahirs and Gujars. The Rajput and Bania castes in particular accordingly had disproportionate influence in the village and appeared to be the most prominent patrons (*jajmans*), while the richest family in the village was Ahir; by contrast, the relatively numerous Bairwas generally had very small amounts of fairly unproductive land. The great majority of villagers were engaged in subsistence agriculture; livestock is an important element of the economy, especially for wealthier sections and for Gujars, whose herdsmen graze village flocks of sheep and goats as far as Uttar Pradesh and Madhya Pradesh for several months of the year once local grazing becomes exhausted. Until about 1982, the elected panchayat head was a Bania, following which a Gujar was elected for the first time. The apparent decline in Bania prominence would seem to be related to their gradual withdrawal from village life as they have established businesses (and in the case of the former headman, a factory) and residences in Kota and Jaipur. Thus although Gujars would seem, among the possible candidates, the most likely to hold a position of dominance and their political prominence seemed to me to be growing, the spread of land ownership and wealth in the village was such that there was no single clearly dominant caste.

During a return visit to the village in 1995, certain changes were evident; there appeared to be sharpening economic differentiation both within the larger castes and along the traditional divide between the 'higher' and 'lower' (clean and untouchable) caste blocs, together with a relaxation on commensal restrictions between higher castes such as the Banias and Rajputs. The Gujar panchayat head had stepped down when the post became reserved for a woman's seat and the election had just been won for the BJP—across caste lines—by the wife of an increasingly wealthy Rajput, whose father was generally socially res-pected. The limited number of educated women had vastly restricted the possible range of candidates and the only rival candidate had been another Rajput wife. Any intention that the reservation of such seats would have an impact on women's social and political status seemed unlikely to be fulfilled, however, since it was universally assumed that the new *sarpanch*'s husband would in fact perform the relevant duties, while the *sarpanch* herself told me that while she would attend public meetings as necessary in order to be adequately informed, her role would be confined to listening as she would naturally remain veiled and silent (see below).

Despite some recent changes, then, Chawandiya is a relatively old-fashioned place in which 'traditional' ideas and practices concerning caste, marriage and other features of social life remain prevalent. This in part is due to fairly low literacy levels (especially among women) and economic status, relative isolation from urban influences and the slow pace of modernisation and infrastructural development in this region of former princely states (attested to in Chawandiya by the lack of facilities such as a road, public transport and electricity at the time of fieldwork, a situation changed only in the form of a daily private bus service—though still no road—and electricity connections to around a dozen houses a decade later. Nevertheless it shares many features in common with numerous other Indian villages and the material dis-cussed in this chapter is as much a part of India's contemporary reality as those places and people that have witnessed more dramatic changes.

All Rajasthani married women practise *ghunghat*, veiling in the presence of the husband and all affinal kin senior to the husband, as well as all males in the conjugal village older than the husband. Beyond the specific respect relationships that this practice denotes, it immediately marks off women who are village 'sisters' (*bai*) and do not veil, from in-married women. Only Rajput women also maintain full *parda* (seclusion from unrelated males) and all except Rajput, Bania and Brahman women participate extensively in agricultural work. Child marriage is customary except among Brahmans and Banias and, increasingly, Rajputs and Lakskars. Other castes tend to marry between the ages of two and fourteen, Gujars and Kumhars having a particular preference for multiple sibling-set and collateral-set marriages (see Kolenda 1978, for an account of such alliances among Jats in Jaipur District). Brides do not normally take up residence in their husbands' households until after the attainment of puberty and brief visits are interspersed for the first few years with long periods of residence in their natal homes. Women's links with their natal homes continue to be valued, and the importance of female labour in all but the highest castes means that a woman may be in demand from both natal and conjugal households at peak agricultural periods (cf. Jacobson 1977a:278-9); enduring ties with the natal home are also maintained throughout most women's lives, particularly through the ritual relations between brothers and sisters (see Jamous 1992 for an account of these relationships among the Meo that is entirely congruent with my own observations from another part of Rajasthan). It is in the context of women's relations with persons from their natal villages that locality-based kinship becomes most visible, and it is primarily through women that village cross-caste ties beyond the politico-economic sphere are articulated for men.

For example, the occasions when village, as contrasted with caste, solidarity, become most evident are those which involve its honour (*gamv ki nak*, literally, 'the nose of the village')—which rests on the behaviour of its women. Among men, supra-caste solidarity is mobilised precisely in relation to their *communal* claims on in-marrying women from other villages. Among Rajasthani Gujars and certain lower castes there is a system of divorce, remarriage and compensation known as *nata*. A woman's first set of affines are compensated by the second set if a marriage fails and the woman remarries, regardless of responsibility. The most common circumstance that precipitates *nata* is some kind of felt incompatibility between the couple at an early stage in the marriage leading to the husband's rejection of his bride, even prior to or most often following the first short conjugal visit. *Nata* following the birth of children is relatively rare, though it may occur after the death of a young husband (any offspring remain with their father's household, to whose lineage they are considered unequivocally to belong). Occasionally, however, a woman rejects her husband by eloping with another man, in a form of marriage-by-capture.

During my stay in Chawandiya, a young Gujar woman from a nearby village absconded with a Gujar man who had been staying there. She was married into a Chawandiya family but had not yet begun residing there (thus, the couple had not consummated the marriage) and was the eldest of four village daughters married in childhood to four sons of Chawandiya. The set included the husband's younger brother, who was married to the eloping girl's younger sister. With remarkable speed a large group of younger village men, armed with heavy sticks, were mobilised and a tractor and flat-bed trailer found (no resident owned such equipment) to transport them in pursuit of the eloping couple. The imperative was to stop the couple and recapture the bride before they reached the man's own natal village. Otherwise they would be unlikely to retrieve the bride for having reached the man's village, it would be considered a matter of *that* village's honour (*nak*) that no woman be taken away. Gujar informants stated that all castes would join in to save 'the village's nose' in such cases. It was also claimed that men from every caste can and do go to fetch back a woman; on the party's return I noticed among the Gujar men a Rajput and a Nai.

Despite the relative caste-specificity of this set of circumstances, the villagers involved in this incident were understood as acting as a single body to defend the honour jeopardised by the elopement.[4] The term for

---

[4] Chawandiya was, to conclude the story, successful; passing through another village to the north, some residents became suspicious and locked the young woman in a room. The village party retrieved the woman and took her back to her natal village. Thinking of another kind of 'honour', I was surprised to find her mother-in-law insisting that the bride would, in due course, be

village honour—*gamv ki nak*, the 'nose of the village'—is well known
but rarely provokes comment or analysis. It seems to rest on an implicit
conception that the village possesses a single moral reputation, or
'face', the integrity of which can be threatened and requires collective
defence. Another somatic image is reported by Lewis who notes that in
Uttar Pradesh village factions are locally known as *dhar*, literally, 'the
upper part of the body' (1969:158). The metaphorical use of another
term denoting a portion of the body to refer to one part of the village
population carries a similar implication that altogether, village residents
comprise the whole, or 'corporate body' (Mandelbaum 1970:334).

The identification with village expressed through such terms may be
linked in turn to the ecological understanding of relations between
person and environment or place that is a central concern of Ayurveda
(Zimmerman 1987) and Indian philosophical traditions (Sax 1990:494).
Villagers attribute importance to the micro-environment that they share,
persons and the water and soil of their particular residence being held to
interact mutually (cf. Daniel 1984). In Rajasthan, notions of appropriateness in relation to the maintenance of health were extremely
important and only the water of one's own village was considered
entirely suited to the bodily constitution of residents. Ill health
following visits elsewhere was frequently attributed to having drunk the
water of other places. Among ethnosociologists much emphasis has
been placed on the concept of 'substance-code' as an illuminating
characterisation of Hindu ideology and a few anthropologists have
considered the idea of a residentially determined code-for-conduct (see
Daniel 1984, and Sax 1990:494-5; 1991:73-7 for a review of work that
considers 'locationism'), but the idea of locality-specific social identity—concordant with substance shared through a common micro-
environment—has generally been de-emphasised since the demise of
village studies. Such locality-related social identity would necessarily
run counter to hierarchical distinctions.

---

accepted into her household as her son's wife, although she did not arrive
before I left the village.

'Fictive' kinship

In rural Rajasthan as elsewhere in north India (cf. Mayer 1960:144-6; Marriott 1969:177-8; Mandelbaum 1970:151-2), kin terms are used to refer to all village co-residents.[5] Beyond this village kinship, institutions of 'fictive' kinship of particular salience to women are of two types: 'fictive' kin relations between married women and all other persons (including women married into the same place) who come from the same natal village—clearly itself an extension of village-based 'fictive' kinship—and formalised adoptive kin relationships between individual married women and otherwise unrelated individual families. The latter type initially became known to me when, on entering the courtyard of a Gujar household one day, I found, to my astonishment, the matriarch of a Rajput family in the village having lunch with the most senior Gujar woman of the house. The Rajput woman (whom I had never before seen outside her home, since she normally kept *parda*) announced that her elderly Gujari companion was her 'mother'. I subsequently learned that the formation of such honorary kinship ties is a well-established practice, especially for Rajasthani women who are married into villages where they do not already have consanguineal relatives. In such cases (and perhaps in others) a fictive kin relationship with another household may be established, apparently regardless of caste. The adoptive mother-daughter tie was particularly emphasised by women informants and the two women involved in such a relationship may share the same *pihar* (natal) village (which would conform to the natal village-derived type of cross-caste kinship to be discussed below and emphasises the salience of locality as a basis for affiliation), but this is not invariably the case. However all members of the adopting household become consanguineal kin of the in-married woman and indeed, when such an adoptive relationship is instituted on the occasion of her marriage, it is the adoptive father who, taking her on his lap,

---

[5] I take this form of generalised 'fictive' kinship among all village co-residents to be common knowledge and so do not describe it in greater detail here. That it may have structural significance is suggested, for example, by Jamous's observation that among the Meo of Rajasthan, 'a man may not marry within his clan, *his village, or his mother's village*' (1992:54, my emphasis).

publicly undertakes to treat her henceforth as his daughter.

These formal adoptive relationshipsare known as *jholi* or *dharm* (see below) and are permanent, extending to subsequent generations and being recognised in ritual transactions and festive occasions that concern other members of both families. An Ahir (Yadav) family's *navan pujna*, the sixth-day naming ceremony and sun worship following the birth of a child, provides one example. A number of women other than the household members, the new mother's *nanad* (husband's sister) and the household's potter, sweeper and barber *kamin*s were present. Following the ceremony, an older Rajput woman followed the new mother to her confinement room carrying a plate containing clothes and toys as gifts to mother and baby. She decorated the doorway by putting a string of silver-coloured paper over the door frame and sticking up coloured paper paintings known as *satya* that commemorate the birth of a child. After presenting the new mother with her gifts, she was in turn presented with a new *orhni* (veil) by the other women of the household. This was, I was told, because she was the mother's *dharm ki bahin* ('honorary sister') as a result of having made this woman's mother-in-law (*sasu*) her own 'mother' (*dharm ki ma*). It was also explained that if a woman has no mother, she can if she wants 'take a mother' (*j(h)oli lena, jholi mem lena*) in this way, the 'mother' being known as *jholi*. (The use of consanguineal kin terms despite the affinal relationship between the two Ahir women is discussed below.)

The standard meaning of *jholi* is 'small cloth bag' or 'pouch'; in Rajasthani it can refer by extension to a cloth slung like a hammock for a baby to sleep in, but is most commonly used to refer to the pouch created by a woman's *orhni* ('veil', 'wrap') when one end is tucked into the skirt at the waist and the material pulled down at the front over the abdomen. The 'pouch' so created may be used to carry handfuls of grain, coins or other small items. It also comes into play on certain ritual occasions, such as the first visit of female affines to their son's bride's village. Following a death in the bride's family, it is appropriate for female affines to attend the *nukta*, a death feast given on the twelfth day after death. On one such occasion, members of the (two-year-old) bride's family clothed each female visitor of the groom's family in a new *lugri* (also 'veil' or 'wrap') and gave each a blouse and five paise, while the young groom was given a turban length. Then the bride's mother placed a piece of *gur* (jaggery) in the 'pouch' (*jholi*) of her daughter's mother-in-law. After pressing her *byanji*'s legs (a gesture of respect), the two women embraced, pulling one another forward. During this exchange men held a towel pulled taut like a rope between them, to prevent the women snatching each other away 'out of affection'. While this exchange could signify the transfer of maternal responsibility alone, the symbolism of the pouch seems fairly explicit; the bride's mother transfers an auspicious (sweet) item into the pouch of her daughter's mother-in-law, just as she transfers the child of her womb into the care of the wife-taker. After this act the affective bond between them is performatively demonstrated. The fact that the women stress this bond while men maintain separation by restraining them, is suggestive of a differential emphasis on affective solidarity and wife-giver/wife-taker inequality and segregation among women and men respectively.[6] The use of the word *jholi* to denote mother-daughter relationships between non-biological kin serves to identify such relationships with the kinship created by procreation.[7]

The informant who sent me the story translated at the beginning of this chapter commented (in Hindi) that, 'The meaning of the story is that in whatever way ties get made, in villages there is a "pouch" (*jholyam*) tradition through which if they wish, [women] may establish a relationship like [that of?] the natal village, regardless of caste or

---

[6] I am grateful to Chris Fuller for suggesting this interpretation, for an observation on the significance of fictive consanguinity, and for other illuminating comments and general support.

[7] Neither Sakariya and Sakariya's Rajasthani-Hindi dictionary nor Chaturvedi's Hindi-English dictionary give this use of the term, though Bhargava's Hindi-English dictionary offers under *joli*, 'companion, associate'. Enquiries about the use of the term to denote this form of adoptive kinship in 1995 prompted references to the fact that in the above-mentioned ceremony the adopting father takes his adoptive daughter 'into his lap' (*godi mem*). Possibly there is some implication here of a connection between this act and the girl's adoption as the 'fruit of his loins'; if so, the association of the term with biological reproduction as proposed above would still obtain although the emphasis shifts to the masculine role.

religion; between Hindu and Muslim too why not if it's desired—in Kacholiya village where I used to teach there is such a tie' (Bhoju Ram Gujar, personal communication). In *jholi* kinship the male adoptive relatives assume the same roles as those of the natal father and brothers in relation to the woman's affines, offering gifts on all relevant life-cycle occasions.Two further brief examples of such relationships illustrate the general social recognition of *jholi* kinship. An elderly widow of the Rajput household in which I lived made special festive foods to be sent as an offering (*bhoj*) to a locally revered *Sati Mata* in a nearby village, in celebration of the birth of a male calf to her water buffalo. After sending the offerings she fed all the village Brahmans, one neighbouring family of Banias with whom her household has 'relations' (*vyahvahar*), the members of her own household and myself, the village Patwari, and the Gujar family whose oldest female member was the *dharm ki ma* (honorary mother) of one of the more junior wives of her own Rajput household. Here, the 'honorary' relatives are clearly classified as kin and treated accordingly (below I consider other cross-caste transactions between households which refer to the more diffuse type of non-genealogical kinship based on locality). Finally, at the marriage of a Rajput girl, a Gujar man of the village acted as 'mother's brother' throughout (see, for example, the mother's brother's essential role in the *mel* ceremony). He had some years previously become the *jholi* 'brother' of this girl's mother, who had no contact with her own natal relatives.

I now turn to a description of the nature and form of the second, more general type of 'fictive' kinship referred to above by way of an ethnographic example. On the day before a child's marriage an occasion called *mel* (lit. 'affection', 'friendship', 'union') is celebrated, in which a party including the child's mother's brother come from the mother's natal village bringing gifts known as *mahera*. Any women of the mother's natal village who also reside in her conjugal village— whatever their caste—are invited to the feast for this party. At a Kumhar *mel*, this included a young Rajput wife (otherwise in strict *parda*) from one of the most respectable families in the village and a Mehtar woman. After eating, the mother's brother's party 'dress' everyone in the family with new clothes, together with any adoptive (*dharm ki*) relatives of the mother (see above) and those women in the village who come from the same *pihar* as the bride or groom's mother and are younger than her.

This occasion exemplifies female cross-caste relationships of the second type, in which kinship between women of the same village is formally acknowledged. Although this form is clearly a direct and logical extension of the widely documented 'village' kinship that obtains between co-residents of a place, to my knowledge no other ethnographic accounts detail kin relationships traced between or through women from the same *pihar* who share a conjugal village but are not related by birth or marriage. This absence itself demonstrates that studies of caste and kinship have generally taken a dominant, male-centred patrilineal view to be the only one. My material demonstrates, in common with other chapters in this volume, that other modes of reckoning social relations exist which may be emphasised or down-played in different contexts by various actors. In particular, the ties established through married women's natal villages are of strategic importance for women residing in their conjugal homes and may also be used by men for political and economic reasons when visiting other villages where their married village sisters reside. It is illuminating to review briefly other descriptions of 'fictive' kinship, including a couple that indirectly point to the importance of kinship established through women's natal village ties.

Mayer's chapter on 'The village as a unit' (1960:132-47) is one of the few detailed ethnographic accounts of the different forms of 'fictive' kinship in a village setting. The most prominent form in Ram-kheri is 'ritual' kinship established through a rite in which groups of young people 'hear Ram's name' together from a guru and are then considered to be ritual brothers (*gurubhai*) and sisters (*gurubahin*); this form of ritual siblingship in central India is also referred to by Jacobson (1977b:72). Mayer notes its importance as a means of support for women in their conjugal villages; recently arrived brides are often participants and through the rite they acquire a network of supportive fictive consanguines. Women themselves are the main organisers of the rite and are responsible for the selection of partners for their sons or sons' wives; indeed, pre-existing friendships among women appear to be the primary bases for selection of the younger participants. Mayer suggests that the importance of the rite to women may explain why the main emphasis is on the brother-sister tie, 'rather than on the equally valid relation between the two ritual brothers' (1960:140), but the parallel relations that presumably exist between ritual sisters go unremarked.

Mayer and Atal (1968:162) also describe a ritual tie made on the last day of a wedding between the bride and a man in the wedding party (not necessarily from the same caste) who becomes her ritual father (*dharam ka bap*). He will thenceforth present clothes at her children's weddings and the bride maintains ties as if of consanguinity with the members of his household as in the Rajasthani institution of *jholi*. A third, widely documented form of 'ritual' kinship, the tying of a thread (*rakhi*) by a woman on to an unrelated man's wrist at the brother-sister festival of Raksha Bandhan, is regarded as a 'minor' ritual kin tie by Mayer (1960:146). Carstairs, in a footnote to the terms *dharm-bhai* and *dharm-bahin*, appears to accord ritual kinship established by *rakhi*-tying more local importance than Mayer finds for it in Ramkheri (perhaps because *guru* siblingship is not found in this region):

This is a form of honorary adoption of a blood-brother, or 'sister of honour', much esteemed in Rajput history and still observed, particularly among the farming and landowning castes of Rajasthan. (Carstairs 1958:236)

Sharma refers to the same means of 'adoption of a ritual brother' (1980:188) in Punjab, and also describes a practice in Himachal in which the married woman who removes the wrist decorations of a newly arriving bride becomes her ritual sister; this would seem to be a regional parallel to the establishment of a *dharm bap* documented elsewhere.

In all these forms of 'ritual' kinship, relationships may be and are established across castes although, in the case of Rajasthani *jholi* specifically, not across the 'clean'/'unclean' caste divide (due—

according to some informants—to the restrictions on commensality entailed). Indeed it is plausible to suppose that among higher castes such as Rajputs, in which considerations of honour are especially important, the establishment of fictive consanguinity for a young wife in a household of a different caste may be actively preferred, since within another Rajput household the relaxation of behavioural norms prescribed for a female affine and the establishment of affective ties that are consequent on the establishment of 'fictive' kinship, could give rise to tensions in intra-caste relations between 'actual' kin. The pragmatic advantages of 'fictive' kinship by and for married women in their conjugal villages also throws an interesting sidelight on the stereotypically oppositional relationship between husband's mother and son's wife, since it is often older women who arrange such supportive relationships for their daughters-in-law.

Both Mayer and Sharma additionally note that close friendships which are expressed in a kinship idiom and include exchanges of prestations appropriate to brother-sister relations come close, in practice, to formally established ritual kinship. In all the accounts of which I am aware, 'ritual' kinship of all types between two individuals and their families is categorically distinguished from the widely documented institution of 'village' kinship, the systematic use of kin terms among co-residents based on a conception of 'the local village community…as consisting of a core of agnatically related males with their in-married wives' (Vatuk 1969:259). Mayer suggests that, where the use of kin terms extends beyond the village to strangers, it 'is little more than a form of courtesy' (1960:145), unlike the attitude towards fellow-villagers, who are called 'village kinsmen' (*gamv ka rista*) and among whom there are certain mutual obligations. Sharma distinguishes more categorically between the two forms by describing the former, in contradistinction to 'village kinship', as 'courtesy kinship…the extension of kinship terms as a matter of politeness to any person whom one meets in the course of everyday activities' (1980:186).[8]

---

[8] Her definition of 'village kinship' is 'the extension of kin terms or (for in-marrying women) affinal terms to all members of the same village, even to people of different caste' (1980:186).

What is missing from Mayer's otherwise insightful account is any discussion of 'fictive' kin relationships between women although if, as he proposes, such ties are particularly important to them, one might expect fictive kinship between women as well as between women and men to be in evidence. Clearly his account is written from a masculine perspective (he notes, for instance, that unlike real kin, ritual kin cannot shave their heads when a ritual brother dies; ego here must be a male, since only men shave their heads in mourning). Sharma suggests that since a woman's 'social personality' is expressed through her position in the 'real' and 'fictive' kinship systems rather than through her name, 'fictive' kinship is more significant for women than for men. There is, she suggests, 'no room for the concept [of female friendship] in the local vocabulary...[so that any independent relations among women] must be assimilated to fictive kin relations of some appropriate type' (1980:190).

Yet ethnographic evidence either for ties specifically between women, or for locality as a determinant in non-genealogical kinship ties established by or through women, is scarce. Of a village in central India, Jacobson observes that, 'In Khalapur, women who are good friends may become ritual sisters' (1977b:72-3), and above Sharma's reference to the establishment of a 'ritual sister' for Himachali brides has been noted. The significance of women's prior locality-based kinship ties in determining forms of 'fictive' kinship in other localities is suggested in two early accounts from north India which focus on patterns of address and reference in kin terms. Vatuk shows that pre-existing 'village kinship' links between female neighbours are used to establish 'fictive' kinship terms of address and reference in one neighbourhood of a north Indian city. The following excerpt from one woman's description of two such relationships is revealing, particularly with respect to how relationships are calculated, since it reveals that calculation rests on the identification of locality-based connections:

It is the same with the professor's wife next door and the woman across the street. The professor's wife's mother comes from my *sasural*, so she is my *nanad* [HZ, i.e., HFZD], and I am her *bhabhi* [BW, i.e., MBSW]. Her children call me *mami* [MBW]. The woman across the street is married into the village of one of my *jethanis* [HeBW], so I consider her my *bhabhi*. Usually when we start to become friendly with someone we ask first of all, 'Where are you from?' 'Where are you married?' Then if we have any connections in those places, we establish relationship [*rista banati hai*] accordingly. (1969:264-5)

Freed's (1963) detailed study of men's use of kin terms in a north Indian village concludes that it is based on the existence of a comprehensive fictive genealogical system. However, he found that the anomalous terms of reference used by several male respondents were due to the tracing of prior 'fictive' kin relationships through women. Two wives of Brahman lineages came from the same village as the original families of these respondents of other castes and so were related to them as sisters of that village; the kin terms of reference used by these respondents for male members of the Brahman lineages were in accordance with this tie. This method of calculating kin relationships resulted in the Brahmans being accorded greater generational seniority than would be expected from the village's fictive genealogical system; Freed therefore interprets it simply as a means of according more honorific kinship terms to castes higher than one's own, and concludes that most discrepancies between expected and actual 'fictive' kin terms are adjustments to the relative prestige of local caste groups. Raheja's material concerning the same phenomenon (Raheja and Gold 1994:106-20) documents the preferential use of kinship terms according to the tracing of relationships through in-married women's natal villages, or even their mothers' natal villages, rather than through their affines and conjugal villages. Some of the cases documented concern cross-caste ties. Rather than being a matter of relative prestige, this preference seems to derive from the situational advantages (such as partial freedom from avoidance practices and availability of extrafamilial support should tensions or disputes arise within the conjugal household) afforded to women by the establishment of putative consanguinity in their conjugal villages through the tracing of links through the natal village. While the advantages gained by such 'alternative' modes of reckoning kinship relationships are clearest for married women, the appropriate terms and associated behaviour are reciprocally employed and acknowledged by the men concerned.

An implicit but pervasive emphasis on the dominant ideology of caste and male perspectives in most ethnographic accounts may explain the paucity of evidence for female-female 'fictive' kin ties, inattention to the broader significance of women's links to two (natal and conjugal) villages and also, in consequence, a general failure to recognise the interrelationship between kinship established through co-residence and that established through ritual adoption. My Chawandiya material suggests that female-centred 'fictive' kin relationships are accorded local recognition and that the categorical distinction generally made between 'village kinship' and 'ritual kinship' is to some degree a misapprehension. Once women move into their conjugal homes, their ties with village sisters from the same *pihar* become ritual ties which are formally acknowledged and affirmed on the appropriate occasions. There are enough sporadic references in other ethnography to suggest that ritual kinship among women is common, that natal village co-identity is one basis for it, and that these kin ties are established and accorded recognition by both men and women.

Describing village factionalism in India, Lewis notes that nonetheless,

if two men of hostile factions have married daughters in the same village, each, whenever he visits that village, must visit the daughter of the other and pay the customary rupee to symbolise the fact that she, like his own daughter, is a daughter of the village. (1969:159)

Raheja reports the same tradition in her recent accounts of *milai* gifts which are said 'to increase unity' (1988:222; 1994:90). *Milai* is given most commonly,

when a brother visits the conjugal village of one of his 'sisters' (his own *sagi bahin*, 'sister of the same womb', a woman of the same *got* as his own, *or a woman of any caste from his own village*). He is then expected to give her a small gift, usually one or two rupees. (1988:222-3, my emphasis)

She also illustrates how on the occasion of a wedding, *milai* from the groom to 'sisters' already married into his future wife's village is considerably larger, including clothes as well as money. Such occasions are complementary to that of the Chawandiya *mel* described above, which preceded the wedding of a son.

In an extensive footnote, Raheja offers a cogent critique of the general tendency to ignore 'indigenously defined "mutuality" among *jatis* within a village' (ibid.:266, n.14) along lines similar to those I detail below, illustrating her assertion by reference to the use of kin terms between members of different castes reckoned according to relative age, and to the practice of ritualised leg massage by younger women for older women of hierarchically lower caste. Raheja's account of prestation types includes several other references to cross-caste prestations relating to indigenously understood 'kin' ties rather than to economic/ritual (*jajmani*) relations. Due to her emphasis on the 'centrality' of the dominant caste and the special character of inauspiciousness-transferring *dan* as contrasted with other prestations, however, the significance of these components of 'mutuality' (following Wiser 1936) among *jatis* is downplayed. Thus with respect to three types of gifts categorised as 'signs of brotherhood' (*bhaiacara ka pratik*), Raheja notes in passing that *nyauta* (lit. 'invitation') refers mainly to gifts, 'that are given by members of one's own *kunba* [lineage] *and people of one's own village, as well as other "relatives"*, at the time of the marriage of a daughter' (1988:220, my emphasis). Both donors and recipients of these gifts are referred to as *ristedar* ('relation').[9] The implications of including among donors and recipients of *milai* and *nyauta* prestations persons who are neither genealogical kin nor perform services, though, remain unexplored in the analysis. Rather, Raheja argues that whereas *nyauta* gifts are given as 'part' of brotherhood, *milai* 'creates mixture' and is the cultural expression not of existing unity but of its creation through joining

[9] These is no room in this chapter to describe in detail other cross-caste relationships in Rajasthani villages not based on village kinship, or economic or ritual interdependence. Ties between individual households of different castes are described as *vyahvahar*, lit. 'relations', all those with whom 'relations' exist being invited to participate in a household's life-cycle ceremonies and eat on other festive occasions. Atal's account of a death feast in southern Rajasthan mentions that invitations are extended to persons with whom the host had *vyohar*, 'family relationships' (1968:162).

(ibid.:226-7). The giving of *milai* or *mahera* to 'sisters' from the same natal village at weddings, though, suggests the reaffirmation of pre-existing locality-based kinship rather than its creation.

Nevertheless, both *nyauta* and *milai* gifts are taken to comprise a single category of prestation type in that they are given to 'one's own' and thereby stand in contrast to *dan* prestations, which are given to those who are 'other'. As Raheja observes, in the work of both Dumont and Marriott, 'analyses of prestation patterns remain tied to the assumption that exchanges of all kinds are linked in all contexts to the system of rank' (ibid.:240). The inclusion, in the context of alliance formation, of inmarried women from a single natal village in the category of agnatic kin by persons from that village, clearly expresses a concept of relationship on the basis of shared locality of origin in relation to which hierarchical caste relationships are irrelevant.

These relationships of shared locality always take the form of putative consanguinity. In a woman's *sasural* where all her kinship ties (both to her husband's relatives and to other village residents) are affinal, 'ritual' and '(natal) village' kinship takes the form of consanguineous relations. Thus in the example from Chawandiya given above of an Ahir woman celebrating the birth of her adoptive mother's grandchild, the new mother was described as her 'honorary sister' (*dharm ki bahin*) rather than her honorary sister-in-law (brother's wife). Similarly Vatuk observed a widespread preference among women in an urban neighbourhood for structuring their relations according to a model of '*pihar* kinship' (1969:266), with women calling one another 'sisters' while their (putatively in-married) husbands call one another 'brothers'. Vatuk commented that this is not in fact a pattern found in the *pihar*, since sisters' husbands and mother's sisters' husbands would not be present there, and concluded that:

The distinction meant here is doubtless that between consanguineal and affinal kinship. The women...explained that '*pihar* kinship' is favored because it connotes more love than *sasural* (affinal) kinship. If one uses affinal terms, one must be on guard to behave with the proper respect among women neighbors. With 'sisters' one can relax, for 'sisters' can live as good neighbours forever. (ibid.:266)

Clearly affinally based kinship precludes the kind of affective solidarity that is created and sustained through consanguineal kinship, thus necessitating an emphasis on consanguinity where such reckoning is possible. An interesting contrast emerges from Mayer's discussion of the creation of ritual kinship, in which he observes that the emphasis is always on brother-sister relationships and comments that:

It is as if the brother tie, as a main feature of patrilineal kinship, were considered to be too exclusive to be thus contracted, in contrast to the brother-sister tie which is primarily one of affectionate co-operation rather than duty. (1960:145)

The 'exclusivity' of agnatic brotherhood suggests that for men it is complementary to the exclusivity of the affinal tie for women.

Kinship, locality and caste

This discussion of my own and others' ethnography of 'fictive' kinship and the role of locality in reckoning such relationships implies a number of difficulties and inconsistencies concealed within the apparently logical progression in sociological knowledge about caste in India. Particularly relevant to my argument are, first, the assumption that within Indian culture, kinship is necessarily secondary to (or encompassed by) caste and second, the emphasis on *jajmani*-type relations in accounting for, then discrediting, the phenomenon of multicaste village 'solidarity'. The social construction of kinship as described in the preceding sections renders the first assumption problematic. The emphasis on *jajmani*-type relations refers back to the debate instigated by Dumont and Pocock (1957; 1970) concerning the social reality of the village. Their repudiation of the notion of the village as a social fact constituted the first assault on the predominant focus on village life in the ethnographies of the 1950s and was to prove highly influential (cf. Fuller 1989:52). Srinivas took particular exception to their critique of his concept of the dominant caste, but his own defence of this concept (1987) clearly reveals how the apparent reality of the village as social unit could be so easily deconstructed.

Intercaste relations in villages have been described primarily by reference to economic relationships and in particular the '*jajmani* system', an economic/ritual model that emphasises occupational role separation and status differences, whether within a model of 'hierarchy' (cf. Dumont 1970a) or one of 'centrality' (cf. Raheja 1988). Srinivas's conception of village solidarity was predicated on the assumption that it resulted from the inter-caste co-operation consequent on patron-client relations. These enduring hereditary relationships were said to lead inevitably to the establishment of emotional ties (1987:43-4). Although he also described the 'ritual unity' of the village at Coorg religious festivals, the grounds for supra-caste relations were held to lie ultimately in economic dependence, a psychological explanation being adduced to account for the existence of 'community' beyond the purely economic interlocking of castes through the 'productive process' (ibid.:57).

Srinivas's concept of 'dominance' to describe the pre-eminence of a particular caste within a local setting was rapidly adopted in the analysis of other ethnographic data. It was therefore a simple matter for Dumont and Pocock to argue (in their 1957 review of Srinivas's and Marriott's edited volumes, *India's Villages* and *Village India* respectively) that the supposed 'solidarity' of the village was in fact contingent on the coercive power of the dominant caste. However, the 'jajmani system' was itself a construct that conflated patron-client based jajmani redistributive relationships with balutedar-village servant relationships (Fuller 1989). The very phenomenon of baluta-type forms, in which village servants and officials linked to the village as a whole rather than to individual households or castes are remunerated on behalf of the whole village, demonstrated the existence of the village as a social unit in some regions.

Secondly, Dumont and Pocock contended that the actual social referent for a village name is not the whole village but merely the local caste group of the speaker within that village. The assumption that the village has 'a social reality transcending caste' (1957:27) was thereby disputed. Yet Marriott's contribution to *Village India* described the use of agnatic kin terms among co-villagers, followed by an account of how villagers classify co-villagers' affinal villages as high or low, thereby recognising 'the fiction of common local descent which binds the residents of each of those other affinal villages, as well' (1969:178).

Logically the social referent must in this case be the villages rather than the component caste group of the speaker.

Thirdly, Gough's (1969) material on inter-village disputes over land that involved the mobilisation of lower castes by quarrelling landlords was used to reinforce Dumont and Pocock's claim that village solidarity was simply a by-product of dominance; they ignored her observation that some inter-village disputes in which various castes participated concerned adultery. In such cases village unity cannot easily be attributed to dominant caste influence.[10] Finally, they chose to ignore the substantial ethnographic data on religious festivals in which the 'ritual unity' of the village is emphasised (see Fuller 1992:128-54, and Mandelbaum 1970:331-4 for reviews and analyses of these data).

Tellingly, Dumont and Pocock began their critique by acknowledging that the *idea* of the village is a pervasive one held by social scientists, Indian villagers, writers and politicians alike (1970:25-6). The basis for this idea was left unexamined but its very existence implies that local identity is an indigenous value and thereby constitutes an aspect of conscious ideology different from that of caste. A review of the wider background to Dumont's sociological exploration of caste and space over the past 30 years illuminates the main reason for the general tendency to disregard locality. Dumont and Pocock's critical review of village ethnographies in the first issue of *Contributions*

---

[10] Elsewhere Dumont and Pocock further suggest that the 'village community' is an orientalist construction: 'these same western ideas of the "village community" seem to be responsible for a recent failure of legislation in India' (1970:14). They describe the establishment of elected panchayat assemblies as a mistaken attempt to transfer the traditional caste councils to the multi-caste village. Certainly panchayats were often, even primarily, caste-specific, but multi-caste panchayats were not necessarily an innovation. In Chawandiya, the division of a Khati (Carpenter) household was overseen by the *panchadmi* (lit. 'five men', the term used to refer to traditional juridical assemblies in contrast to the State panchayat system). At the house during the morning, six or seven elderly Khatis and three Gujars discussed each household item extensively as they divided the goods into three. I was told that any adult senior households could partipate in *panchadmi* and heard that later on, representatives of practically all castes were present to help decide the division of the house, courtyard, cow byre and sawmill. In another context I was told that in intracaste disputes, the *panchadmi* of that caste is called to settle matters; in general village affairs a *panchadmi* of senior men of all castes, also referred to as the *gamv ke panch*, is called.

signalled the advent of a structuralist approach in the sociology of India. They were quite explicit about their intention not only to bring sociology and Indology together for a sociology of India, but also to advance (through the comparative method) sociology and social anthropology as a whole. The further development of a relational or structural approach was part of this aim. A comment in Dumont's preface to the French edition of Evans-Pritchard's *The Nuer* is particularly revealing:

there is certainly room for distinguishing a territorial dimension or a territorial attribute in the case of certain groups, but one could, I believe, without taking anything away from the real content of *The Nuer*, avoid treating this attribute as a substance, the principle of a sub-system in its own right. In this case, there would be only one system instead of two: a system of unilineal descent groups without a territorial dimension. (1975:340)

This, precisely, is what he accomplished in *Homo hierarchicus*, in which acknowledgement of Evans-Pritchard's influence immediately precedes the introduction of 'The fundamental opposition' (1970a:42) of the pure and the impure as the basis of caste. Recognising that the pursuance and refinement of the structural approach in social anthropology required a shift away from the territorial grounding and micro-contextual approach of village studies in India, Dumont found it necessary to repudiate the prevailing understanding that villages had any kind of sociological (as contrasted with substantive) reality. In 'A note on locality in relation to descent' (1964) Dumont attempted to render locality subordinate to kinship. Yet he was forced to admit that locality is not reducible, in the Ramkheri case documented by Mayer, to an attribute of descent. He concluded that:

At any rate we have to avoid the alternative of speaking *either of* space, locality, territory, *or of* lineage, descent, etc. The question is of losing sight of neither and specifying more precisely their relation: to this end, the necessary terminological refinements may be introduced. (1964:76; original emphases)

Reviewing both my own ethnographic data and that presented in the numerous studies of Indian villages, it requires a conscious effort of will *not* to see there an indigenous value associated with locality, expressed through such forms as the Rajasthani institution of *jholi* (in which co-residents of a woman's conjugal village become 'consanguines'), the attribution of 'fictive' consanguinity among those born in the same place and the notion of 'village honour', not to mention numerous religious institutions and practices that cannot be discussed here.[11] The idea of the village (as Dumont and Pocock themselves noted) and more generally, of personal and social identity as bound up with a particular place of origin, is a ubiquitous notion in Indian consciousness. This is perhaps most obvious in relation to relatively 'traditional' village contexts but the principle of belonging as a relational criterion of group identity is pervasive. It is, however, only one component of social identity. In India as elsewhere, identification with *jati*, kin group, village, language, religion or region corresponds to the particular level in focus. The observation that, for example, the relative significance of caste, kinship (indigenously defined) and locality may vary according to gender and context should seem unexceptionable and the suggestion that villages are sociologically 'real' might sound little short of anachronistic. Nonetheless, despite the long demise of structuralism, most sociologists of India still appear to be engaged in the search for a single (encompassing?) principle through which to characterise their findings, whether it be hierarchy, centrality, substance-code or kingship. My discussion offers a corrective to the predominant approach.

I have suggested that in conventional characterisations, the treat-

---

[11] A few examples from Chawandiya include the village-specific 'mother' deities revered by all castes; obeisance by new brides to the guardian deities of their husband's village immediately after marriage; intercaste village boundary rituals focused on *Ghans Bhairu* (cf. Atal 1968:164-5) and protective rituals for livestock, now falling into decline, involving all the village deities in which every resident must participate for the success of the ritual (cf. Mandelbaum 1970:333-4, Sax 1991:98-104 on Garhwali pilgrimage); and analogous practices such as, in Rajasthan, *mor cuga* in which a communal 'offering' of grain collected from village households is passed over the village boundary, and the process repeated from one village to the next (cf. Chauhan's (1967:227) account of communal village charity through grain collection to feed pigeons and household rotating duties to fill animal watering troughs).

ment of caste and kinship has been coloured by a systematic male bias. A review of the history of theoretical approaches to the analysis of social structure in the sociology of India has revealed certain Dumontian deletions that prompted a general inattention to locality. As a result, the literature has obscured the fact that there clearly are socially sanctioned and ritually affirmed relationships within and between residential localities which cannot readily be accounted for by reference to caste, patrilineal kinship, political dominance or economic ties. These relationships are clearest among women, for whom agnates and affines are not only conceptually but spatially differentiated and as such they bear closer examination, for they seem to imply that views of caste and place may differ according to gender and situational context. Yet this differentiation has been widely ignored. Thus even where locality is recognised as socially significant, as in Fuller's statement that, 'For the majority of Indians, including many urban migrants, the village where they were born and brought up or have lived for a long time is home in the full sense of the word' (1992:129), an apparently uncontentious statement becomes questionable in view of the fact that for most women, 'home' means two villages rather than one (if not throughout their lives then for a large part). Indeed, in northern India the continuing identification of married women with their village of origin is indicated by the use of proper names for women in their conjugal villages that are derived from the names of their *pihar*. Thus the matriarch of a Gujar household in Chawandiya was known ubiquitously as 'Sodali Ma' or 'Sodali Babu' because of her natal home in the village of Soda; Jacobson reports the same phenomenon from central India (1977a:275) and Vatuk from an urban neighbourhood in Uttar Pradesh (1992:82).

My view, however, is not so much that gender must be accorded more importance but more generally that locality—and its expression in the social construction of kinship—is a component of social identity which cannot in all contexts be taken as secondary or subordinate to caste. Through women, it exists as a component cross-cutting caste allegiance for men too, but it is only by taking a gendered perspective on the available ethnographic material that this dimension emerges with particular clarity. As suggested in my account of an event in which the notion of 'village honour' is articulated, some of my ethnographic data suggest an indigenous recognition among men of social identity based on common residence that is not explicable in terms of established understandings of intercaste relations as either hierarchical or patron-focused.

This identity again becomes most explicit in relation to women, but village-based kin ties traced through females may have strategic import for men too. Although these ties may be of particular value as sources of social support to women in their conjugal homes, the general recognition of locality-based kinship also points to the existence of inter-caste networks through men's kinship with out-married village sisters that are ritually acknowledged by men on the occasion of visits to these women's conjugal villages. Raheja (Raheja and Gold 1994:119-20) interprets the privileging of married women's *pihar* ties over their husband's patrilateral ties in calculating kin relations within the conjugal village, as evidence of women's resistance to patrilineal ideology. However, men too not only acknowledge in-married women's 'fictive' and *pihar*-derived kin ties as legitimate, but also reciprocally employ the relevant terms of address and reference, and indeed themselves ritually legitimate 'fictive' kinship relations for in-marrying women as adoptive fathers. These observations might mitigate the claim that this alternative mode is strictly an expression of resistance and suggest, rather, that it is generally available in the cultural repertoire for specifying social relations.

A paper on segmentary caste systems (Carter 1975) argued that hierarchy and 'kinship amity' are not opposed but rather interpenetrate, with either principle being stressed depending on the context. Carter concluded that, 'Kinship amity as well as individualism may provide the basis for relations of equality' (1975:135). The sociology of India might be further enriched by incorporating approaches that emphasise situated multiplicities of meaning as well as feminist anthropological advances in the 'engendering' of ethnographic knowledge (Caplan 1988). The analysis of caste is rewarded by attention to situation and context in determining its meaning and relative importance as just one component in the construction of social identity and the classification of persons. It is important not to assume that there are entirely discrete men's and women's constructions, for just as women can and often do adopt an androcentric perspective in their views of the world, so too men can and do see the world from a 'female' perspective. It is the interpenetration of these alternative constructions which I have sought to reveal in this chapter.

References

Atal, Y. 1968. *The changing frontiers of caste*. Delhi: National Publishing House.

Caplan, P. 1988. 'Engendering knowledge: the politics of ethnography.' *Anthropology Today* 4, 5:8-12 [Part 1], 4, 6:14-17 [Part 2].

Carstairs, G.M. 1958, *The twice-born: a study of a community of high-caste Hindus*. Bloomington: Indiana University Press.

Carter, A. T. 1975. 'Caste "boundaries" and the principle of kinship amity: a Maratha caste Purana.' *Contributions to Indian Sociology* (n.s.), 9:123-37.

Chauhan, B. R. 1967. *A Rajasthan village*. New Delhi: Associated Publishing House.

Cohen, A. 1986. 'Of symbols and boundaries, or, does Ertie's greatcoat hold the key?' In A. Cohen (ed.), *Symbolising boundaries: identity and diversity in British cultures*. Manchester: Manchester University Press.

Daniel, E. V. 1984. *Fluid signs: being a person the Tamil way*. Berkeley: University of California Press.

Dumont, L. 1964. 'A note on locality in relation to descent.' *Contributions to Indian Sociology* 7:71-6.

———. 1970a (1966). *Homo hierarchicus: the caste system and its implications*. London: Weidenfeld and Nicolson.

———. 1970b (1966) 'The "village community" from Munro to Maine.' In L. Dumont, *Religion/politics and history in India*. Paris: Mouton.

———. 1975 (1968). 'Preface by Louis Dumont to the French edition of *The Nuer*.' In J.H.M. Beattie and R.G. Lienhardt (eds.), *Studies in social anthropology: essays in honour of E. E. Evans-Pritchard*. Oxford: Clarendon Press.

Dumont, L. and D. Pocock. 1957a. 'Village studies.' *Contributions to Indian Sociology* 1:23-41.

———. 1970 (1957b). 'For a sociology of India.' In L. Dumont, *Religion/politics and history in India*. Paris: Mouton.

Evans-Pritchard, E. E. 1940. *The Nuer*. Oxford: Clarendon Press.

Freed, S. A. 1963. 'Fictive kinship in a north Indian village.' *Ethnology* 2:86-103.

Fuller, C.J. 1989. 'Misconceiving the grain heap: a critique of the concept of the Indian jajmani system.' In J. Parry and M. Bloch (eds.), *Money and the morality of exchange.* Cambridge: Cambridge University Press.
———. 1992. *The camphor flame: popular Hinduism and society in India.* Princeton: Princeton University Press.
Gough, E. K. 1969 (1955). 'The social structure of a Tanjore village.' In M. Marriott (ed.), *Village India: studies in the little community.* Chicago: University of Chicago Press.
Henderson, C.. 1994. 'Famines and droughts in western Rajasthan: desert cultivators and periodic resource stress.' In K. Schomer *et al* (eds.), *The idea of Rajasthan: explorations in regional identity,* vol.2. New Delhi: Manohar.
Jacobson, D. 1977a. 'Flexibility in central Indian kinship and residence.' In K. David (ed.), *The new wind: changing identities in South Asia.* The Hague: Mouton.
———. 1977b (1974). 'The women of north and central India: goddesses and wives.' In D. Jacobson and S. S. Wadley, *Women in India: two perspectives.* New Delhi: Manohar.
Jamous, R. 1992. 'The brother—married-sister relationship and marriage ceremonies as sacrificial rites: a case study from northern India.' In D. de Coppet (ed.), *Understanding rituals.* London: Routledge.
Kolenda, P. 1978. 'Sibling-set marriage, collateral-set marriage, and deflected alliance among Annana Jats of Jaipur District, Rajasthan.' In S. Vatuk (ed.), *American studies in the anthropology of India.* New Delhi: Manohar.
Lambert, H. 1989. 'Medical knowledge in rural Rajasthan: popular constructions of illness and therapeutic practice.' Unpublished D.Phil. thesis, University of Oxford.
———. 1994. 'The homeless goddess: cosmology, sickness and women's identity in Rajasthan.' *Journal of the Anthropological Society of Oxford* 25, 1:21-30.
Lewis, O. 1969 (1955). 'Peasant culture in India and Mexico: a comparative analysis.' In M. Marriott (ed.), *Village India: studies in the little community.* Chicago: University of Chicago Press.
Mandelbaum, D. G. 1970. *Society in India.* Berkeley: University of California Press.
Marriott, M. 1969 (1955). 'Little communities in an indigenous civilization.' In M. Marriott (ed.), *Village India: studies in the little community.* Chicago: University of Chicago Press.
Mayer, A. C. 1960. *Caste and kinship in central India: a village and its region.* London: Routledge and Kegan Paul.
Raheja, G. G.. 1988. *The poison in the gift: ritual, prestation, and the dominant caste in a north Indian village.* Chicago: University of Chicago Press.
Raheja, G. G. and A. G. Gold. 1994. *Listen to the heron's words: reimagining gender and kinship in north India.* Berkeley: University of California Press.
Sax, W. S. 1990. 'Village daughter, village goddess: residence, gender, and politics in a Himalayan pilgrimage.' *American Ethnologist* 17:491-512.
———. 1991. *Mountain goddess: gender and politics in a Himalayan pilgrimage.* New York: Oxford University Press.
Sharma, U. 1980. *Women, work, and property in north-west India.* London: Tavistock.

Srinivas, M.N. 1987 (1975). *The dominant caste and other essays.* Delhi: Oxford University Press.

Vatuk, S. 1969. 'Reference, address, and fictive kinship in urban north India.' *Ethnology* 8:255-72.

——. 1992 (1982). 'Forms of address in the North Indian family: an exploration of the cultural meaning of kin terms.' In A. Ostor, L. Fruzzetti and S. Barnett (eds.), *Concepts of person: kinship, caste, and marriage in India.* Delhi: Oxford University Press.

Wiser, W. H. 1969 (1936). *The Hindu jajmani system.* Lucknow: Lucknow Publishing House.

Zimmerman, F. 1987. *The jungle and the aroma of meats: an ecological theme in Hindu medicine.* Berkeley: University of California Press.

Chapter 5

THE URBAN DYNAMICS OF CASTE:
A CASE STUDY FROM TAMILNADU[1]

M.L.Reiniche

Tiruchengodu (hereafter TCG), a medium-sized city with about 70,000 inhabitants in 1991 and the headquarters of a taluk in Salem district, is located in the Salem-Coimbatore cotton-weaving belt about 10 to 20 kilometres from the Kaveri river bend.[2] Until 1965, when TCG became a municipality, it was a small commercial centre for the surrounding villagers of this dry and rocky area, but it also enjoyed a degree of fame as an ancient sacred centre. A temple, dedicated to the uncommon form of androgynous Shiva, Lord Ardhanarishwara, is located at the top of the hill which overlooks the town and the countryside; the town at the bottom has been built, according to the classical design, around the four walls of the Lord Kailasanatha (Shiva) temple.

The sacredness of the site may explain why TCG is at the junction of a network of seven roads, but they are of local importance only. TCG has not benefited from the main national communication routes built by the British.[3] Moreover, for its trade in textile goods, TCG has mainly to rely on Erode, 20 kilometres to the west and on the other side of the Kaveri. This does not bother the citizens of TCG very much. As some of them explain, they are the best entrepreneurs and are well-known in

---

[1] The study of Tiruchengodu, Tamilnadu, is a project of the French Institute of Pondicherry, in association with the Ecole Française d'Extrême-Orient and the Centre d'Etudes de l'Inde et de l'Asie du Sud (Paris), entitled 'Urban configurations and trading networks'. For the politico-economic information, I am indebted to my colleagues and friends, who are members of the team: Professor Amitabh Kundu (Jawaharlal Nehru University), Brigitte Silberstein, Loraine Kennedy and Philippe Cadène.

[2] The town had 12,322 inhabitants in 1931 and 21,386 in 1961. It jumped to 36,990 inhabitants in 1971 and 53,941 in 1981, the decadal rate of growth being respectively 72.96% and 45.83%.

[3] The railway and the Salem-Coimbatore trunk road cross Sankagiri, 10 km north of TCG, and the north-south trunk road coming from Bangalore bypasses it as well.

northern India, and they dream that TCG will be selected, instead of Namakkal, as the headquarters of the new district that the government intends to create by subdividing Salem district. It is perhaps surprising, however, that the high opinion of TCG citizens about themselves is confirmed by the statistical data showing that TCG, although a medium-sized town, 'has got linked with the national market and is experiencing rapid economic and population growth' (Kundu 1992:7).

This success, which still remains liable to economic setbacks, is partly the result of history, as well as of a fortuitous conjunction of circumstances, and is partly to be credited to different categories of local people who have found ways to seize opportunities in order to make the best of them.

The town

Like many other places in Salem district, TCG was a settlement of cotton weavers. Before the twentieth century, this weavers' settlement was probably not much more important than those in some other large villages in the area, from where many of the present TCG weavers' families seem to have come during the first half of the century. In TCG, the Mudaliyar weavers used to reside outside the four Car streets surrounding the temple, at the north-east corner near a large space called *pavadi* used for warping (*pavu*). Outside the four Car streets were also located Muslims, several groups of people with Telugu or Kannada origins (Naidu, Virashaiva-Jangama, etc.), oil-mongers, barbers, and much further out, untouchables (Scheduled Castes); at the foot of the hill there was a cluster of families of the former peasant caste (Padaiyatchi-Vanniyar) who are still resident there. Along the four Car streets, mostly settled on the south, were the Shaiva Brahman priests' families for both temples; on the west there were Smarta Brahmans (one or two families today), and on the north and east mainly families of different kinds of Chettiyar traders. In the first half of the century, except for one or two families, the Kongu Vellalar, the most representative peasantry of the area, were not settled in TCG.

This earlier settlement pattern has undergone changes.[4] Within the

[4] Compared with other south Indian towns built around a temple, some

boundaries of the municipality, drawn in 1965, there are small villages and agricultural lands. The ambitions of those who wanted the TCG municipality to become an urban area seem not to have been completely fulfilled yet. However, the town has grown outwards along the main roads through the development of industrial areas (workshops and textile industries) and new residential areas. Among the latter, there are colonies of weavers who no longer had enough space in their old *pavadi* ward, settlements of Scheduled Castes and other poor migrants of mixed origin, and fully residential areas with individual bungalows for Kongu Vellalar settled in the town, wealthy weavers who have become businessmen, and other middle-class people. However, the most significant changes, which are not immediately visible, have mainly affected the trading Chettiyar castes.

Economic evolution

Some of the circumstances that have contributed to the present growth of the town may be briefly mentioned. At the beginning of this century, Mudaliyar weavers migrated to Ceylon to work on tea estates. Their descendants, who belong to a few of the leading families of the 1950s and 1960s, each claim that their grandfather or father was a *kangani* (recruiter and supervisor of workers), and that some *kangani*s, after having come back to TCG, organised cloth-trading with Ceylon through the family members still remaining there. For these people, that was the source of their wealth. Along with a few others, these Mudaliyar then began yarn-trading, and also acted as master-weavers who gave out piece-work to handloom weavers and then sold the product. The Mudaliyar with the means to do so, also used to be moneylenders.

A most important development in the 1930s was the growth of a co-operative movement, closely related to the policy of the Congress Party, for peasants as well as weavers. In 1930 wealthy farmers foun-

---

features of the TCG settlement pattern are atypical. In particular, nobody recalls a ward belonging to the Asari craftsmen. As jewellers, Asari are piece-rate workers for other non-Asari people; as carpenters or blacksmiths, they are mostly newcomers working in the lorry workshops. Although everywhere in Tamilnadu, carpenters and blacksmiths are usually in charge of the temple cars, the Padaiyatchi-Vanniyar claim that they were purposively settled in TCG with exclusive rights to the work.

ded a Marketing Co-operative Society for selling commercial crops (oil seeds and cotton) and to help the peasants with credit facilities. In spite of the ADMK government's seizure of it in 1976, this Society is still flourishing—which is exceptional in Tamilnadu. The staple-food grains of the time, mainly locally grown millets, were traded through the network of regional weekly fairs (candai). Paddy, which was not grown on a large scale in the area, was brought from afar (South Arcot or elsewhere). The Vellan Chettiyar had already engaged in this trade in the 1940s, when some Mudaliyar began to be involved in the paddy and rice business;[5] the paddy was husked in Chettiyar rice-mills in TCG, and most of the rice was sold in large cities like Coimbatore. The Chettiyar then became unable to keep control of the business.

For the handloom industry, however, the co-operative movement was crucial. Weavers of the whole district were involved (Mines 1984) and one of the TCG Mudaliyar was a leading figure in it. The first Handloom Co-operative Society was opened in 1938 in TCG, followed by others in the surrounding villages. The masterweaving system and the Co-operative Society continue to coexist. Moreover in the 1960s, the substitution of handlooms by powerlooms was initiated by the council members of the Handloom Co-operative, who belonged to some of the leading TCG Mudaliyar families. (Today most of the powerloom fabric is still sold and exported as handloom.) The first spinning-mill in TCG was built in 1938, but the local Mudaliyar were unable to keep control of it. Later in 1982, seven of them, all related by kinship and marriage and acting in partnership, opened their own Cenguntar spinning-mill, and other mills have since been founded. From the 1960s onwards, many small units of 10 to 20 powerlooms

[5] As a supplementary occupation, Mudaliyar women were already buying some paddy at the weekly fair, to husk it and to sell rice at home. The development of the paddy and rice trade also reflects the change in staple diet from millet to rice, which at first was much in demand in large cities. In Salem district, the main Chettiyar group involved in the paddy and rice business are the Komutti Chettiyar. There is a fascinating coincidence here: no Komutti Chettiyar dare live in TCG because, people say, having offered to the god a dress which was not purified, they were cursed by Lord Ardhanarishwara, together with the washermen who, since that time, have not had the right to live inside the city.

began to be built in TCG and the surrounding area,[6] and many sizing mills also opened to supply the powerlooms. Although these textile enterprises were initiated by Mudaliyar, they were soon followed by Kongu Vellalar coming into the textile business, sometimes in partnership with Mudaliyar, who put powerloom units in villages. During the same wave of mechanisation, the textile workers began to be recruited from the low-income groups of every caste, including Scheduled Castes.

The peasant Vellalar were heavily involved in other kinds of entrepreneurship, in which we also find some Mudaliyar and other people. At first, they were interested in transport, investing in lorries and buses. An Asari craftsman from elsewhere had the idea of creating a workshop for lorry-body building, such an industry having already started in the next important town, Namakkal. Many workshops then developed, whose owners were mainly Asari and Vellalar. During the 1970s, someone—several people claimed to be the first—brought to TCG a mobile rig unit for boring wells, manufactured near Hyderabad. A big business then started, and the rig units from TCG and the surrounding areas are being sent to bore wells everywhere in India, mostly in Maharashtra, Rajasthan and Madhya Pradesh. Profits seem to be large, but so are the risks.

The development of all these enterprises (including textiles) could not be realised except in partnership; the money invested was pooled through private finance agencies, with one businessman, if influential, controlling several of them. Ways to make the best out of every law and every governmental concession are well-known, and relationships with political parties are useful. At the same time, everyone tries to diversify his activities as well as his allegiances. Last but not least, many enterprises work with sub-contractors at different levels.

If TCG today is no longer a small market-town, it still partly remains what it used to be: a regional religious centre, a market place for the area with its bazaar and weekly fair, and an administrative head-

[6] This dispersed industrial development has been helped by the closure, following strikes by textile workers, of the large units in Bombay and elsewhere in northern India, and by the sale of their machinery to small-scale industries (Kundu 1992; Silberstein 1991).

quarters. But a bridge was crossed with the mechanisation of its textile industry and the development of mechanical workshops, as well as with its managerial involvement in transport and the operation of mobile rig units. All these activities have positioned TCG at the centre of a communication network much more extensive than the network of its secondary roads. They have also generated many other businesses by creating ancillary units for production, repair work and commerce.

Nonetheless, according to popular opinion, TCG's presiding god— with his patrons, priests and annual festival—still remains today one of the main symbolic agents for partially integrating the multiple social heterogeneities which exist not only in the town but also in the surrounding countryside. Although it explains nothing in itself, it is still true and important that the presiding deity of the area attests to the divine sovereignty's permanency over and above social and political fluctuations, and that it acts as an embodied ethical reference which enables anyone, privately or publicly, to be involved in the sustainment of an ideal citizens' kingdom. People partly find in the Lord of the place a criterion for defining a global TCG identity. Partly only, however, since everyone continues to explain what his own forefathers have offered to the temple and what his own caste members still go on doing, in order to claim that his caste group is the one that, from time immemorial, has been the most closely acquainted with the god.

We cannot ascertain what was the main factor of integration in TCG in the early twentieth century, nor whether there was any overlap between the leading people of the time (who might have been the Chettiyar) and those who then controlled and managed the temple. Today, TCG people express a TCG identity of which they are proud in many different ways. Reference to the Lord of the place has not disappeared, but it is not spontaneously to the fore. What people feel proud of, and what is somehow expressed by public opinion as the TCG identity, is the economic success of the last three decades. Shared identity, however, does not mean that the population's socio-economic integration has been perfectly realised, as it is shown by a few limited slum areas, as well as by the poverty of many people in the rural dry area just next to the municipality.

Influential castes in TCG

Understanding the nature of a shared urban identity is another question, since, in itself, it is just the stereotypical expression of a more or less self-satisfied feeling about being an inhabitant of TCG. When we try to go deeper, we only find multiple identities, and some particular ones seem to monopolise TCG identity itself. This takes us to the question of caste and what it means in the urban context of TCG today.

My analysis will concentrate on three main castes. First, among the artisans, I shall focus on the Tamil weavers, the Kaikkolar,[7] who are called the Cengunta (Sengunthar) Mudaliyar today; other artisans, such as carpenters, who have started mechanical workshops, are not considered in this chapter. Secondly, among the traders, the Nagarattu Chettiyar (a caste of the 'Thousand Vaishya') and the Vellan Chettiyar will be discussed; except for the one family of Nattukkottai Chettiyar from Ramnad, I cannot cover the many others with the title Chetti, who are making a living from local trade or are engaged in other tertiary occupations. Thirdly, among the peasants, I shall look at the Kongu and Nattu Vellalar;[8] every peasant of the area (except very poor ones of Telugu origin called Naicker and those from the Scheduled Castes) is called Kavuntar, a title that includes Vettuva Vellalar (formerly 'hunters' not residing in the town), and Padaiyatchi-Vanniyar.[9]

Our analysis is mainly focused on the Mudaliyar, who are tentatively compared with the Vellalar and Chettiyar. The Mudaliyar are conspicuous in TCG. This comes from their demographic weight

[7] In Salem district, we find also Devangar weavers, taking the title of Chetti, who were migrants from Karnataka. None of them appears to reside in TCG.

[8] Nattu Vellalar form a subcaste of the Kongu Vellalar. From the outside there are no apparent distinctions between the two subcastes and they share the same clan names as the Kongu Vellalar. However, the Nattu Vellalar, mostly living in an area to the north-east of TCG, claim that their ancestors were formerly kings ruling TCG from a village 8 km away. Hereafter, when discussing Vellalar, we will not distinguish between them.

[9] The Padaiyatchi-Vanniyar are anciently settled in TCG. A few families among them are well-to-do, but none of them seems to have been able to do business like the Vellalar. However, their weight in the town is not to be underestimated, since they have control of the town co-operative bank and nowadays a strong political connection through a young Vanniyar of TCG who, after winning the 1991 legislative elections, has become a government minister.

(around 30 per cent of the population)[10] and from the fact that they are still mostly living in clusters, the main one remaining the congested *pavadi* ward not far from the bazaar. Somehow they retain a central position in the town, compared with the Vellalar newcomers who reside at the periphery; this is not only an empirical fact but is also related to the Mudaliyar's centripetal conception of life. In contrast, even the Vellalar settled in the town have a centrifugal way of life. Usually open-minded and spontaneous, they are nonetheless resourceful at escaping enquiries, which is helped by the fact that they are dispersed in the countryside or live at the edge of the city. Compared with both the Mudaliyar and the Vellalar, the Chettiyar have been losers in the economic game during the last decades, but they are still able to master every kind of interaction.

The Cengunta Mudaliyar

If the co-operative movement was decisive for the weavers of Tiruchengodu, that was not mainly because it brought some help to the handloom weavers, although it was aided by the consistent policy of the Indian government after independence to promote handloom fabric and small-scale industries. For TCG Mudaliyar, and precisely for those who, in the 1930s, had already got some wealth and some control over handloom weavers, the co-operative movement and its links to the Congress seemed to have awakened in them an awareness of a genuine strength and an anticipation of further economic betterment. For years they monopolised the Board of the Handloom Co-operative Society, reinvigorating, at the same time, the community feeling among TCG Mudaliyar expressed through the old institutions.

Traditionally, TCG is supposed to be the chief territory (*maha-nadu*) of seven Mudaliyar settlements (*elu karai* or *nadu*) in the Salem district. It is difficult to ascertain the type of relationships which originally linked the seven settlements. However TCG had a judicial power over the others which continues to be expressed ritually even today: a panchayat, with a representative from each of the settlements,

---

[10] The Mudaliyar claim to constitute 60% of the population, but that is no longer true.

is held at the time of the annual festival to Lord Ardhanarishwara at TCG, and the *pavadi* (that is, the local panchayats) of each of the seven *nadu* are supposed to pay a tax for the celebration. Through that panchayat organisation at different levels (*pavadi, nadu, maha-nadu*), TCG is the highest caste council for the Cengunta Mudaliyar of the south-eastern part of Salem district; it was supposed to settle disputes among them and might have formerly managed relationships regarding the work and trade of the weavers (Mines 1984).

The leading personalities among the TCG Mudaliyar between the 1940s and 1960s seized the opportunities given by the Congress and the co-operative movement, managing at the same time to strengthen an ideal co-operation with the TCG weavers in order to maintain the tradition of the panchayat—at a time when such institutions were disappearing everywhere—so that in some respects it is still working today. Two factors helped in this. One is the ritual connection between the caste council and the festival of the sacred site. The second is related to the significance for all weavers of the *pavadi*, which is highly symbolic, as well as emotional and practical. The *pavadi* is where, as handloom weavers, they were for generations obliged to come in the early morning to work at warping in close co-operation with other weavers. It was also the place for local panchayat meetings and worship. Although there was progressively less need for manual warping, as weavers gave up handlooms for powerlooms, the *pavadi* site remained a centre: a panchayat building was erected, followed by a spacious marriage hall, which is the biggest in the town (an earlier smaller one is located in the bazaar), and then a third hall. All the halls are rented out for marriages and other meetings, even to non-Mudaliyar. The remaining space is rented to traders in a vegetable market, and shops have been built for rent as well. The Mudaliyar community as a whole is now very wealthy.

Mines has explained very well (1984:94, 117ff.) how the introduction of powerlooms by the handloom co-operatives was paradoxical, because it went against the handloom-weavers' protection policies followed by the modern caste association (the Cengunta Mahajana Sangam, 1927-1979). That partly reflects (ibid.:118) the diversification of interests among the well-to-do Mudaliyar and the 'overlapping roles in the production process' of weavers, who were members of the co-operative, but also worked for masterweavers according to market conditions. However, the behaviour of the TCG Mudaliyar leaders of the time also partly reveals their centripetal interest in building a strong corporate Mudaliyar caste group. How far the Mudaliyar caste of TCG actually is corporate is another matter to which we shall return later, but we may say that the leaders have succeeded in creating a TCG Mudaliyar identity.

This probably occurred in the late 1960s or early 1970s, when support by the Congress party was no longer helpful, and also when the shift to powerlooms undercut the working co-operation of the weavers in warping. The TCG Mudaliyar panchayat then took a decision. Under the pretext of preventing forbidden marriages between families related by kinship, who might have forgotten their relationship owing to the growth of population and migration, it was decided to create *gotra*s, that is, 'clans' between whose members alliance was possible. Married men (with living wives) were then listed, in a register kept by the panchayat, under their lineage (*kudumbam* or *vidu*) names, and all the lineages related by kinship were grouped under a *gotra* name. Thirty-one *gotra* names—which were so many different names of the god Murugan—were selected, regrouping a total of 95 lineage names and 839 married couples at the time of the registration. What is probably highly relevant is that those Mudaliyar who belong to one of the 31 *gotra*s think that they are genuine Tiruchengodu Mudaliyar and used to have the initial letter T for TCG in front of their names. The pedigree 'TCG Mudaliyar' was then certified and so, at the same time, was TCG Mudaliyar identity.

What might have been the need for such a pedigree, beyond the desire to avoid wrong marriages? As an explanation that desire has little weight, when we consider how many other castes lack the double reference of clan and lineage. Our enquiries also show that the registration has never been completed; some people were not in TCG at the relevant time and many of them were not really interested, even if they nowadays refer to their *gotra*. Among the lineage names, approximately a third refer to a place located outside TCG, which leaves open the question of a genuine TCG origin,[11] and some other names, which we have got from enquiries, were never registered. Among the 31 *gotras*, one of them has nobody registered for it, three others have only one couple, and seven *gotras* have between 39 and 111 couples' names (many more than the others). It is not very surprising to discover that the leading figures between the 1940s and 1960s belong to these seven *gotras* and also to particular lineages within them; this is still more or less true today, even though some other Mudaliyar have been able to improve themselves. It also means that those people who had control of the Co-operative Society, as well as of the caste panchayat, were seeking to ensure their roots through the label of TCG Mudaliyar.

In fact, this label could not coincide with the subcaste itself, because many marriages are celebrated with non-TCG Mudaliyar, even if there is a very strong tendency for the TCG Mudaliyar, particularly those from the present leading families, to marry amongst themselves. Thus we may tentatively hypothesise that the TCG pedigree was partly a statement of enhanced status by the Ciru Tali Mudaliyar, the TCG subcaste who used to give a *pariyam* ('bride-price') of 25 rupees and are non-vegetarians; they are considered inferior to the Periya Tali Mudaliyar, who are vegetarians and give a *pariyam* of 35 rupees. Among the latter, only a few families reside in TCG, and during the 1950s a few well-to-do Ciru Tali Mudaliyar gave them their daughters in marriage, contrary to custom, in order to distinguish themselves. These alliances have not been perceived as successful and TCG Mudaliyar eventually chose to consolidate their TCG status. Finally, moreover, the pedigree was a way to prohibit non-TCG Mudaliyar, who have no *gotra*, from becoming council members of the panchayat (although some attempts were made and were followed by suits filed in the court).

The apparent constitution of a corporate group has been relevant for

---

[11] People explain that their forefathers shifted to a village because of some calamity and later they came back to TCG; the other names refer either to a great-grandfather's name, or to an office (accountant, priest), or to some other characteristics related to occupation, type of house, etc.

the creation of a TCG Mudaliyar identity, which, to some extent, is also shared as a TCG identity by the town's population, because in the town Mudaliyar represent the exemplary image of economic fulfilment through 'business' promotion. It is also an acknowledgement of Mudaliyar power, since for years the Municipal chairman was a Mudaliyar.

The Chettiyar

By comparison with others, the position of the different Chettiyar—as they themselves see it—looks more or less depressed. As is usual nowadays, some individuals have found non-trading jobs. However, the several categories of Chettiyar in the town mainly continue with trading, which is mostly related to the rural production of numerous types of oil seeds, and is often directly connected with the trades carried on in the TCG and surrounding weekly markets. The most well-to-do Chettiyar were (and in a few cases still are) those who were carrying on a wholesale trade (*mandi*), sometimes running a ginning and oil mill, and were at the same time involved in moneylending. In this latter occupation, they became 'shroffs' (a word now understood as 'owner of a jewellery shop'), who exchanged coins to certify their value in standard coins, and then keepers of cash, and eventually private bankers. If there is a continuum from local, rural production-based trade to banking, it appears to be because these different levels of 'traditional' trade were in the hands of different kinds of Chettiyar, who had some overlapping functions but were still organised in a kind of division of labour.

In the early twentieth century, private banking, as such, was in the hands of two newly-arrived families of Nattukkottai Chettiyar. In the 1930s, these families had to close their banks, probably as a consequence of the recession. A few years later, another Nattukkottai, who had had to leave Burma, settled in TCG with his son. His grandson continues to run a private bank, which is part of a supra-regional banking network of close relatives, and he is the banker of the wealthiest Mudaliyar who need loans for maintaining a working capital. Beyond the needs of his business, the Nattukkottai banker does not really take part in the socio-economic confrontation going on among the different categories within the TCG population.

Yet that is not exactly so for the Nagarattu Chettiyar, who claim the higher status of Vaishya. They wear the sacred thread, are vegetarians, and have *gotras* with *rishi* names; the Association of the 'Thousand Vaishya', which includes several trading castes among which Nagarattu seem to be influential, patronise a monastery in Periyar district with a Brahman guru. The kinship relationships among the TCG Nagarattu extend to Salem, Coimbatore and Periyar districts. Many of them have left the area—for some traders' sons with a modern education have found better opportunities elsewhere—but those who have remained in TCG (approximately 15 to 20 mostly joint families) cannot forget the days when the Nagarattu Chettiyar houses and businesses were sited all along the Chetti street, which the Mudaliyar have dared to rename 'North Car street'. At present only two 'shroff' families remain (one of them being a wealthy jeweller employing 10 to 15 Asari goldsmiths), together with one family living in a conspicuous house including a oil seeds *mandi*, and a few others. With the opening of the Co-operative Marketing Society, the competition was too severe for the private wholesale trade in oil seeds and cotton.[12] A few Nagarattu were probably yarn merchants in the early twentieth century, but the Mudaliyar have finally been able to take control of this market. Even in the field of money-lending, competition is everywhere nowadays.

Thus the Nagarattu Chettiyar feel that the Mudaliyar, who, they say, only settled in the town a hundred years ago, have superseded them. This is expressed by how they talk about the affair of the bus stand. In the 1970s, the Municipal Council, whose chairman was a Mudaliyar, decided to build a large bus stand on a site located at the end of North Car street, where the Nagarattu Chettiyar owned a flower garden near a small temple dedicated to Ganesha. Compensation has been paid,[13] but since the price of the urban land has increased a lot, the Nagarattu think that they were cheated.

[12] Many of the *mandis* have disappeared. The Nagarattu still retain two of the five or six remaining, and claim that many farmers come to them because they do not like going to the Marketing Society.

[13] The Municipality proposed Rs 34,000. Then the Nagarattu filed a suit and won compensation of Rs 300,000. Around their Ganesha temple, which has been protected, they have a building with shops from which they get Rs 6,000 per month.

The Agaram Vellan Chettiyar are supposed to come from a place of origin located in TCG taluk itself. They are constituted by nine *gotras*, and their kinship network extends over a small area. They are non-vegetarians, but patronise a Brahman guru whose seat is near the river Kaveri. They are still numerous in the town (about 200 families); traditionally, they were mainly engaged in the oil seeds and cotton trade, and two or three of their *mandi*s are still working. In the 1930s and 1940s, a few of their leading families extensively engaged in the paddy and rice trade and they opened six rice and oil mills, as well as ginning factories. After the 1950s, they disposed of everything, selling the mills mainly to Mudaliyar.

Explaining their fate, both groups of Chettiyar will recall that Mudaliyar and Vellalar have received loans from the government, when they themselves never got any help. They will add that the Chettiyar retain their customs, being honest, speaking truthfully and openly, and giving the right measure of goods: 'to do business they have just to be seated, and the customer will confidently come to them because their fathers had a good reputation'. However, Mudaliyar for their own part will argue: 'the sons of these Chetti have just remained sitting and eating, not being taught anything, and, moreover, how can they improve, since no Chetti can join two threads together?'

These stereotypical statements are rather contradicted by the facts, since one Nagarattu owns a mobile rig unit and a Vellan Chetti has opened a sizing mill. However, there is a kind of integrated Chetti identity in relation to the type of occupation for which they are suited. For example, a Nagarattu father proudly announced that his young educated son had opened a cardboard factory, explaining that it was the first time that someone from their community had succeeded in entering this type of enterprise. The son, on being interviewed, explained that everything was going all right, but he felt that manufacturing goods was too risky compared with trade transactions. He was already expecting to make a comeback in a more secure business field, to which he was accustomed by familial tradition, by opening a textile dealership in partnership with a friend.

The Kongu Vellala Kavuntar

Compared with the Mudaliyar and Chettiyar, the Vellalar are characterised by quite another type of personality. The Vellalar are found both inside and outside the town, since they tend to reside at the periphery, and many of them, who come to the town daily, actually live in the countryside. Moreover, the Vellalar network extends beyond the Kaveri all over the Kongu country through kinship links, relations with lineage temples and the maintenance of a traditional type of organisation with specific offices. The Vellalar are also mobilised through a modern caste association, and they have an awareness of their political strength and economic interests. As a result, their importance in the town is much greater than their numbers (10 to 15 per cent of the population) would suggest.

The Vellalar of the TCG area are subdivided into several *kuttam*s, 'clan'. Beck (1972) has shown that the kin organisation of the Kongu Vellalar corresponded to socio-territorial settlements (*nadu*) with lineage temples at different levels. A deeper enquiry would probably enable us to confirm Beck's findings. However, it is not certain that the systematic territorial organisation described for the 1970s by Beck has remained as it was. In the TCG area today, the notion of *nadu* is more or less forgotten. Moreover, when the members of any one *kuttam* have dispersed, a *kuttam* is often subdivided in relation to several goddess temples located in different places. Nonetheless, these temples remain centres of identification corresponding to areas of peasant dominance which have social implications. It is interesting to note that educated and urbanised Vellalar, who have never completely cut their rural ties, involve themselves fully in maintaining these temples, collecting money for renovating them, and ensuring that worship and festivals are not interrupted. This implies that Vellalar identity, as defined by some kind of authority over people in the rural area, is still meaningful.

Some Vellalar lineages also had a relationship with the god of TCG. The chief priests of Lord Ardhanarishwara, as their gurus, formerly used to visit the Vellalar villages where they were paid respect and received gifts. A relationship of guruship with Vellalar families still remains, as does the latters' participation in the annual festival. The first Vellalar to build second houses in the town were some of the large landowners who had been selected by the British as zamindars responsible for collecting the rent from several villages of an area, and who were later often involved in the Congress nationalist movement. As such, Vellalar carry with them an aura of political authority. The last president of the Union Panchayat of TCG was a Vellalar.

Many of those who subsequently settled in the town were only peasants, who very often claim, like the Mudaliyar, that their families were poor. If many Vellalar have now become well-to-do, this is—they claim—just because they are used to very hard work, for there is no other way to make a living in a dry area like that around TCG. In the town, the Vellalar have mostly involved themselves in transport, mechanical workshops and, above all, in mobile rig units. None of these enterprises would have been feasible without pooling resources, which have often come from credit given against land by national banks, and then increased through private finance agencies. Furthermore, everything is done in partnership, as among the Mudaliyar, but unlike the latter, kinship and alliance relationships are not the only basis for it, because the Vellalar are also able to enter partnerships with different kinds of people, even from other castes.

Competitive images of TCG castes today

Nowadays, it is common to hear someone explaining that the Vellalar, through operating mobile rig units, bring more wealth than the textile industry to the town and its area. Whether or not this is actually the case, the Vellalar and Mudaliyar have acquired a competitive image in the eyes of local people. There is real competition in several fields. One well-to-do Vellalar, chairman of the Union Panchayat, has opened a private technical college in his own name. Then the Mudaliyar, collectively supporting the initiative of one of their number, the chairman of the municipality, established their Cengunthar College some years later. Nevertheless, competition until today has been limited and it tends to express itself as a complementarity between two types of behaviour which reflect something of the way of life and nature of each caste.

Vellalar and Mudaliyar are ready to acknowledge each other's respective achievements. Beyond that, the Vellalar are said to be cordial, frank but somehow rustic in speech, ready to work day and night, earnest and diligent, and yet also sturdy and ready to take any risk. The Mudaliyar are said to be clever and cunning, if not crooked, but physically neither strong nor sturdy, and unable to maintain a business for long. The Mudaliyar will explain that although many of them practise money-lending (and then make black money), they have not succeeded in managing private finances well, whereas if Vellalar have flourishing businesses, it is because they are ready to recover money even by violent means.

From the point of view of the Mudaliyar, the Vellalar are only interested in money. 'If they earn Rs 100, they will spend only 10, while a Mudaliyar will spend 500.' The Vellalar are successful in the well-boring field, not only because they are physically strong, but also because they are ready to leave their families for months, enjoying life and drinking. In contrast, the Mudaliyar cannot stand the idea of living outside the family, and they are also the most inclined to co-operate for the welfare of their community, whereas Vellalar, say Mudaliyar, do not care about the laws and bonds of their own community. On the other hand, the Vellalar are satisfied with themselves because, generations ago, they began to act according to current norms of family planning: their men marry late (at about 30) and each family has only two or three children. They also marry their daughters with the required jewels and dowry. According to them, the Mudaliyar do not do things correctly, since they celebrate the wedding at the bridegroom's place. But the Mudaliyar prefer to keep to their customs.[14] They more or less

[14] Mudaliyar customs do not appear particularly orthodox. Probably Virashaivism has been influential, even if only a few Mudaliyar are actually Virashaivas. This influence is present in their funerary rituals; for many of their lineages, death pollution does not last more than three days. The question of purity/impurity does not seem to bother them very much either. I have seen a Scheduled Caste man, an ex-serviceman and owner of a small mechanical workshop, attending a Mudaliyar wedding, which may be normal today. But at the end of the celebration he got up on the marriage platform with other personalities to give his blessing to the couple, which is more unusual. For marriage rituals, they very often call a Mudaliyar, a retired teacher, who acts like a Brahman priest.

avoid the modern evil of dowry,[15] and they strengthen their community
ties by marrying within TCG as far as possible.

Partial simplifications though they may be, these stereotypical
statements are interesting from several points of view. They distinguish
the nature of each caste (as a species), but at the same time they do so
through opposition, by stressing that each caste identity has then to be
defined relative to another. Thus Vellalar are sturdy, Mudaliyar are not,
but they are cunning—this latter qualification recalling that craftsmen
in Tamilnadu are usually supposed to be cunning. Reference to
behaviour is also a way to talk about moral qualifications, as well as
about the status ascribed to the other or to oneself—even if, in TCG,
questions of relative purity are not so much at stake and the emphasis is
eventually put on how weddings are celebrated. These statements were
made in interviews that were mainly concerned with the present
economic growth of the town, which people usually feel has been
'tremendous', to the credit of both Vellalar and Mudaliyar. If the
Vellalar, whose nature as well as activities are outwardly oriented, are
diametrically opposed to the Mudaliyar, who are inwardly oriented and
care more for their families and community, economic development is
nevertheless perceived as the joint result of the two castes' efforts.

Their respective ways of developing a strategy for self-improvement
are also implied by these statements. Vellalar are bold and even violent;
they are supposed to have no problems in dealing with people, in
controlling them and in managing any enterprise. In other words, they
have the authority to get different kinds of people working with and for
them.[16] That is not really so for the Mudaliyar, who prefer to rely on

[15] As a Mudaliyar businessman explained, he did not give dowry to his
daughters. For his daughters-in-law, he did not ask for dowry, and even the
weight of gold that they brought as jewellery was much less than what he gave
for his daughters. Moreover he selected his daughters-in-law from families
whose standing was a bit lower than his own—a better way, he said, to control
them.

[16] This was asserted by a Vellalar rig-owner describing his trips to Madhya
Pradesh to bore wells. He, or his partner, has to accompany the team of workers
in order to control them. In Madhya Pradesh, he has to deal with gang leaders,
each of them protecting his own territory. A heavy tax is paid at the beginning
and the gang leader of the territory where wells are bored also gets half-the
money paid by the customer.

their own caste members to a greater extent. According to Vellalar, Mudaliyar do not know how to manage things for long; according to themselves, however, Mudaliyar are generous, 'know how to join two threads together' and know how to manufacture goods, unlike Chettiyar who mostly feel secure only in commercial transactions.

What people state about themselves and others largely complies with a sort of traditional image, a kind of 'natural' identity: members of a dominant peasant caste are 'powerful', artisans are 'clever and cunning', but traders are seen just 'sitting and waiting'. Although the status position and wealth of some of the Chettiyar are acknowledged, the Vellalar and Mudaliyar have largely infringed upon the Chettiyar's ascribed prerogatives in the sphere of trade and financial transactions. In this busy town, emphasis is clearly put on the spirit of 'business' enterprise. It is thus surprising to discover that, in a reflection of the natural identities attributed to castes, something germane to what we call the caste system and the social division of labour implied by it, still seems to hold good. We may ask how far this is fiction and how far reality, because there are many examples of Mudaliyar who are bold men or rig owners, Vellalar who are poor peasants or powerloom workers, and so on and so forth. Answering this question is not easy however, in so far as caste as a species apparently remains endorsed through caste endogamy.

Caste as a process of differentiation

Our research was concerned with the economic development of the town, and many of the people interviewed were successful businessmen. Leaving aside details about particular events in their lives and activities, we are left with generalising statements about Mudaliyar, Vellalar and others. Moreover, successful people tend to speak as if they were exemplary representatives of the whole.

Yet the study of what is going on within a single (local) caste category reveals differences and distances among people of the same caste which are quite antithetical to the idea of a common nature and a shared identity. Concerning the Mudaliyar, we already know that the caste's main morphological features are its subdivisions into *gotra*s and lineages: according to the Mudaliyar, there is no hierarchical ranking among the segments of either kind of subdivision. However, at the time of registration under *gotra* names, some Mudaliyar families tended to be much more in evidence, owing to their leadership positions. Within the *gotra*s and lineages, a dynamic process of evolution is at work, which is tending to produce differentiation through lineage segmentation. Although the workings of such a process are well-known (being comparable to many societies with unilineal descent), difficulties begin to arise when we try to analyse its present and future implications in any specific case, as the data then needed would be accurate samples with some historical depth. For a tentative interpretation, however, some material can be taken from genealogies which were collected for information on kinship and alliance relationships and also, as far as possible, for other details, such as occupation and place of residence.

As usual in Tamilnadu, the depth of the genealogies is shallow: five generations at the most descending from a great-great-grandfather whose collateral relatives have been forgotten, but very often memory does not go beyond the grandfather. A lineage segment, starting from ego's grandfather, might be much extended if ego were to remember all the brothers and sisters (including their spouses and children) of his grandfather, father and himself. But nobody is endowed with such a memory, which is understandable, if we consider that a generation or two ago there were often six, eight or even more children in a family. More interesting is that people's memories are more or less purposely selective, even at the level of their fathers' and their own generations.

Although there is great variety among the cases, the information shows that potential and actual conflicts between brothers are frequent, even in several joint families in which married brothers seem to live in harmony together under an authoritative and enterprising father; in families in which the father is not a 'big' man, partition is usually decided upon when he is still alive. It always looks as if two brothers cannot treat each other on an equal footing. At best, they keep a distance between each other, or some of the brothers acknowledge the success of one of them and assume a secondary position; otherwise, less successful brothers leave the town to take their chances elsewhere, or they search for closer co-operation with affinal relatives.

All these facts taken together suggest that competition between individuals for the leadership of their own lineage segments is anticipated in each generation. In other words, the analysis of genealogies makes it clear that each male ego is implicitly forced into a confrontation with others in which he has to prove his mastery by any means, and current economic opportunities have stimulated men's ambition for money and some sort of power. Success of this kind does not come to everyone. As the Mudaliyar will say, it depends on hard work and luck. Luck is a part of every human's fate and is related to the many circumstances of familial and individual life which cannot be controlled. Hard work seems more specific, but it is something more than the mere fact of working hard (which a majority of Mudaliyar do), or even of being well-trained in new fields of business (which was not possible for those who grew up in the 1960s). What is required is some mastery over co-operation derived from kin and marriage relationships and over caste interactions. Hence we may hypothesise that the Mudaliyar 'hard worker', who has nowadays become a big business-man, is someone who has succeeded in differentiating his own lineage segment from the others in the contemporary context. The invention of *gotra* by the successful Mudaliyar in the 1960s may be explained as a way of consolidating the leading position that they acquired within the segmentary process.

Thus, even if segmentation is nothing new in caste society, its use to enhance differentiation between lineage segments is probably not exactly the same as it was when the Mudaliyar were mainly handloom weavers. Economic and political mastery over caste relationships—by being a master-weaver as well as a person of authority—were as important then as they are today, but they were probably used more to emphasise relative differences of status. Now, although many Mudaliyar tend to stress their honesty and religious merit as proof of status, the youngest ones are often more cynical: for them, money is status and power. Since their grandfathers' time, occupations have become far more diversified within the same field of activity, as well as in the many other fields opened up by the development of the town or by education.

All these changes have some consequences for the internal organisation of the local caste. Especially striking is the economic differentiation among Mudaliyar still living in TCG, and we may guess that it has drastically increased in the last few decades. Differentiation mainly tends to follow the lines of segmentation from a single grandfather; in each generation, ego's opportunities for promoting himself and his line in the segmentary process remain open. As a result, there is apparently no commensurability between, on the one hand, a handloom-weaver,[17] a powerloom worker, a clerk or a tea-shop owner and, on the other, his cousins (parallel or cross) who are owners, even in partnership, of a sizing mill plus many powerlooms together with, as the case may be, a cinema, a finance agency, or some other business. Yet notwithstanding such gaps, when a wedding is celebrated everyone—according to the extent of the kindred defined by classificatory relationships—will attend, including the big men and members of the panchayat who, according to Mudaliyar tradition, have to witness the new alliance and give their blessings. Despite the increased differentiation between lineage segments, and moreover despite its increasing socio-economic heterogeneity, the TCG Mudaliyar community still proclaims, through its well-to-do representatives, the unified identity of their caste within an organic whole.

Caste today

TCG, as its citizens assert in using the English term, has become a 'business' place. That is corroborated by the conspicuous notice-boards of the private finance agencies located near the local branches of national banks. All the main businesses have their own regional associations (for lorry- and bus-owners, powerloom and sizing-mill owners, etc.). Membership of these associations is, as the case may be, combined with membership of the Rotary or Lions Club, and with many other caste, political, religious and cultural associations.

In other words, TCG has become a society that may be characterised as urbanised in so far as a degree of heterogeneity prevails, which is

---

[17] In TCG itself about 150 handloom weavers remain, mainly settled within the limits of the municipality.

correlated with fragmented interactions and, to a certain extent, with some loss of face-to-face relationships (Wirth 1938). All this is one of the normal consequences of population growth, and like any city TCG has grown through the immigration of many newcomers from the surrounding areas, as well as of those who still sometimes come from further afield. However, this heterogeneity cannot be opposed to any imaginary homogeneity existing in TCG in the early twentieth century. Heterogeneity has surely become much more important and definite than it ever was in the past, but this must be qualified, for it is still possible to argue that any south Indian small town, past or present, or indeed any large multicaste village, was never a homogeneous whole from the point of view of caste understood as *jati* ('species'). We are reminded here of the unfinished discussion about rural-urban continuity. In contrast to the west, rural life in India cannot be opposed to urban life on the basis that the population is homogeneous, rather than heterogeneous.[18] To be brief and to generalise unwarily, we may say that the integration of caste heterogeneity in a village, when it was accomplished, worked through symbolic and practical links to gods and rituals at different levels, and through relations constituted by the local caste system and by dominance. From a relatively abstract point of view, therefore, heterogeneous differences are integrated as specialised activities within the overall social division of labour.[19]

However, what about a modern urban setting? To what extent is TCG peculiar, as an example of a town in transition where caste categories within the population are still easily identified?[20] What is fasci-

[18] Everywhere in Tamilnadu, for many centuries, migrants from the Telugu and Kannara regions have settled in towns as well as in the countryside. Although these migrants have been assimilated among the Tamil population, they keep up their differences, especially by continuing to speak their mother-tongue among themselves.

[19] The 'organic social ethics' that, according to Weber (Stern 1971), characterise Indian society, anticipated the specialisation and complex division of labour attributed to the modern industrial world in Durkheim's evolutionary thought.

[20] Such identification is perhaps not always so easy in cosmopolitan cities. Nevertheless, the Naidu population of Coimbatore is considered the principal agent of development in this large city; the Brahmans, who were very influential early in the century in Madras, are far from being completely lost among other categories of the population; no doubt other examples also exist.

nating in TCG is the people's awareness about the growth of their town; they feel they have an active role in it and many of them expect, on their own level, to share in the efforts and fruits of that development. This common opinion seems to express in itself a shared TCG identity and, depending on the point of view, that identity may also be related to the unifying and authoritative moral symbol represented by the presiding deity of the site.

I have tried to show that this shared identity is multi-faceted or, at least, dual: the two main agents of TCG's growth in recent decades are the complementary, but also opposed models of an expectation of betterment. With some qualifications, these two models combine into one model of politico-economic dominance. In practice, Vellalar and Mudaliyar are the people to be approached in order to get a job, for moral and political support, for help for an individual or a donation for any social or religious enterprise, and so on. However in actual networks of relationships, Vellalar and Mudaliyar do not enjoy an exclusive dominance and control over the locality at all, because opportunities for behaving as a 'big' man are nowadays open at many different levels of caste interaction, as well as to the many individuals who engage in business, or who are in a position to practise moneylending or bribery. Moreover, political intervention from outside may be called upon if necessary. The idea of dominance still works as a caste-based model for identification. Yet the reality of its operation at the local level of the town is no longer absolutely pre-eminent (if it ever was), for it tends to be more and more fragmentary.

In discussing caste, I have given at least three meanings to the term: as a 'species' (Parry 1979:85-7), expressed as an identity in relation to different and opposite ones; as a 'corporate group', constituted by those who have succeeded in being acknowledged as representatives of the local 'species' and who have control over its subdivisional network; and as a process of differentiation that relies on segmentation. This segmentation process is crucial, since it involves—from and through each (male) individual—a potential dynamic for achieving mastery over relationships at different levels, which is correlated with the rate of politico-economic achievement, more or less inflected by religious

merit and recognised wisdom. Through this dynamic, as we have tried
to show, those who have successfully differentiated themselves and
their own lineage segment may embody, and at the same time mobilise,
the apparently united front of their caste. They can do this even though
each caste's shared identity in relation to occupational skill (especially
in the case of the weavers) has become obsolete, and socio-economic
differentiation within the caste may become prejudicial to unity in the
long run.

Nevertheless, the 'spirit of caste' is still operating along the three
dimensions that we have analysed, which seems to hold good for every
caste (with qualifying differences in each case). My hypothesis, therefore, is that caste today is not so different from caste yesterday, except
for the fact that a crucial process involving the individual person in the
dynamics of differentiation has been invigorated, for better or worse.
This has occurred in principle by the modernisation associated with
democratic laws, and in practice by the opening of new fields of activity and economic opportunities that are accessible according to
people's circumstances. In other words, the incentives for personal
enhancement and action, which rely at every level on the morphological
processes of caste, may be the main factor giving coherence to the
shared identity, defined in opposition to others, of a caste as a species
(whose boundaries as a supposedly closed group are never of course
known).[21]

The question remains: what has happened to the caste system? At
first, we may say that it no longer exists as such anymore. But to what
are we referring when speaking of the 'caste system'? If it is to the (abstract) concept of a global society, in an appropriate relation to the cos-
mos, as an organic whole, then something of this concept remains in the
idea of castes as species different from one another even in an urban
setting, but the concept's coherence seems to have been lost. Yet is this

[21] For these proposals, which remain my own, I am nevertheless indebted to
Henri Stern, for the importance, that he has always emphasised, of individual
action associated with self-mastery in Indian society, as well as to Raymond
Jamous for his analysis of the process of segmentation in a very different
society. I am further grateful to Chris Fuller for his careful reading of this paper
and his comments.

loss of global coherence really new and a consequence of modernisation? Empirically, in many places in India it is still possible to observe the workings of a local caste system through a structure of ritual and social relations, mostly connected with agricultural production. Nevertheless, the organic concept of the caste system has in fact included within its own operation a contradictory movement: the Hindu aspiration for salvation within the world, open to every individual on equal terms with all others. It may be that settings larger than villages were always more favourable to the individual quest for salvation. But this crucial quest, whatever 'salvation' finally means, is still crucial in TCG today.

References

Beck, B.E.F. 1972. *Peasant society in Konku: a study of right and left subcastes in south India*. Vancouver: University of British Columbia Press.

Kundu, A. 1992. 'Industrial dispersal and integration of medium sized towns in the national economy—the case of Tiruchengodu (Salem District) of Tamilnadu, India'. Unpublished paper presented at the European Conference of Modern South Asian Studies, Berlin.

Mines, M. 1984. *The warrior merchants: textile, trade and territory in south India*. Cambridge: Cambridge University Press.

Murton, B.J. 1979. 'The evolution of the settlement structure in northern Kongu to 1800 AD.' In B.E.F. Beck (ed.), *Perspectives on a regional culture: essays about the Coimbatore area of south India*. New Delhi: Vikas.

Parry, J.P. 1979. *Caste and kinship in Kangra*. London: Routledge and Kegan Paul.

Silberstein, B. 1991. 'The textile line of production as viewed from Tiruchengodu: continuity with the past and recent decisive change.' In *Urban configurations and merchant networks in south India: a workshop* (Pondy Papers in Social Sciences, 9). Pondicherry: French Institute.

Stern, H. 1971. 'Religion et société en Inde selon Max Weber: analyse critique de *Hindouisme et bouddhisme*.' *Informations dans les Sciences Sociales* 10, 6:69-112.

Wirth, L. 1938. 'Urbanism as a way of life'. *American Journal of Sociology* 44:1-24.

Chapter 6

CASTE IN CONTEMPORARY INDIA[1]

André Béteille

Meaning and legitimacy of caste

The subject I have selected is a very large one, and I am anxious therefore to indicate at once the limits within which I shall try to confine the discussion. Caste has been a subject of continuous interest to ethnographers, historians and sociologists for the last hundred years, and attempts have been made to identify its fundamental structure, either in terms of a set of enduring groups and the enduring relations between them (Mayer 1960; Berreman 1963), or in terms of some principle of opposition, for instance between purity and pollution (Dumont 1966; Marriott 1990). I have myself written on the subject from time to time (Béteille 1969a; 1991a), opposing some views and supporting others, but I will not enter into an extended discussion here of the social morphology of caste or the cultural oppositions on which it is based.

My primary concern will be with questions of meaning and legitimacy. What does it mean in India today for a person to belong to a particular caste or subcaste? What demands can it make on him or her and in what contexts, and to what extent is he or she prepared to meet those demands? We know very well that individuals do not always meet the demands made on them, that they are subjected to contradictory pulls and pressures, and that they sometimes subordinate social obligation to personal interest. We know also that there are sanctions of various kinds against the violation of prescribed or generally accepted

[1] A first, very preliminary version of this paper was presented as a lecture at the University of California, Berkeley, in April 1992 where Professor G.D. Berreman, who was in the chair, made a number of observations from which I have greatly benefited. I am grateful also for the many helpful comments I received when it was presented in London in July 1993, and would like in particular to thank Professor Jonathan Parry and Dr. C.J. Fuller for their comprehensive written comments which have helped me in making extensive revisions.

codes of conduct. What are the sanctions available to the caste or subcaste today to ensure the conformity of the individual with the codes prescribed or acknowledged by it?

It is quite obvious that being a member of a caste or subcaste does not have the same meaning today for all individuals everywhere, if it ever did in the past; nor do caste sanctions operate with the same force in all sections of Indian society. I shall not attempt to provide a key to the understanding of caste as a whole or as a 'total social system' in either the past or the present, being mindful of the fact that such attempts have usually come to grief. I shall confine myself largely to urban Indians in what may be described as modern occupations, leaving aside, except for occasional comments, the large majority of Indians who inhabit the rural areas and derive their livelihood from agriculture and related occupations. This does not mean that my argument does not have some implications for the latter, but those implications are not as yet fully clear.

I do not wish to circumscribe too narrowly the class or section of society on which I seek to focus attention. It may be referred to loosely as the 'urban middle class' or even the 'urban middle classes'. More recently, the terms 'intelligentsia', 'professionals' and 'service class' have been employed to refer to roughly the same category of persons (Rudra 1989; Bardhan 1984; Béteille 1989; 1991b). These terms are useful, not because they are accurate, but because they draw attention to the growing importance of this class or stratum in contemporary India. Here numbers are important but not necessarily decisive. If we adopt a narrow definition and take into account only civil servants, managers and higher professionals, we will still be dealing with a population that runs into hundreds of thousands. If we extend the conception to include schoolteachers, clerks and other white-collar workers, as some are inclined to do, we will have a much larger category, numbering 50-75 million persons or more. Of course, these distinctions have to be made much more carefully if we are to achieve precision, but I am not now in a position to do so.

There is a reason why it is necessary to have some sense of the numbers involved even when it is not possible to give precise numbers.

It is sometimes said that the underlying structure of caste remains what it was, and that if there are changes in caste practice, they are superficial and confined to a handful of urban, or educated, or Westernised individuals who are in any case not truly representative of Indian society and culture. I wish to emphasise that the class or stratum that I am talking about, whether conceived broadly or narrowly, does not comprise a mere handful of individuals, and that socially, if not demographically, it is a very important part of contemporary India.

Again, I am anxious to avoid the impression of making too large a claim for my argument. What needs to be stressed as much as the social significance of the class or section in question is its great social diversity in terms of language, region and religion—and, what is as important, in terms of wealth, occupation and education. Limiting ourselves only to the professionals, there is all the difference in the world between a senior member of the Calcutta or Bombay bar and a small-town advocate; or between the research scientist in the Indian Institute of Science and the science teacher in a mofussil college. The stratum as a whole is so large and so diverse that any statement made about it could be either wholly true or wholly false for at least some of its individual members. Caste cannot possibly have the same meaning or the same legitimacy for all the individual members of such a large and diverse population, but that in a sense is the point I wish to make against those who would represent it as a kind of uniform medium that constrains all individuals in the same way.

Growing ambivalence of upper strata

In viewing the section or stratum of society referred to above, whether narrowly or broadly conceived, we observe a characteristic ambivalence in the orientation to caste as it exists today. It is very marked among academics—sociologists, political scientists, historians, economists, and so on—but may be noted also among judges, lawyers, journalists and others, and is probably very widespread and extends beyond the section of society with which I am particularly concerned. The ambivalence is easy to recognise and not difficult to describe, but it has not received the scholarly attention it deserves. It can lead the same individual to deny any significance to caste at one time and to give it exaggerated importance at another.

European and American visitors to India often remark that when they ask educated Indians about caste, they are told that it does not exist any more. It would be a mistake to think that this is always an act of conscious deception. There is certainly an element of self-deception here, and we must ask why this form of self-deception is so commonly encountered. Of course, educated Indians know that caste exists, but they are unclear and troubled about what it means for them as members of a society that is a part of the modern world. No one can say that it is easy to give a clear and consistent account of the meaning and significance of caste in India today.

In a presidential address of 1957, entitled 'Caste in modern India', M.N. Srinivas (1962:15-41) drew attention to the continuing if not increasing importance of caste in public life. The *Times of India* of 21 January 1957, commenting editorially, said that the role of caste had been greatly exaggerated in the address. It was pointed out that caste barriers were falling, both in ordinary interchanges among persons and in ceremonial life. However, the same newspaper reported shortly afterwards that caste loyalties were being extensively used for mobilising political support in the second general election that followed in a few weeks.

Facts on the ground aside, Srinivas's view of caste was not in tune with the general intellectual climate in India in the wake of independence. I may say on the basis of personal experience in both Calcutta and Delhi, that the intelligentsia in general then had its mind on other things than caste. The preoccupation of the social anthropologist with the subject was on the whole viewed with disfavour by all those who believed that India was on the move, and that the eye should be to the future and not upon the past.

At the time of independence, most reflective Indians felt that they had come to a watershed on the other side of which were many new possibilities which it was up to them to seize and turn to the country's advantage. They had a new Constitution, a new Five-year Plan, and they felt that, given the will-power, they could do many things to bring about justice, equality, growth and well-being for the people of India. Certain things needed to be put out of the way in order to achieve these objectives: poverty, hunger, malnutrition, illiteracy, ignorance and superstition. The caste system too was counted among the obstacles in the way of progress. Certainly, it would be fair to say that those who fashioned the Constitution and the Plans did not wish to give a new lease of life to caste.

Caste proved to be much more obdurate than it was judged to be. Perhaps the will-power was not adequate to the task of its removal or containment. But we can also say now, with the advantage of hindsight, that there was a basic misperception of its strength among Indian intellectuals. It is important for us today to examine, honestly and with the maximum possible detachment, the reasons behind this misperception.

We have to go back to the period immediately preceding independence in order to form an idea of the different perceptions of caste and the changes in those perceptions. Caste had become a subject of debate and discussion before independence, and more than one view was formed regarding its pervasiveness and strength. At the risk of some oversimplification, I will pick out two among them that were in many ways the opposite of each other. There was the view of the colonial government and its many able administrators that caste was not only the pre-eminent institution of India, but that it permeated every area of life, and the idea that caste could be dispensed with was wishful thinking. As against this was what I may call the nationalist view, to which Indian intellectuals by and large then subscribed, that the importance of caste had been greatly exaggerated by the colonial administration, that it was clearly on its way out, and that its decline would be greatly hastened once India became independent. Here I must point out that a change in the orientation to caste had come about in the course of the nationalist movement itself. Indian intellectuals did not condemn caste as widely a hundred years before independence as they were ready to do when independence came.

The Indian perception of caste at the time of independence had been shaped, at least to some extent, by the dialectic between the colonial and the nationalist views regarding its place in the present and future society of India. For the Indian intellectual, it had become a matter of pride to confute the colonial view that, however eloquently they might talk about democracy and development, Indians were and would remain under the grip of caste with its exclusiveness, its hierarchy and its ineluctable fragmentation of civil society.

But the misperception of caste among Indian intellectuals was not based solely on national pride; it had another more tangible, if not more credible, basis. Indians could use the evidence the colonial administrators themselves provided to argue, with some plausibility, that caste was definitely and irreversibly in decline. The predominant western view was that caste was basically a matter of religion and ritual, and educated Indians could see that that side of caste was withering before their eyes.

Religious definition of caste

The centrality of caste in Indian society and the religious definition of it became a part of the conventional wisdom of comparative sociology, so that social stratification—or, if one prefers, social hierarchy—was perceived as being essentially a religious phenomenon, emanating somehow from the very nature of Hinduism. This became the predominant view of Indian society among those who were specialists on India and also among those who were not. Nirad C. Chaudhuri (1979:7) has written bitingly about the 'Western legend of Hindu spirituality', and argued that many educated Indians found it convenient to acquiesce in the legend and even to promote it. It gave them a kind of comfort in the face of India's manifest economic and political inferiority to the west to feel that they were spiritually superior. Chaudhuri's own erudite work on Hinduism, marked as it is by many angularities, pays very little attention to caste.

Émile Senart, who published an influential book on caste at the end of the nineteenth century, wrote, 'Hindu society is regulated by religious custom, and the law-books are essentially collections of religious precepts' (1930:91). Henry Maine (1931:14-17), writing in the second half of the nineteenth century, had found it difficult to detach Hindu law from Hindu religion, and the belief became widely established that

Hindu society was unchangeable because it was rooted in immutable religious observance.

Max Weber, perhaps the most outstanding comparative sociologist of all time, clearly defined the social identity of the Hindu in terms of caste, and of caste in terms of ritual. 'Caste, that is, the ritual rights and duties it gives and imposes, and the position of the Brahmans, is the fundamental institution of Hinduism. Before everything else, without caste there is no Hindu' (Weber 1958:29). Even those who would broadly accept this view might point to significant exceptions: Hinduism always had a place for the renouncer, and the *sannyasi* might still be considered a Hindu, although without caste or clan.

Like Weber, Bouglé too was an outsider to Indian studies for he had not done fieldwork in India or learnt any of its classical or modern languages. Yet his work on caste has had great influence among scholars. Pointing to the remarkable historical continuity of the system, he wrote, 'The caste system allows all regimes to pass over its head: it alone remains' (Bouglé 1971:65). He drew attention repeatedly to the inseparability of caste and Hinduism. 'All observers are agreed on this: caste is basically a religious institution' (ibid.:65). And again, 'Hinduism is defined more by the observance of caste rules than by fidelity to some precise dogma' (ibid.:66). Louis Dumont (1966) has carried Bouglé's perspective further forward and greatly enriched it by his mastery of Indian ethnography as well as his knowledge of Indian languages, both classical and modern.

The assumption about Hinduism in much of the early sociological writing is that in it religion and social structure are inseparable so that Hinduism stands not only for a particular religion but also for a particular social structure, that structure being caste. Western writers on religion, including western sociologists, rarely make such an assumption about Christianity, for they see quite clearly that Christianity as a system of beliefs and practices has a certain autonomy in the sense that it can be transferred, more or less easily, from one social or historical context to another. On the other hand, we are shown a somewhat peculiar feature of Hinduism that makes it appear quite different from Christianity, Islam or Buddhism. This poses an intriguing problem for the sociologist of religion. To be sure, there is everywhere some relationship between religion and social morphology, but why should the two be inseparable in only one particular case? This assumption of inseparability leads directly to the question whether Hinduism is at all a religion in the true sense of the term.

The 'Western legend of Hindu spirituality' was more a creation of nineteenth-century Orientalists and Indologists than of twentieth-century ethnographers and sociologists. By the time ethnographic studies came into their own in the early decades of the present century, the legend of Hindu spirituality had largely evaporated. It was displaced by a view in which ritual observances of every conceivable kind were given pride of place. The view of Hinduism that dominates the ethnography of the late nineteenth and early twentieth centuries may be best summed up in the words of Herbert Risley (1969:233) as 'magic tempered with metaphysics'. Today's anthropologists have learnt to become more circumspect than the civil servants and missionaries who were their predecessors, but if we look closely into their accounts of Hinduism, we will encounter Risley's ghost at many places.

The evidence on which anthropological accounts of caste and Hinduism were based was impressive. The British had built an administrative system in India which was remarkable in its own way. One of its permanent achievements was the decennial census, now more than a hundred years old, and the massive apparatus associated with the ethnographic mapping of the country. From the end of the nineteenth century onwards, a voluminous body of literature began to be built up which described extensively and in detail the castes and tribes in the different parts of the country (Risley 1892; Thurston 1909; Enthoven 1920-2). The official accounts of the civil servants were supplemented by accounts by missionaries. This whole body of literature is an invaluable record of the customs, usages and practices of the people of India.

The I.C.S. ethnographers, if the phrase be permitted, included men of considerable scholarship such as Ibbetson (1916), Risley (1969), Gait (1913), Blunt (1931), O'Malley (1932), Hutton (1946), and many others. They were in India not merely to collect taxes and maintain law and order, but also to observe, describe and interpret, with patience and care, and not always without sympathy, the new social world they had come to inhabit. In addition to the detailed descriptions of particular castes and tribes, they provided a number of general accounts of caste as the framework of Indian society.

These detailed and voluminous accounts repeatedly bring caste to our attention, and do so in their own distinctive way. There is a continued emphasis on the religious basis of caste, so that the system appears to be pervaded by a general aura of ritual and ceremonial. Even when such subjects as endogamy, exogamy, division of labour, occupational specialisation, craft practices and so on are being discussed, we are never far away from the world of religion, magic and superstition.

Description and analysis are saturated with accounts of purity and pollution, and the manifold taboos or interdictions associated with them. These struck the attention of administrators, missionaries and others in the nineteenth century, and every successive generation of I.C.S. ethnographers tried to dig a little deeper in order to get to their roots. Most of them gave a central place to the rules relating to food and drink in their accounts of caste. These rules were so elaborate and so complex that one could fill volumes merely by listing them. Another favourite topic was the maintenance of distance and the avoidance of physical contact between members of different castes and subcastes.

Since many of the I.C.S. ethnographers had antiquarian interests, their accounts of caste, apart from the general stress on ritual, purity, pollution, taboos, interdictions and so on, carried a certain archaic flavour. Now, educated Indians in the 1930s and 1940s naturally felt that if this was the essence of caste—*kacca* food and *pakka* food, 36 paces between Tiyan and Nambutiri, 12 paces between Tiyan and Nair, and so on—then, going by their own experience and observation, caste was clearly in retreat. These manifold customs which had been practised in the past, though perhaps not exactly as described in the ethnography, were rapidly losing their meaning and significance among educated Indians, and those who continued to practise them, at school or at work, were sometimes ridiculed by those who did not. Dwelling mainly on the ritual side of caste, it did not appear too implausible to maintain that it was irretrievably in decline.

Thus, the misperception of caste common among the Indian intelligentsia at the time of independence was due partly to the misplaced emphasis on ritual in accounts of it by civil servants and others in the preceding decades. Was there a misperception among the latter as well, and how can we account for it? Whatever place religion may have had in it in the past, the future of caste lay not with religion but with politics. I think that on the whole—for different reasons, and with notable exceptions—both sides failed to read the signs of the future. The I.C.S. ethnographers like Hutton failed to read them because, before independence, they were themselves too closely involved in preparing the very ground on which caste was taking its place in politics. And if, immediately after independence, the Indian intelligentsia failed by and large to dwell on the future role of caste in politics, wishful thinking had something to do with it. They knew that it was there, but hoped that it could be made to wither away—through rapid economic development, through the spread of education, and through science and technology.

Erosion of legitimacy

The concentration in the anthropological (as against the Indological) literature on Hinduism, as I have shown, has been on ritual, purity, pollution, taboos, interdictions, and so on—what pertains largely to magic rather than religion in the proper sense of the term. There is also another side of religion, concerned with morality, that has received rather less attention. It is characteristic of educated Indians today that they find it difficult to acknowledge, not only before outsiders but also among themselves, that caste might have had something to do with morality. N.K. Bose (1975; 1967) was one of the few anthropologists who, despite his deep antipathy to caste, tried to understand and interpret its moral and ethical basis in the traditional social order. But he also pointed out that that basis was being irrevocably undermined.

Indians have not always been shy of writing about the moral basis of caste. It was expounded in the nineteenth century by such men as Bankimchandra Chatterjee (1961); and as late as in the 1930s, Gandhi

(1962) wrote in support of the morality of caste, at least in the form of *varna*. Gandhi favoured *varnadharma* to the extent that it stressed the community rather than the individual, co-operation as against conflict, and duties rather than rights. His conception of *varnadharma* was somewhat remote from reality as it did not take into account considerations of superior and inferior rank.

The student of comparative sociology, on the other hand, views caste society as above all a hierarchical society, in fact the prototype of all such societies. There social distinctions of certain kinds not only exist, but are widely acknowledged as right, proper and desirable. Law, religion and morality all serve to strengthen and reinforce the subordination of the individual to the group and the ranking of groups as superior and inferior (Lingat 1973). In such a society, the individual has certain obligations to the group of which he is a member by birth, and the group as a whole to other groups according to their respective ranks.

It is true that religious reformers from Buddha to Chaitanya and after have questioned the significance of these distinctions, and have asked what meaning they have for man's dignity and worth, and for his inner life (Bose 1975:116-36). There were continuous fluctuations in the force and significance of caste, and it was not the inflexible, invariant and unchanging system it has often been made out to be. Nevertheless and despite these fluctuations, it retained for many centuries a very distinctive character. There is no other way to account for the correspondence between representations of caste in the ethnographic record of the late nineteenth and early twentieth centuries, and in the record of classical Indology (Bose 1975; Dumont 1966).

The point to stress here is that when we first encounter caste in the writings of nineteenth-century observers and scholars, we encounter it as a more or less complete system. We encounter not only the existential order of caste, as something that might be observed on the ground from the outside, but also its normative order, as something regarded by its individual members as both meaningful and morally binding. This is not to say that there was perfect consensus regarding the values of caste, but that caste distinctions were considered significant and legitimate by most members of society, and particularly by those belonging to the upper castes whose descendants in contemporary India are precisely the ones who are most ambivalent and troubled about its meaning and legitimacy today.

Since the Indian intelligentsia is today most troubled about the hierarchical distinctions of caste, it needs to be emphasised that in the past and up to the middle of the nineteenth century, those distinctions were, at least among the Hindus, acknowledged, upheld and reinforced by law, religion and morality. Things began to change thereafter, as a result of the British presence as well as the Indian response to it. It would be seriously to misrepresent the dialectics of that change if we were to attribute it solely to the colonial intervention and ignore the nationalist response to it (Ganguli 1975). As I have noted elsewhere, Indians probably learnt more about equality from the colonial practice of inequality than from the British theory of equality (Béteille 1979).

Caste undoubtedly exists in contemporary India, and I shall speak in a while of its continuing influence in marriage and its marked, if not increasing, presence in politics. It does not, however, exist as a complete system any more, but—if the phrase be permitted—as a truncated system. The first and most decisive casualty has been the legal basis of caste (Sivaramayya 1984). No two texts can be more divergent in their orientation to caste than the Manusmriti, which we may take as the charter of traditional Hindu law, and the Constitution of India, which may be regarded as the charter of contemporary Indian law. As we have seen, comparative sociologists from Weber to Dumont have dwelt on the intimate connection between caste and Hinduism, regarding it as the social expression of the Hindu religion. But many of the modern proponents of Hinduism, such as Vivekananda, have attacked caste instead of defending it. There are very few contemporary proponents of Hinduism who would be prepared to argue that caste has to be saved in order to strengthen the Hindu religion.

The question of caste morality is more difficult to dispose of briefly, for the evidence is often unclear and sometimes contradictory. One of its principal components was the sense of obligation that the individual carried towards the caste into which he was born, to abide by its customs, to adhere to its style of life and to pursue the occupation allotted to it. Perhaps that sense of obligation, though not easily articulated, is still quite strong among cultivators, artisans and others in the rural areas. But it has weakened considerably in the urban areas and among those sections of contemporary Indian society to which I said I would largely confine this discussion. The compulsions of occupation operate rather differently in the different sectors of the Indian economy. Among engineers, doctors, scientists, civil servants and managers, the obligation to one's occupation exists independently of the obligation to one's caste and to some extent displaces it. The schoolteacher, the clerk or the electrician no longer feels very strongly that he has a duty to encourage his offspring to persevere in his own occupation or the occupation of his forefathers as the village blacksmith, carpenter or potter might have felt in the past.

Nothing could be more mistaken than to believe that caste was something that for two thousand years Indians merely lived by, without giving thought to its meaning or its rightness, that it existed merely as practice and not as theory. We must not lose sight of the intellectual tradition of India in which theoretical reflection and dialectical skill were used for describing, explaining and justifying the distinctions of caste by generations of intellectuals. Dumont (1966:56) was right in drawing attention to the systematic thinking on which caste observances were based; but he was plainly wrong in suggesting that 'Hindus of today and of past times' think about caste in the same systematic way. Until the nineteenth century, Hindu intellectuals could argue with force and conviction about the significance and value of caste. Their counterparts of today, who are still mainly of upper caste, have lost the capacity not only to explain and justify caste, but even to describe it coherently.

Endogamy and reproduction of identity

It is often said that no matter how loudly Hindus might proclaim their indifference or even hostility to caste, when it comes to marriage, all of them—educated and uneducated, urban and rural, professional and peasant—turn to caste. Many have in fact maintained that the

regulation of marriage and the social exclusiveness associated with it—
something akin to a sense of race—are what make caste what it is.
Risley stressed this aspect of caste far more than religion: 'Race
dominates religion; sect is weaker than caste' (1969:80). Obviously, we
cannot associate caste with race as a biological fact, as Risley was
inclined to do, but only with a sense of race more or less widely felt in
society.

It will be of little avail to argue about the decline in the legal,
religious and moral basis of caste if it turns out that on such an
important issue as marriage, nothing has changed at all. One hears both
kinds of arguments among the intelligentsia today: some say that
intercaste marriages are now quite common while others maintain that
they are rare and exceptional. Sometimes one hears a person argue
vehemently that intercaste marriages are impossible in Indian society,
only to learn that he himself has married outside his caste. More
common perhaps is the man who declares himself passionately against
caste in every form, but nonetheless opposes strenuously the marriage
of his children outside his caste.

Some changes are in fact taking place in marriage rules and practices among educated Indians in the higher occupational strata, but we
are hindered in our assessment of them by the paucity of systematic
data. People frequently take recourse to casual empiricism, selecting
one or another set of examples to argue for and against the same proposition. No clear conclusion can be reached in the absence of statistical
data that tell us something about rates and frequencies. But rates and
frequencies are not enough; for where it concerns marriage, we have to
attend not only to practices but also to rules and to enquire whether
these rules continue to carry the same sanctions and the same meanings
as before.

In a recent interview with the editor of the *Times of India*, M.N.
Srinivas noted the changing role of caste in marriage. 'Equally significant as regards pan-Hinduism, Professor Srinivas says, is the diminishing importance of caste in marriage. Inter-caste, inter-regional and
even inter-religious marriages are on the rise' (Padgaonkar 1993).
What is remarkable about the observation is not that Srinivas is India's

leading sociologist, but that he has repeatedly cautioned the Indian intelligentsia against underrating the strength and resilience of caste.

Similar observations were made thirty years earlier by C.T. Kannan in the only satisfactory full-length study of intercaste marriage.

Just twenty-five years ago the instances of intercaste marriages were very few; and those individuals who dared to marry outside the caste had to undergo truly great hardships. Today the situation is altogether different. Not only has the prevalence of intercaste marriage become considerable, but even the difficulties the intercaste marriage couples have to face have become comparatively quite mild. (Kannan 1963:vii)

Kannan limited himself to 200 couples formed by intercaste unions (and 50 others formed by inter-community unions), and therefore his study cannot tell us very much about rates and frequencies that is statistically significant. At the same time, it does draw attention to significant social processes that had been set in motion at least a decade or two before his study was published.

In discussing these questions we must remember that not all inter-caste marriages are of the same kind. A marriage across two sub-subcastes of Smarta Brahmans would be an intercaste marriage in some sense, but it would be very different from a marriage between any Brahman and an Adi-Dravida. In an earlier paper (Béteille 1966), I had suggested that there are ambiguities in the very idea of intercaste marriage. There I had drawn attention to the slow and gradual way in which even for arranged marriages, the horizons of endogamy were being extended from sub-subcaste to subcaste, and then to caste among the Tamil Brahmans. I am not suggesting that there never was any ambiguity in the past, but the ambiguity over what constitutes the unit of endogamy has almost certainly become more pervasive now, particularly among the upper castes.

It is possible that a more permissive attitude towards caste in the selection of spouses is being accompanied by a greater attention to other restrictions such as those relating to education, occupation and income. Many different criteria are taken into account in the selection of a spouse, and in the case of someone who is highly desirable on a number of important counts, one may overlook the traditional

restrictions of caste if the person belongs to a different subcaste of the
same caste or even to a different but cognate caste. It is only rarely that
caste considerations are ignored altogether.

One can get a good sense of the diversity of the categories at play
by looking at the matrimonial advertisements in the Sunday papers.
These advertisements are classified, but not according to any single or
consistent plan. The categories of caste are very prominent, but those of
religion, such as Sunni, Sikh and Muslim, and of language, such as
Sindhi, Bengali and Tamil, are also found. Cheek by jowl with these
are categories belonging to other sets, such as 'doctors', 'engineers',
'MBA/CA', 'postgraduate' and 'cosmopolitan'. One should not be
misled, however, because caste is frequently indicated, directly or
indirectly, even under 'cosmopolitan'. But then again someone may
indicate his own caste, in case the other party finds it relevant, even if
he writes, 'Caste, dowry no bar', to show that he does not regard it as
relevant for himself.

To be sure, even in the past, people took many factors into account
in addition to caste, but those factors were taken into account after
keeping caste constant. One always looked for an appropriate family in
seeking a match, but one took it for granted that such a family would be
of one's own caste. An advertisement in the *Sunday Times* of 19
December 1993 reads, '32/167, C.K.P. well-settled businessmen from
educated family seeks alliance from good-looking, cultured girls with
good family background. Caste no bar'. (The man was 32 years old,
167 cm in height and of the Chandraseniya Kayastha Prabhu subcaste.)
I have been much struck by the insistence on 'good family', 'cultured
family', or 'status family' even in advertisements that do not give any
specification as to caste.

I would like to return very briefly to the traditional rules of marriage
through which the identities of caste, subcaste and sub-subcaste were
maintained and reproduced. As is well known, there was not one single
rule, there were several rules. Of these, two are of particular significance, the rule of endogamy and the rule of hypergamy. The rule of
hypergamy not only distinguishes between castes (or subcastes) but
also ranks them, and on that ground it has sometimes been regarded as

even more distinctive of caste than the rule of endogamy (Dumont 1966:152-61). It should be pointed out that the rule of hypergamy (or *anuloma*) was not universally or even extensively observed in all places in all times (Karve 1961:16), although it was clearly acknowledged by the shastras whereas its opposite or *pratiloma* was universally condemned.

Where intercaste marriages do take place among the intelligentsia, ignoring for the moment the question of frequency, such marriages are in general as likely to be of the *anuloma* (or sanctioned) as of the *pratiloma* (or unsanctioned) type. More than that, in some areas where hypergamy was widely prevalent, the rule appears to have lapsed altogether. I can say from personal knowledge that many Bengali Brahmans, of both the Rarhi and the Barendra castes, well-known until the middle of the nineteenth century for the observance of hypergamy (associated with the notorious system known as Kulinism), have now little or no knowledge of the traditional rule and its implications. The attack on Kulinism in nineteenth-century Bengal and its gradual disappearance throw an interesting light on the relationship between caste, hierarchy and marriage rules.

It seems clear to me that Kannan's assessment of the weakening of collective sanctions against intercaste unions in urban India was on the whole the right one. His data show that the collective pressure of the caste or the subcaste against intercaste unions among the urban middle classes is neither very strong nor very effective. In risking a wrong alliance, the primary focus of anxiety is the family or perhaps the 'kindred of co-operation' (Mayer 1960), itself more restricted in the city than in the village, whereas caste figures only dimly in the background. There are of course exceptions, and these must be noted. Newspapers sometimes report instances of brutal violence in small towns or villages against certain unions, typically where the woman is of a high caste and the man a Harijan or a Muslim. These acts are reminiscent of the lynchings that took place in the American South until forty or fifty years ago when a black male sought union with a white female. Otherwise, intercaste marriages in metropolitan cities are not accompanied by any significant public violence, although there is no lack of urban violence in contemporary India.

Political uses of caste

I mentioned earlier that in the 1950s, most Indian intellectuals believed that caste was on the way out, while only a few said that it was there to stay. Even those who said that it was gaining a new lease of life could point to evidence from only a single domain, that of politics, to support their argument. No one could seriously maintain that, to use the language of Hutton, the strictures and sanctions of caste were becoming stronger; or that the many ritual injunctions and interdictions relating to food and physical contact were gaining in strength; or that the association between caste and occupation was growing closer; or even that the rules of endogamy were being more strictly defined and observed. In all these domains, caste was growing weaker, very slowly, almost imperceptibly in some cases, more clearly and noticeably in others.

It is only when we turn to politics that we get a very different picture. When Srinivas argued in his 1957 address that caste was getting a new lease of life, all of the evidence that he provided, or almost all of it, came from the domain of politics. But only a few years earlier, Radcliffe-Brown (1952:x), reflecting the views till then common among anthropologists, had observed as follows in his Foreword to Srinivas's book on the Coorgs: 'A caste is in its essence a religious group, membership of which entails certain ritual observances. The rules of caste behaviour are rules of religion'. Clearly, some changes were under way which had not come to the attention of Radcliffe-Brown, although he had registered his interest in political anthropology as early as in 1940.

Caste did not enter politics all at once with independence, but it made its presence strongly felt in the first general election, and increasingly with each successive election. Although the subject of caste and politics was initially of interest to only a handful of social anthropologists, it soon attracted the attention of political scientists and others (Kothari 1970; Frankel and Rao 1989-90), and there is now a large literature on it. Even after the subject had been taken up by scholars in various disciplines in the 1960s and 1970s, some differences remained between the ordinary run of social scientists who saw and stressed the importance of caste in politics, and what are called 'left intellectuals' who were inclined to treat it lightly. Today, many more scholars, both Marxists and non-Marxists, acknowledge the importance of caste in politics, although they draw different policy conclusions from it (Centre for Social Studies 1985; Béteille 1992).

It will not be possible for me in the brief space remaining to review or even summarise the principal findings of the very large literature that we now have on caste and politics. I will only draw attention to certain processes that are known to be quite widespread, and indicate very briefly how those processes are viewed, explained and justified by some of the principal actors who participate in and give shape to them.

In an essay written more than 25 years ago (Béteille 1969:152-69), I had, after making a distinction between problems of distribution and problems of process, tried to identify the basic processes through which caste becomes involved in politics. The loyalties of caste are used for the mobilisation of political support in a number of ways: by a generalised appeal to caste sentiment, by activating networks of kinship and marriage, and by the organised activities of caste associations. Studies conducted in the last 30 years have shown the extensive use of caste for the mobilisation of political support during elections and in between elections, although there are significant regional variations.

As Srinivas showed, caste came to be used in the electoral process from the first general election, and indeed it had entered the political arena even before. But the question is not simply of the extent of the use of caste in electoral politics, but also of its meaning and legitimacy for the different sections of Indian society. Clearly, those who yielded to the appeal of caste loyalty and voted for candidates of their own caste, could not have all thought that it was a bad thing to vote according to caste. By and large, the intelligentsia showed an ambivalent attitude. They were troubled by 'casteism' in politics even though they might support someone from their own caste. They were inclined to treat this kind of caste preference more as an aspect of Realpolitik than of political morality.

In the 1950s and 1960s, the leaders of all political parties condemned in public the use of caste in politics. Politicians freely acknowledged that caste was being extensively used in the politics of post-independence India, but they said that it was being used by other parties, not their own. When it was shown that their party too was using caste, their reply was that they did not start the process but were being forced to accommodate caste in order to survive, for in politics, or at least in Indian politics, one could not afford to be too idealistic if one wished to remain in business. In other words, they sought to defend the use of caste (unlike, for instance, the use of class) on tactical rather than ethical grounds.

A change in the orientation of political leaders, and with them of other members of the intelligentsia, appears to have started in the 1970s when the politics of backwardness took a new turn with the installation of the first non-Congress government in New Delhi in 1977. It began to be argued that caste needed to be given a place in public life not so much on grounds of Realpolitik as on grounds of social justice. The lower castes had been stigmatised and exploited in the past, and they should be given special protection through extensive quotas in every domain of public life. The argument was not new; it had been an important component of colonial policy in the decades preceding independence (Irschick 1969; Béteille 1992). What was new was its increasing appeal to social justice and its increasing vehemence.

Again, I cannot enter into a discussion of the principal features of the politics of backwardness on which I and others have written extensively, but would like to point out that it has acquired a markedly ideological tone since 1990. The ideological tone was given a new articulation when the left parties decided to join hands with Mr. V.P. Singh's Janata Dal in pressing for the extension of caste quotas in the cause of social justice. This made it in effect impossible for any party openly to oppose caste quotas, so that caste has, at least for the time being, strengthened its grip over politics. But it still is an unsteady grip, for neither the supporters nor the opponents of caste quotas say that caste itself should be revitalised. In fact, the strongest supporters of caste quotas are, paradoxically, also the strongest opponents of caste as a hierarchical system.

Ethnicity and the metaphor of caste

Those who are given to moralising sometimes observe that democracy
has been debased in India by the pernicious influence of caste. The
issue for the moment is not how caste has altered politics, but how
politics is altering caste. Edmund Leach (1960:6-7) had already asked
more than thirty years ago whether castes cease to be castes when they
compete with each other for political power. My view then (Béteille
1969b) was that there were obvious and significant continuities
between the castes of the present and those of the past; something so
complex and deeply-entrenched as caste does not cease to be itself as
soon as one or even a few of its basic characteristics change. I would
now like to examine some of the shifts that are taking place in the ways
in which caste identities are defined.

As is well known, conventionally caste has had at least two distinct
(though related) meanings: *varna* and *jati*. While it is true that most
Indians recognise both meanings of caste, they now think of it more as
jati than as *varna*; that would be consistent with the shift in emphasis
from religion to politics in matters relating to caste. In an influential
paper, Srinivas (1962:63-9) had drawn attention to the distinction, and
argued that caste has been frequently *mis*represented as *varna*.
Srinivas's own argument was perhaps one-sided, but it was timely, for
it came at a moment when educated Indians were probably beginning
to think of caste less as *varna* than as *jati*. They probably thought of it
as *varna* much more commonly until after independence when the role
of caste became increasingly prominent in politics. A few years before
the publication of Srinivas's paper, the historian Niharranjan Ray
(1945) wrote a book on caste in Bengali which he entitled *Bangali
hindur barnabhed*,[2] meaning distinctions of *varna* among Bengali
Hindus. He was following a well-established usage for the
representation of caste, a usage which was, however, changing.

There are other ambiguities besides those that might arise from the

---

[2] In transliterating Bengali words, I have gone by the sounds of spoken
Bengali, and not followed any consistent scheme. Thus, I have written
'Barendra' and not 'Varendra', and hence '*barna*' and not '*varna*' which is the
more common north Indian form and also closer to Sanskrit.

confusion of *varna* and *jati*, for there are collective identities that are not identities of caste in the strict anthropological sense, but are nevertheless represented as such. Though most frequently paired with *varna* in the ethnographic (and Indological) literature, the term *jati* (or the more colloquial *jat*) has other associations as well. It is commonly used to cover a series of identities of increasing degrees of inclusiveness from sub-subcaste through caste to religion and language.

Those who use data from large-scale censuses and surveys have often to deal with lists of castes (or *jatis*) that are very heterogeneous indeed. While conducting a survey in 1958 for the Indian Statistical Institute in Giridih town and its surrounding villages in Bihar, I encountered in the entries under 'caste', in addition to the names of castes in the restricted sense, such terms as 'Marwari', 'Oriya', 'Jain' and 'Muslim'. Later, in 1963 and 1964 in the villages in Burdwan district in West Bengal, I was told that the inhabitants included Brahmans, Baidyas, Sadgopes, Aghuris, Bagdis, Santals and Muslims.

We have moved some distance away from caste as *varna* when we are dealing on the same plane with such disparate groups and categories as Baidyas, Sadgopes, Telis, Bagdis, Santals, Oriyas and Muslims. The disparate assemblage of clans, sects, castes, tribes, religious communities and linguistic groups that can all, according to context and situation, pass as *jatis* fits at best awkwardly into the clear and symmetrical design of the four *varnas*. It would be unwise to declare that these modes of representation are all new, without any roots in past social experience and practice. At the same time, new perceptions of collective identities are forced upon people by the political process which uses the distinctions of language, religion and caste in the same way for the mobilisation of political support.

The operation of caste along with language and religion in the political arena has led some to speak in a rather inclusive sense of 'ethnic groups', 'ethnic identities' and 'ethnic loyalties'. This is to signal a shift in the meaning of caste brought about by its increasing role in a new field of activity. Srinivas has recently been quoted as saying, 'In the future, too, caste will remain a predominant feature of Indian life. But it will be conceived more in terms of ethnicity' (Padgaonkar 1993).

The movement from caste as *varna* to caste as ethnic group has been seen by some as the 'substantialisation of caste' (Dumont 1966:280; Deliège 1993:107-10). This may be somewhat misleading in so far as the notion of substance conveys a sense of homogeneity, whereas in fact each caste is becoming progressively differentiated in terms of occupation, education and income. Clearly, some shifts are taking place in the meanings that people assign to caste. When journalists and political commentators refer to castes as ethnic groups, they have in mind not so much hierarchical distinctions of status as differences in bargaining power and in life chances in general.

Few will deny that caste has become increasingly salient in the political arena, or that in that arena hierarchical distinctions of status count for less than differences in life chances. Does that mean that distinctions of status are losing their meaning and significance for Indians? It would be rash indeed to answer that question categorically in the affirmative. For one thing, we cannot say for certain what meaning and significance the innumerable ritual restrictions of the past had for distinctions of status among persons; the ethnographers have tried mainly to explain either the origins of those restrictions or their formal structure, but rarely asked what they meant for those who applied them or to whom they were applied. For another, distinctions of status continue to enjoy a luxuriant life among all social strata in contemporary India.

Some of the best accounts of distinctions of status and their meaning (or lack of meaning) in contemporary Indian life are to be found in literary as against ethnographic writing. V.S. Naipaul (1964) has left a memorable account of his encounter with rank and status in settings that are characteristic of modern India. Naipaul's *An area of darkness* caused much resentment among educated Indians, no doubt in part because many of them found something of themselves in his account.

Contemporary Indian life provides numerous occasions for the play of status in the factory, in the office, in hospitals, in laboratories, and in banks; in work and outside work; and in both public and private places. I am speaking now not simply of the distinctions of rank that are an inherent feature of every modern association, institution and organisation, but of patterns of deference and invidious distinction that grow within and around them in great and sometimes unexpected profusion. It is this luxuriance of status distinctions that some are inclined to regard as the characteristically Indian part of modern Indian life. They point out that all the professions of equality in the Constitution and the laws are but words in the face of the Indian's undying preoccupation with hierarchy, rank and status.

It is natural to ask about this preoccupation with rank and status in contemporary Indian life whether it is anything more than a new manifestation of the old hierarchy of caste. The concept of caste has always been elastic, and the concept of status even more so. It is of course possible to speak of caste both literally and metaphorically, and in the latter case to describe every form of invidious distinction and social exclusion as a form of caste. But then one must be careful to note when one is speaking of caste in the restricted sense of distinctions of status based on specific ideas of purity and pollution, of birth and inherited bodily substance, and when one is speaking of it in the broad and general sense of rigid and elaborate social distinctions.

Even when an Indian is acutely conscious of his own caste and also of his status, he may not make distinctions of status among others solely or even mainly according to their caste. The social world of the professional, the civil servant and the executive in the large metropolitan city is different from the social world of the village or even the small town. It would be rash to declare that the city is less animated by a concern for status than the village, and, indeed, from the villager's point of view, the case may appear to be the opposite. That apart, the definition of status, its symbolic form and its social expression are not the same for the two. There are innumerable tales of persons from the village or small town being bewildered by the intricate conventions of status among their upper-class relatives in the metropolitan city.

In addition to caste, the things that count for status in the sections of society about which I am writing are education, occupation and income, and the subcultures of the profession, the office and the association. The latter are by no means unrelated to caste in the traditional sense, but they can hardly be regarded merely as aspects or expressions of it. The social world created by education, occupation and income, the office, the firm, the law court and the laboratory cuts across the social world of caste. The social circle of the Brahman judge, diplomat, engineer, civil servant or manager is not the same as that of the Brahman clerk, schoolteacher or cook. Particularly among the higher occupational strata, many relationships are formed that cut across caste, as may be easily seen from the patterns of residence in large metropolitan cities where housing goes directly with occupation and income, and only indirectly with caste.

There are, to be sure, many continuities and linkages between the new status distinctions prominent among the intelligentsia and the old ones based largely on considerations of purity and pollution. Different criteria of status, different symbols of distinction and different strategies of exclusion now co-exist in various sectors of Indian society. It is clear that they do not all fit neatly into a single, unified hierarchical design; whether and to what extent they did so in the past are questions that cannot be addressed here.

If we are to reach a proper understanding of variation and change in contemporary Indian society, we have to be on our guard against the unreflective switch from the literal use of the term caste to its metaphorical use as, for instance, in the phrase that the Boston Brahmans are an acutely caste-conscious set. It is of course well known that western writers from Alexis de Tocqueville (1956) to Michael Young (1961) have used the metaphor of caste while commenting on their own societies. No great confusion or misunderstanding is likely to result from the metaphorical use of caste to describe status, the sense of distinction or the strategies of exclusion in western societies; few readers are likely to think that the court of Louis XVI or the playing-fields of Eton were teeming with Brahmans of different kind, carefully calculating what kinds of boiled vegetables they might share and with whom without serious risk to the purity of their bodily substance. Yet such misunderstanding repeatedly arises when the metaphorical use of caste is extended to contexts in contemporary India where caste in the traditional sense has ceased to have its old significance.

Conclusion: imputed meaning and actor's meaning

I began by pointing to the highly ambivalent attitude to caste among certain influential sections of Indian society, and some will no doubt object that I have ended by trying to show that caste no longer has any legitimacy at all. How can certain identities remain so manifestly durable if they have no meaning and no legitimacy for their bearers?

I would like to state clearly and firmly in conclusion that I do not believe that caste has disappeared or is likely to disappear from even the sections of society about which I have written; but I do believe that shifts are taking place in the meaning and legitimacy of social relationships and social activities among many members of it. We are likely to miss the significance of those shifts if we continue to think of caste—or, indeed, Indian society—in the old way, relying mainly on the ethnographic record of village studies or the Indological record of the classical texts. The problem in the past has been that anthropologists often came to India in search of the eternal, and that is why so many of them were drawn, instinctively as it were, to the remote village and the classical text. I have tried to redress the balance somewhat, but there is always the danger of going to the opposite extreme and, by focusing attention on a relatively small though very influential section of society, losing sight of the larger body of people.

The exercise I have undertaken above has to be seen primarily as an effort to redress the balance among anthropologists. To draw attention to the growing ambivalence towards caste is not to say that caste has become or is becoming meaningless, but to indicate that there are now both positive and negative components of evaluation that sit uneasily together. The negative components of evaluation have not in my view received sufficient attention from social anthropologists who study caste, and that is why I have dwelt on them at some length. It is of course true that meanings do not always lie on the surface but may be latent or hidden, and meanings that appear inconsistent on the surface may in fact be resolved at a deeper level. Psychoanalysis and some forms of structural analysis deal with these latent or hidden or imputed meanings, whereas my concern has been more with the empirical or observed meanings (Kolakowski 1982), or the meanings that actors themselves assign to their actions (Weber 1978). All that I can say is that if caste today has a single or homogeneous meaning, I have failed to discover it either in my own observation and experience or in the writings of other anthropologists.

It would be strange if something that occupied such a central place in society were to lose all positive significance for its members simply because they have changed their laws, or acquired a different system of education, or taken to new occupations. Evidence of some positive attachment to caste may be found in almost every sector of Indian society, among doctors, lawyers and scientists, not to speak of administrators, managers and businessmen. I said at the very beginning that the statement from educated Indians that caste does not exist any more should not be taken at face value. The attachment to caste may lie very deep indeed, so that a person may not even be fully aware of it; but then it might find expression suddenly and unexpectedly when, for instance, a daughter declares that she wants to marry a man from a very low caste, or when a man of a different caste boasts about the achievements of that caste. Much patience and care are required for collecting such evidence in a systematic way, and going back to the village or the classical texts cannot be a substitute for it.

It is easy enough to show that caste has both a positive and a negative significance for many members of contemporary Indian society. What is difficult is to weigh and measure these different components and draw an accurate balance sheet. Where the evidence is contradictory and points in different, even opposite, directions, the sociologist is very likely to draw on it in accordance with his own bias, and that bias may lead him either to exaggerate or to underrate the contemporary significance of caste. For the last twenty-five years, I have been told by anthropologists in London, Cambridge and Chicago that I ignore evidence of the significance of caste in contemporary India, and by scientists, economists and others in Calcutta and Delhi that I exaggerate it, and, indeed, that as a sociologist I am paid to do so.

In 1990, Indian intellectuals became deeply divided over the significance of caste in contemporary Indian society. The division was over an issue of policy, that of caste quotas in education and employment (Béteille 1990; Guhan *et al.* 1990). It has been said that those who opposed quotas minimised the significance of caste, sometimes deliberately. But it must not be assumed that those who supported quotas thought that caste was a good thing which ought to be strengthened; on the contrary, they said that caste was an evil but believed that the best way of doing away with it in the long run was by having quotas in the short run. No doubt personal interest played some part in this, but it would hardly be reasonable to suppose that Indian intellectuals are unique in the world in supporting or opposing policies solely on the basis of personal interest. At any rate, those who supported the quotas belonged to diverse castes, and Indian intellectuals, who are predomnantly of upper caste, both supported and opposed the quotas.

If among the intelligentsia, individuals differ in their perception of caste or in the significance they give to it, it may well be that these differences have some relationship to the differences in their positions in the hierarchy of caste. Where some individual mobility is possible, the burden of caste may weigh more heavily on the lower- than on the upper-caste person. In certain contexts, caste might matter more for Harijan than for Brahman intellectuals as race seems to do more for black than for white intellectuals in the United States (Carter 1991; West 1993). But this again would be a kind of reversal of the traditional order where caste matters were ultimately the responsibility of the upper and not the lower castes. That at least is my reading of the literature relating to village India and to classical India. If we are to understand what is happening to caste in contemporary India, we will have to look for new types of data, devise new concepts, and, above all, approach the subject with a more open mind that does not seek either to ignore the distinctive features of Indian society or to maximise the difference (Molund 1991) between India and the west.

References

Bardhan, P. 1984. *Political economy of development in India*. Oxford: Basil Blackwell.

Berreman, G.D. 1963. *Hindus of the Himalayas*. Berkeley: University of California Press.

Béteille, A. 1966. 'Closed and open social stratification in India.' *European Journal of Sociology* 7:224-46.

———. 1969a. *Castes: old and new*. Bombay: Asia Publishing House.

———. 1969b. 'The politics of "non-antagonistic" strata.' *Contributions to Indian Sociology* (n.s.) 3:17-31.

———. 1979. 'Homo hierarchicus, Homo equalis.' *Modern Asian Studies* 13:529-48.

———. 1989. 'Are the intelligentsia a ruling class?' *Economic and Political Weekly* 24, 3:151-5.

———. 1990. 'Caste and reservations.' *Hindu*, 20 October 1990.

———. 1991a. *Society and politics in India*. London: Athlone Press.

———. 1991b. 'The reproduction of inequality.' *Contributions to Indian Sociology* (n.s.) 25:3-28.

———. 1992. *The backward classes in contemporary India*. Delhi: Oxford University Press.

Blunt, E.A.H. 1931. *The caste system of northern India*. London: Oxford University Press.

Bose, N.K. 1967. *Culture and society in India*. Bombay: Asia Publishing House.

———. 1975 (1949). *The structure of Hindu society*. Delhi: Orient Longman.

Bouglé, C. 1971 (1908). *Essays on the caste system*. Cambridge: Cambridge University Press.

Carter, S.C. 1991. *Reflections of an affirmative action baby*. New York: Basic Books.

Centre for Social Studies. 1985. *Caste, caste conflict and reservation*. Delhi: Ajanta.

Chatterjee, B. 1961 (1888). 'Dharmatattva.' In *Bankimrachanabali*, vol.2, pp.584-679. Calcutta: Sahitya Samsad.

Chaudhuri, N.C. 1979. *Hinduism*. London: Chatto and Windus.

Deliège, R. 1993. *Le système des castes*. Paris: Presses Universitaires de France.

de Tocqueville, A. 1956 (1835, 1840). *Democracy in America* (2 vols). New York: Alfred Knopf.

Dumont, L. 1966. *Homo hierarchicus*. Paris: Gallimard.

Enthoven, R.E. 1920-2. *The tribes and castes of Bombay* (3 vols.). Bombay: Government Central Press.

Frankel, F.R. and M.S.A. Rao (eds.). 1989-90. *Dominance and state power in modern India* (2 vols.). Delhi: Oxford University Press.

Gait, E.A. 1913. *Report on the Census of India*. Calcutta: Government Printing.

Gandhi, M.K. 1962. *Varnashramadharma*. Ahmedabad: Navjivan.

Ganguli, B.N. 1975. *Concept of equality*. Simla: Indian Institute of Advanced Study.

Guhan, S. *et al.* 1990. 'South India and reservations: a reply to André Béteille.' *Hindu*, 27 October 1990.

Hutton, J.H. 1946. *Caste in India*. Cambridge: Cambridge University Press.

Ibbetson, D. 1916. *Panjab castes*. Lahore: Government Press.

Irschick, E.F. 1969. *Politics and social conflict in south India*. Berkeley: University of California Press.

Kannan, C.T. 1963. *Intercaste and inter-community marriage in India*. Bombay: Allied Publishers.

Karve, I. 1961. *Hindu society*. Poona: Deshmukh Prakashan.

Kolakowski, L. 1982. *Religion*. London: Fontana.

Kothari, R. (ed.). 1970. *Caste in Indian politics*. Delhi: Orient Longman.

Leach, E.R. (ed.). 1960. *Aspects of caste in south India, Ceylon and north-west Pakistan*. Cambridge: Cambridge University Press.

Lingat, R. 1973 (1967). *The classical law of India*. Berkeley: University of California Press.

Maine, H.S. 1931 (1861). *Ancient law*. London: Oxford University Press.

Marriott, M. (ed.). 1990. *India through Hindu categories*. New Delhi: Sage.

Mayer, A.C. 1960. *Caste and kinship in central India*. London: Routledge and Kegan Paul.

Molund, S. 1991. 'Sociology as critical understanding: an interview with André Béteille.' *Antropologiska Studier* 48:31-47.

Naipaul, V.S. 1964. *An area of darkness*. London: André Deutsch.

O'Malley, L.S.S. 1932. *Indian caste customs*. Cambridge: Cambridge University Press.

Padgaonkar, D. 1993. 'In conversation with M.N. Srinivas.' *Sunday Times of India*, 12 December 1993.

Radcliffe-Brown, A.R. 1952. 'Foreword.' In M.N. Srinivas, *Religion and society among the Coorgs of south India*. Oxford: Clarendon Press.

Ray, N. 1945. *Bangali hindur harnabhed*. Calcutta: Visvabharati Granthalaya.

Risley, H.H. 1892. *The tribes and castes of Bengal*. Calcutta: Bengal Secretariat Press.

———. 1969 (1908). *The people of India*. New Delhi: Oriental Books.

Rudra, A. 1989. 'The intelligentsia as a ruling class.' *Economic and Political Weekly* 24, 3:142-50.

Senart, É. 1930 (1896). *Caste in India*. London: Methuen.

Sivaramayya, B. 1984. *Inequalities and the law*. Lucknow: Eastern Book Company.

Srinivas, M.N. 1962. *Caste in modern India and other essays*. Bombay: Asia Publishing House.

Thurston, E. 1909. *Castes and tribes of southern India* (7 vols.). Madras: Government Press.

Weber, M. 1958 (1916-7). *The religion of India*. New York: Free Press.

———. 1978 (1922). *Economy and society*. Berkeley: University of California Press.

West, C. 1993. *Race matters*. Boston: Beacon Press.

Young, M. 1961. *The rise of meritocracy*. London: Thames and Hudson.

Chapter 7

THE MEO AS A RAJPUT CASTE
AND A MUSLIM COMMUNITY

Raymond Jamous

The Meo are a community of more than 300,000 people scattered throughout approximately 1,200 villages in Mewat (across Haryana, Rajasthan and Uttar Pradesh). They form one-quarter of the total population of this area. This chapter examines different aspects of the two dimensions, caste and Islam, which characterise this community as it was observed during fieldwork in 1982-3, and ten years later in 1992-3.

There is an apparent contradiction between the hierarchical values of the caste system and the egalitarian ideology of Islamic religion. Each system seems mutually exclusive, which means that we have to analyse the community according to either one or the other principle of political and religious organisation. It is as if we had to show that the Meo were a Rajput caste and false Muslims or, on the contrary, that they were Muslims and not a real caste. In fact, the Meo case is not so simple: they are both a Rajput caste and a Muslim community. This does not mean that they have found some mysterious way of harmoniously fitting the two kinds of identity together. Islam is not reducible to normative rules: Muslim communities all over the world can and do interpret the Islamic faith in their own way and they have adapted it to their local or regional systems. In this sense, one can say that among the Meo, caste and Islam are not only compatible but are articulated with each other. The normative aspects of Islam—the principles of equality and of participation in the Muslim Community of the Faithful—can under certain circumstances take specific forms and contradict local or regional identities. Such a situation is, again, very widespread among Muslim communities. Yet we can say that a growing tension has developed in recent years between the Meo's identity as a Rajput caste and their participation in an Islamic reform movement. But as I shall try to show, no definite choice is being made. (Who could

180

make such a choice consciously?) The Meo live out this tension daily and try to keep it under control. My purpose is to analyse this dilemma. First, I discuss aspects of caste among the Meo, and then their Islamic features as I observed them in 1982; finally I will analyse the situation that existed in 1993.

Aspects of caste

There are several ways to define caste in the Indian context. It is not my purpose to look at the different theories in order to compare their respective interpretative merits. My aim is more modest. It is instead to look at two aspects of the caste system among the Meo: their particular position in the system as a Rajput caste, and thus the different types of relationships in terms of separation and interdependence which they have with other castes, and, secondly, the internal organisation of their caste, which will mostly be about the kinship and territorial structure. To do this, we will have to consider the Meo's own representations of their status as a warrior caste and compare them with anthropological observations.

The Meo as a Rajput caste

In Mewat, the Meo claim to be members of the second *varna*, the second 'category' or 'class' of the Kshatriyas from which the Rajput caste came forth. The Meo are proud of their warrior tradition. There are numerous legends which tell how they attacked caravans going from Delhi to Rajasthan, or how they raided the Mughal capital several times. Songs also tell of the courage of those who faced violent death without hesitation in order to demonstrate their warrior status.   ·

The Meo had to submit to the Mughal administration, and pay taxes to the Rajput state of Alwar or to the Jat state of Bharatpur. But this does not mean that they recognised the legitimacy of those external authorities. There is no tradition among the Meo of considering their political leaders as representatives of an outside power. Fighting with those external polities was treated in the same way as submitting to their military superiority (and consequently their coercive and admini-strative authority); it was merely a function of the circumstances. To put it differently, the Meo thought that they had a status equivalent to any one of those external groups, and that war and peace with them were two aspects of the same type of political interaction.

The Meo conceive themselves and are perceived locally as a 'high caste' (*unci jati*), like the Hindu priests (Brahman) and traders (Baniya). These three castes distinguish themselves from the 'service castes' (*kamin jati*) who have a low status; some of them are Muslims (like the barbers, washermen, bards and funeral priests or fakirs, who are equivalent to the Hindu Mahabrahmans),[1] whereas others are Hindus (like the potters, jewellers and different untouchable groups).

In multicaste villages, the Meo generally occupy separate quarters located in the western part of the residential area, while the other high and low castes share the central part, and the untouchables live in the eastern part of the village. The Meo bury their dead in their own cemetery (*kabristan*) and other Muslim castes share a separate cemetery.

This spatial separation from other castes is related to the problem of contact as a mark of differentiation. The Meo are non-vegetarians, but they are very sensitive about questions of purity and impurity. They differentiate between *kacca* and *pakka* food, and between everyday and ceremonial food. They accept cooked food from the high castes or those assimilated to the high castes, like the barbers, but they refuse to take food from all other castes. On ceremonial occasions, they generally use clay pots as vessels for the Meo guests and throw them away afterwards. Only the sweeper can take the pots away. The funeral priests (the fakirs), but also the sweepers and the washermen, will not enter Meo houses because of their impurity. We can therefore say that for the Meo, purity and impurity mark their separation or differentiation from other castes.

The Meo are locally the 'dominant' caste. They have the preeminent right over the land in the villages where they live. According to legend, when their ancestors settled in a village, they took the land and distributed it among their descendants. Some add that since the

---

[1] Muslim fakirs and Hindu Mahabrahmans are supposed to take care of the dead body and dispose of all the impure objects connected with the deceased or his family (see Parry 1979:65).

Brahmans accompanied the Meo in their migrations, they also received some pieces of land. There was a sort of jajmani system working in the area in 1982. In this context, the Meo patrons are called *jajman*s, and are at the centre of the economic and ritual organisation. Each Meo family with a share of the land uses the economic services of specific families from different castes, which are their 'service castes'. For their work, the latter mostly receive a share of the crop during harvesting. The relationship between *jajman*s and service castes is also a ritual one because the same families participate in Meo ceremonies; they offer their services and receive ritual payments or honoraria (*neg*). Thus economic and ritual relationships in this jajmani system were closely connected. The one implied the other, but it is because Meo used the ritual services of families of different castes that they had to use their economic services during harvesting, and not the other way round. A few wage-labourers are engaged for agricultural work and they receive a salary. Labourers have a contract for one season, whereas the service castes have an indefinite contract, which can be broken only if the *jajman* or his clients have failed to discharge their ritual or economic duties.

The Meo do not use the ritual services of the local Brahmans. But they do have Brahman genealogists who live outside Mewat and come every two or three years to a village to record the birth of children in their *jajman*s' families. The genealogies are recorded in books kept by the Brahmans, who are the only people who can read them. The Meo do not know the exact content of the written documents. They have a very poor knowledge of genealogical links within their patrilineal lineages and wider clan groups. But they think that their genealogists are knowledgeable and that is enough for them. More specifically, the Meo believe that these Brahmans know the identity of the ancestor who first settled in the village and founded the lineage, where he came from, how he is related to the ultimate ancestor of the clan, how this ultimate ancestor is related to other similar Hindu ancestors inside the' vast Rajput clans, and finally which Hindu gods or heroes 'created' this ultimate ancestor. The local bards (*mirasi*) make up songs and are supposed to know the history of their *jajman*s. But they never go upwards beyond the third or fourth generation of their living patrons. The bards' knowledge is local and partial in comparison with the more global knowledge of the Brahman genealogists who are supposed to understand the implications of the social and cosmic order, so that they can establish the temporal and spatial dimensions of social groups (that is the movements of clan ancestors and their descendants within the territory), the legitimacy of the Meo's Rajput status, and the relationship between the gods and human beings. In this context, genealogy is not a simple matter of kinship, but also an intercaste feature. For their services, genealogists receive *neg*, which is also the name for the ritual honorarium given to the service castes. Among the local Hindus, Brahmans are ritual specialists. They offer their services at different moments of life-cycle rituals (birth, marriage, death). But no one can understand the meaning of the Sanskrit words they utter and why they make particular gestures. Nevertheless, their presence is essential and everybody must invite them. The Brahmans' actions are considered to be beneficial in terms of purity and more generally as life-giving. In this sense, there is a similarity between the ritualist Brahman and the genealogist Brahman. Both have global knowledge (social and cosmic) whose meaning is not understandable by their *jajman*s; both are specialists in the matter of life-giving. But the analogy is not complete identity. Recording genealogy is ritualist activity, but not ritual action in the strict sense. Yet it has to be interpreted through the ritual code, even if it is not strictly ritual specialisation, so that the genealogists' activity can be considered as ritual work of a particular kind.

I should add that the Meo do not imagine that they can use the services of the literate Muslims who live among them, notably the Sayyid families who are descended from the Prophet and are settled in Mewat. The Sayyids are considered to belong to the service castes with whom they live and share a cemetery. Despite the respect that the Meo have for the Sayyids and their religious knowledge, they consider them as 'foreigners' (owing to their supposed non-Indian origin), who cannot in any way act as their genealogists. If the Meo had used Muslim specialists as genealogists, it would have meant that this activity were integrated into their Islamic social universe. But this is not the case.

The genealogists are Brahmans and genealogical recording is a caste activity, which can therefore be interpreted as part of the local caste system.

The internal organisation of the Meo caste

To analyse any caste is also to look at its internal organisation. In this respect, there are important similarities among many castes in India, in relation to caste or subcaste endogamy and the existence of unilineal descent groups. But there is also a lot of variation due to any particular caste's position in the hierarchy and there are regional differences as well. Two points will be considered here. First, when a caste is dominant, it implies that its kinship structure and territorial organisation are related, and also that the intercaste relations defined in political terms are important. Secondly, marriage institutions lead us to contrast south India with north India: in the latter region there is a wide set of marriage prohibitions and marriage alliance, when it exists, is related to hypergamous distinctions between wife-givers and wife-receivers. My book (Jamous 1991) mostly focused on these issues, and here I will present some of the findings which are relevant to this paper.

The Meo constitute an endogamous caste and they do not marry outside their own community. They neither accept nor give women from or to other Rajput groups or any other Muslim communities. One legend narrates the story of a Meoni (a female Meo), who was forcibly abducted as a concubine by the Mughal emperor. A Meo called Bahar went to Delhi, entered the imperial harem and rescued the Meoni whom he married. For years, he was searched for by the imperial army. When he was caught, judged and executed, his body was left to rot outside the capital's wall. A merchant from the Baniya caste of Mewat brought him back to his village for a decent burial. The Meo gave this Baniya the honorary title of *chaudri*. To my informants, the action of the Mughal emperor was unacceptable, and the fact that he was a noble and a Muslim is irrelevant. Caste endogamy had to be respected. That is why Bahar is considered to be a hero and his name is remembered. The action of the Hindu Baniya shows how intercaste relationships were reinforced in those circumstances in opposition to an external Muslim power. We will come back to this point later.

The endogamy rule seems to be generally observed and I came across only one case of a Meo who married a non-Meoni. He was a lawyer established in a city outside Mewat and I was told that he could not come back and settle in his village of origin unless he divorced and married a Meoni.

The Meo are divided into a certain number of *got* or patrilineal clans. Informants say that the mythical founding ancestor of each clan is considered to be the descendant of Hindu divinity or hero.[2] In general, however, they do not know the names or life stories of those ancestors. As I said earlier, it is enough for them that the Brahman genealogists know. This is a very typical characteristic of Meo ancestry and genealogy. There are different levels of clan segmentation and at each level it is assumed that an ancestor founded the segment, but very few people remember or are even aware of their names, their stories, and the causes of fission. No site or shrine is established for the ancestors.

Thirteen of the patriclans are attached to, and give their names to, the thirteen territorial sections of Mewat. A legend recounts that this territorial division was decided upon by the Meo themselves, and not by any outside authority. On the contrary, the decision was taken in order to end division among the Meo in the face of external aggression. Each territorial unit is called a *pal*. There is a contrast made by the Meo between the *pal-got*, the territorial clans, and the *nepalya-got*, the non-territorial clans whose lineages are scattered across one or several *pal* territories. The empirical reality is somewhat different, because there are more territorial units than the legend mentions. Informants recognise this, but do not consider it relevant (see Jamous 1991); for them, the fixed number of thirteen and the mythical division are what count, even if we have to consider a more complex reality.

The relation between the agnatic and territorial principles is somewhat similar to that found among the Nuer, as analysed by Evans-

---

[2] The *got* system is a Brahmanical institution which the Meo adopted in the past and adapted for their own use.

Pritchard. Some clans give their name to a territorial section but that does not mean that all members of the clan live there, nor that the members of other clans who do live there have an inferior status. No-one changes his clan affiliation on moving from one *pal* to another. The unilineal principle is independent of the territorial one. At the same time, it is the idiom of patriliny which is used to denote the territorial structure.

Each *pal-got* is divided into a certain number of sub-clans which are also sub-territorial units called *thamba*. Generally, these units each comprise an original village established by the common ancestor of the sub-clan, plus different 'satellite' villages founded by different descendants of this ancestor. In each village, there are one or several lineages which are segments of the sub-clan. But it is also possible for yet other lineages to trace their origins from different *nepalya-got*, the non-territorial clans. In territorial terms, people of the latter class are members of the *thamba* where they live, but in agnatic terms, they are members of their own clans.

It is important to note that in the *pal-got* territories, one finds not only Meo but also members of Hindu groups of the same status, such as Jats, Thakurs or Gujars. According to their location, their villages are included inside one or another *pal*, which means that they are integrated into the Meo *pal* system. The territorial organisation can be seen as a structure of interrelationships between Hindu and Muslim castes of the same status. This has important implications, as we shall see later.

Traditionally, each *pal-got* and each *thamba* had a chief, a *chaudri*, who was chosen from specific families within the dominant clan. In principle, the *chaudri* would occupy his position until his death and his eldest son ought to succeed him. But this rule has not been observed and it is very difficult to recognise an 'eldest line' which has a monopoly over the chieftainship. The *chaudri*'s authority came under the control of the clan 'assembly' or panchayat, and he was the first among equals. In the past, he was a war leader mobilising his *pal* or *thamba*, as a territorial unit against units at the same level. The rule of political affiliation was territorial, not agnatic, which meant that people from the same *got* or patriclan, but who lived in opposed *pal* or *thamba*, should give their support to their co-residents, not their agnates. The *chaudri* could ask such people to follow him when he conducted a raid or a reprisal against another *pal* or *thamba*. But if he was not sure about their fighting spirit against their agnates, he would accept their neutrality and use them as intermediaries when he wanted to conduct negotiations with a rival unit. It was up to the *chaudri* to find a satisfactory solution and if he were to fail, his position would be weakened and the assembly could apply a range of sanctions against him: for example, by obliging him to correct his mistaken action, or to take on a good assistant, or even by forcing him to resign. Some chiefs were killed by the enemy and this was considered a good death for them. In brief, a *chaudri* was a man who knew how to conduct war when necessary and how to settle for peace when that was required. The same was true of his relations with an external authority. The chief was supposed to conduct raids against such an authority or negotiate for peace, but he could neither be the representative of the Maharajas' authority, nor accept any legitimate subordination to the latter. This was the situation until India's independence. In 1982, the *chaudri's* authority was very weak and mainly honorary.

There was no traditional chief or ruler of the whole Meo community. In this respect, the Meo stress their difference from other Rajput groups which have a political stratification system like that in the states of Alwar or Jaipur, or indeed in the Jat state of Bharatpur. As I said earlier, different sections of Mewat were under Alwar or Bharatpur state jurisdiction until 1947, but the Meo never adopted their political structure. They consider themselves to be all equal and they do not accept internal or external rule by a prince. Meo kinship and territorial organisation are locally defined and legitimised through Brahman genealogists, not through external political authority.

The Meo have a marriage system which is similar in certain respects to that of Hindus in north India, but it is very different from that of other Muslim communities. Marriage prohibitions are very extensive: at the group level, no-one can marry inside the patrilineal clan or village.[3] At the individual level, no-one can marry any parallel cousin, any patrilateral cross-cousin, or a matrilateral first cross-cousin. No-one can take a spouse from the natal village of the mother, which means that no-one can repeat the father's marriage, but it is possible to repeat the paternal grandfather's marriage.

Yet this does not outlaw an asymmetrical marriage alliance system. First, I must stress that a wife-giver can never be a wife-receiver. No reciprocity is possible and no reversal of alliance is accepted; the orientation of marriage corresponds to the orientation of 'gifts' or *dan* in general and the *kanyadan* or 'gift of the maiden' in particular. Secondly, marriage alliance has to be considered at both group and individual levels. At the group level, the units of reference are the *thamba* (considered from the agnatic point of view) for the *pal-got*, and the village lineage for the *nepalya-got*.[4] For Meo belonging to one of these units, the equivalent units which are their wife-givers or wife-receivers since time immemorial are distinguished.[5] In this system, there is no concept of a beginning and an end to the marriage alliance. Each marriage between two units is considered to be a repetition of a preceding one, even if it occurred one or two generations ago. The marriage units are equals and matrimonial alliance is isogamous at this level.

At the individual level, the asymmetrical marriage alliance is considered from the woman's point of view: it is said that a niece should follow her paternal aunt. A married woman is supposed to find a

---

[3] Frequently, lineages of different *got* live in the same village as a result of past intermarriage: a man and his lineage segment will come to live with his affines. But the very fact of becoming co-residents in a village means that marriage between these lineages is prohibited.

[4] If ego belongs to unit A of *got* X, he could be a wife-giver to unit M of *got* Y and a wife-receiver to unit N of the same *got* Y. This does not mean that *got* X and Y are in a exchange relationship. The *got* is not a marriage partner and for that reason, it would be a mistake to refer to reciprocity at this level. In fact, the pertinence of both the notions of exchange and of reciprocity have to be questioned when considering the Meo marriage system.

[5] Meo do not go beyond this; their system is intransitive and there is no idea of closing the circle: for example, the wife-givers of my wife-givers could be my wife-givers or my wife-receivers or neither. My relationship to that category of people is direct and not dependent on my relationship with my wife-givers.

husband for her brother's daughter; suppose that she belongs to patriline A. Since her own son, of patrilineal segment B1, could not marry his matrilateral first cross-cousin, she has to find an agnate from another patrilineal segment B2 who could marry her brother's daughter. Such a match is considered by Meo as the preferential marriage. A generation later, the marriage alliance will continue when a women of patriline A can marry a man of B1 to renew the marriage established two generations earlier. This means that a line of wife-givers is related to two lines of wife-receivers, and that there is a correlation between asymmetrical marriage alliance and alternate generations. Moreover, such an alliance has a beginning, when the paternal aunt of A arranges the marriage of her niece, and it will have an ending, when the patriline B stops intermarrying with A. Finally, marriage at this level has a hypergamous tendency. A wife-receiver is considered to be ritually superior to a wife-giver, and it is during and through the marriage ceremonies that this superiority is established. This has to be related to the fact that a woman and her dowry are considered as an oriented gift, a *dan,* and that *dan* circulates from inferiors to superiors.

One can also consider isogamous and hypergamous tendencies in the kinship structure as a manifestation of caste. Caste or subcaste endogamy mean that a person's status comes from both the father and mother, who are equivalent sources of status. The ritual superiority of wife-receivers over wife-givers has to be connected with the hierarchical aspects of intercaste relations.

The asymmetrical relationship between wife-receivers and wife-givers is also connected with the brother-sister relationship, which is very important in marriage ceremonies. After being given as *dan,* a married woman becomes the ritual priest in her brother's house. Following Vatuk's formulation (1975), she is the active subject after having been given as an 'object'. She must officiate when her brother has a child, circumcises his son, or marries one of his children. For her services she receives a ritual honorarium (*neg*). In this context, she is the most important religious authority and is assisted by her paternal nieces, her brother's wife, and different representatives from the service castes, principally a barber and his wife. A mother's brother of the bride must bring the important ceremonial prestations known as *bhat*. He is received by his sister and transmits the gift through her. As we can see, the married sister/brother relationship is similar in this ritual context to that between sacrificer and sacrifier, or Brahman and Kshatriya.

To sum up this section, the Meo are recognised as Rajputs and participate in the regional caste system, and they have economic, political and ritual relations with Muslim and Hindu castes of the area. Within this context, however, their kinship and territorial structure is locally defined and it distinguishes them from other Muslim communities.

The Meo as a Muslim community

The Meo were converted to Islam a few centuries ago. No historical data are available to explain exactly when this happened or why. The Islamic dimensions of Meo social and cultural life can be considered from two opposing points of view, the internal and the external.

Islam as an internal part of local social structure

Various different Islamic features and rituals are part of the Meo caste and kinship structure, and in this section I outline them briefly.

The marriage contract, the *nikah*, is the only Islamic element among the various marriage ceremonies that are very similar in form and content to the Hindu ones in this part of north India. The principal elements of marriage include the betrothal, or *sagai*, accompanied by gift-giving from the bride's side to the groom's side; the marriage proper, which includes the ritual preparation and consecration of the bridal couple (when they take a ritual bath and go in procession, and are elevated to the status of a purified king and queen); the ritual service by the paternal aunt, who replaces a Brahman among the Meo; the gift of the ceremonial prestations, *bhat*, by the maternal uncle; and various ceremonies in which the groom comes forward to take, as *dan*, his future wife and the dowry.

The Muslim circumcision rituals are conducted like the marriage ceremonies: different castes participate and offer their ritual services; the father's married sister is the presiding 'priest'; and the maternal uncle brings the *bhat*.

Meo death rituals are different from the Hindu ones, for their dead are buried in accordance with Islamic rules and the pollution rules are not very restrictive. But it is important to notice that the Meo funerary priest, the fakir, resembles the Mahabrahman. The fakir has to take care of the tombs of the dead, and he receives the deceased's household goods and bed, which are considered to be impure. Since he is connected with death, danger and impurity, the fakir cannot enter a Meo house and no Meo can enter his house. Finally, the fakir should be given some *khir* (cooked rice and milk mixture) weekly for a whole year, and when he eats this food, he is also giving food to the deceased during his journey to heaven. At the end of a year, the obligations towards the deceased are over and no more offerings are given to them; they disappear from the social scene and their tombs are not the object of any regular visits. As among Hindus, the Meo dead are vanishing 'ancestors'

Moharram is a Shia celebration of the battle of Kerbala, during which a son of Ali—the fourth Khalif who married Fatima, the Prophet's daughter—was killed. Locally, however Moharram is treated as a *mela*, a festival, and until recently Hindus and Muslims participated equally in it. At Moharram, a cenotaph is constructed and then treated like a Hindu image; starting from the centre of a village, the cenotaph is taken round in a circle to different places in the village before being thrown into one of the village ponds. This ritual renews the strength of the village and, from a Hocartian perspective, it can be considered as a life-giving ceremony

Among the Meo, the mosques mostly belong to lineages. The Muslim service castes share one mosque and do not go to the Meo ones. Finally, as mentioned above, the Sayyid families are treated like people of the service castes and they are considered to have a lower status than the Meo.

Islam and participation in the wider Muslim community

From the mid-1930s, the Meo began to come under the influence of the Tablighi Jama'at (T.J.), a Muslim 'reformist' movement founded in

Delhi by a religious personage, Maulana Ilyas, whose purpose was to make the Meo 'better' Muslims.[6] Although the movement started its campaign in the mid-1930s, it was only after 1947 that it became very active in Mewat.

After 1947 a group of T.J. members regularly visited Meo villages, where they stayed in the mosques and started to spread the 'good word'. They asked the Meo to pray regularly, to fast during Ramadan and to abandon all non-Islamic elements in their social and religious life, which implied non-participation in Hindu religious festivals and an end to the worship of Hindu gods and even Muslim saints. In these respects, their action was generally successful, even if sometimes not in the way expected by the T.J. Thus the Meo no longer celebrate Hindu religious festivals like Dasara or Holi, and very few of them still visit Hindu shrines. On the other hand, although mosques were constructed in large numbers, many of them are owned by lineages and visited only by their own members. More and more Meo are becoming devout Muslims, who pray regularly and fast during the whole month of Ramadan, but this change has to be treated as the effort of individuals; one may notice that in the same family, some members spend several hours a day reading the Quran at home or in the mosque, while others are erratic in their religious practices. Yet such differences in behaviour have not produced any tension between the two types of people. It seems that in this context, Islamic devotion occupies among the Meo the place of *bhakti* among the Hindus. The Meo have generally abandoned the annual celebrations (*mela* or *urs*) for the different Muslim saints whose mausoleums (*dargah*) are located in Mewat. Since those sanctuaries were visited in the past by Muslims and Hindus, the end of visits to the saints has widened the distance between the two religious communities.

The T.J. wanted the Meo to abandon their kinship system, particularly their clan organisation, because the clans' ultimate ances-

---

[6] Unlike some other Muslim reformist movements, the Tablighi Jama'at was not a militant political organisation. The movement's leaders claimed that their aim was religious, not political, but this does not mean that they had no political influence.

tors were considered to have been created by the Hindu gods, and their marriage prohibitions, so that parallel-cousin marriage could be allowed as in other Muslim groups. In this respect, the T.J. completely failed, for the Meo flatly refused to accede to such demands. This is understandable, because it would have implied the destruction of what has been called the 'social fabric' of the Meo community. To keep their kinship structure also implied for the Meo retention of their status as a Rajput caste. Thus in one sense, Meo were becoming 'better' Muslims without abandoning their caste and kinship systems. It is important to note that the T.J. have now given up their campaign for reform of these aspects of Meo culture.

The T.J. also tried to attract the Meo to their centre in Delhi, where they could receive religious training. It was expected that they would then return to Mewat, spread the good word and become active members of the movement. This would be a way for them to participate in the Community of the Faithful. Some Meo followed this path, but in 1982, the vast majority were only passive members of the movement in the sense that they did accept some of the religious injunctions introduced by the T.J., but they went no further than that.

In short, therefore, the two forms of Meo identity, defined by caste and Islam, were interconnected and yet at the same time mutually opposed. The Meo did not accept that they had to choose between them, but that meant that they had to live with the resulting tension. Owing to the insistent campaign of the T.J., the Meo were becoming more and more conscious of their Islamic identity. As a result, the distance between them and the Hindu communities was widening, although it had not become conflictual, at least by 1982.

The Meo and the Mewat in 1992-3: the aftermath of Ayodhya

Ten years later, some weakening of the economic interdependence between castes is noticeable, although ritual relationships are still strong. Several mosques have been constructed in the area, and a large number of Meo are becoming devout Muslims and are active members of the T.J. The movement is enhancing its influence through a network of *madrasas* (Quranic schools). The tension between the two major forms of Meo identity, given by caste and Islam, has increased and the animosity between this Muslim community and some of the other Hindu groups has grown dangerously. To understand the current situation, it is important to reflect on the recent past and to compare it with what has happened in the area since the destruction of the Ayodhya mosque on 6 December 1992.

From 1932 until 1947, a series of conflicts pitted the Meo against the Bharatpur and Alwar states. The origin of these conflicts was both economic and religious. The Meo rebelled against an increase in land taxes. But the agrarian conflict also took a religious turn, because the Jats of Bharatpur and the Rajputs of Alwar represented Meo resistance as antipathy between Hindus and Muslims. The Arya Samaj and the Rashtriya Swayamsevak Sangh (RSS), two militant Hindu movements, had an influence in the area and also over the ruling dynasties, and some Muslim movements started to express their religious solidarity with the Meo. In 1947, the conflict took a tragic turn. There was an attempt to reconvert the Meo to Hinduism, and their refusal led to a massacre (Mayaram, n.d.; Siddiqui 1986). A lot of Meo fled the area and went to Pakistan. But some of them returned and resettled in the area without any renewed major conflict. Indeed, the Meo revived the strong ties that they had had with the Jats, mostly those living in Mewat.

During this period, the conflict was simultaneously political and religious. It mainly opposed local 'dominant' castes, the Meo on one side, and the Hindu Rajputs and Jats on the other. The economic aspect of the conflict, the question of taxation, was related to agricultural resources.

From the mid-1980s onwards, the situation changed. The Hindu nationalist movement—in the form of the RSS and the Bharatiya Janata Party (BJP)—became active in Mewat through the Baniyas, the trading caste established in the local towns. On the other hand, the traditionally dominant Hindu castes in the locality, the Jats, were opposed to the nationalist movement. The economic situation has also changed in the last ten years. In 1982, the Meo were mostly peasants working on their land, and they did not modernise their agriculture like their neighbours the Jats. In their search for alternative employment, they mostly looked for military or police posts. Very few of them entered into trade. The situation has now changed, and the Meo have moved to the towns, which were becoming prosperous, to open shops in every line of business. In one town that I have started to study, a rough census showed that more than 400 out of 2,000 shops were owned by Meo, mostly opened in the last five years. The Meo have started to become a serious threat to Baniya domination; the Baniyas still have important commercial connections with the major cities, but they are gradually losing a large number of their Muslim clients to Meo traders.

On 7 December 1992, some young Meo attacked Hindu temples in various Mewat towns, including the one I am studying. Some were destroyed, others damaged. In retaliation, the Hindus attacked mosques. The government imposed a curfew on the local towns. In the villages (except for one or two of them) there was no destruction of temples or mosques. But there was tension. On the same day, in the village where I stayed, some young Meo approached the Hindu quarters apparently intending to burn the Hindu temple, which had been constructed a few years earlier and was run by Baniya villagers. The older Meo reacted very quickly, gathered around the temple and easily persuaded the young people to abandon their dangerous plan. Nevertheless, people felt that violence could erupt again and that in the future it could not be stopped so easily. They compared the situation with that at the time of India's independence and were afraid that massacres could start again. The Meo accused the Baniyas settled in the town of starting communal uprisings, and those Baniyas in turn accused the Meo of doing the same thing.

On 10 December, in the same Meo village, an invitation to an engagement (*sagai*) ceremony in a Hindu Jat village arrived. The two villages belonged to the same territory, the same *pal*, and were *bhai*, 'brothers'. The Meo decided to go to the ceremony, even though they knew that there was a curfew in place. I accompanied them and we were very warmly received. The Meo sided with the groom's group, the hosts, and received some gifts from the bride's group. On our way back, the Meo stressed that they enjoyed very good relationships with the Jats and contrasted them with the bad ones that they had with the Baniyas. They added that under normal conditions, they would have responded positively or negatively to the Jats' invitation according to how busy they were. But conditions were not normal and they had to attend. Every event, ritual or visit was used afterwards to reinforce the traditional solidarity between the two groups.

The relationships between neighbouring Meo and Jat have changed in the last forty years. After the period of strains and tension between 1930 and 1947-8, a kind of political solidarity was gradually reasserted through the traditional channels of the kinship and territorial system. A recent example will show it clearly. The Jat villages which were part of a Meo *pal* had to choose a new *chaudri* or chief from among them. There was a dispute between two contestants. No decision could be reached. The chief of the *pal*, a Meo, was invited by the Jats to find an acceptable solution. A meeting was held in one Jat village, with the participation of the Meo chief and several other Meo old men. The mediation was successful and it was decided that the two Jat contestants would occupy successively the position of *chaudri*. For the Meo informants, this case showed clearly that their relations with the Jats were close. The invitation to the *sagai* has to be interpreted as part of this process of reinforcing relationships between the Meo and Jats.

The T.J. movement increased its activities during the next couple of months in 1992-3. Its members visited the villages more often, insisted that the Meo pray for 'peace' and explained to them that their salvation lay in Islam. Everybody understood that the T.J. was pressing them into abandoning all hope of regional solidarity and into becoming fully committed Muslims. In the villages, the Meo felt that they had to pray regularly and listen to the T.J. preachers. In this context, new Quranic schools opened in different places. One example will illustrate the circumstances. In a Meo quarter in one village, the plan to open a Quranic school had been unsuccessful for two major reasons: there was no building to receive the children, and people were not ready to pay for hiring it and the teachers. This had been going on for years. In mid-January 1993, a few weeks after the Ayodhya incident, the problem was suddenly solved. One rich Meo offered his abandoned house as a place

for the Quranic school. A local kazi offered his services as the teacher.
Each householder agreed to pay for the school, and to inaugurate it,
each family sent its contribution and some tea, cake or cooked food for
the children. All this was done under the pressure of the T.J. But the
Meo insisted that they wanted to control their new school completely
and not be dependent on the T.J. It was on this condition that some
families hostile to the T.J. agreed to contribute. According to my
informants, however, the Ayodhya incident was crucial for people's
decision-making.

During this period, tension continued between the Meo and the
Baniyas. After the curfew was lifted, an attempt was made by the Meo
to renew their relationships with the Baniyas. They tried to reassert the
old ritualised 'brothers' relationships that they had had with the traders
who came from the same village. In one village I was shown how two
families, one Meo and one Baniya, had very strong 'kinship' relations
with each other, which were marked by a series of prestations and
counter-prestations. In another village, I was told that the *dargah*, or
mausoleum, of a Muslim saint had been built by a trader who became
his devotee. Once again, I heard the legend of the Meo hero whose
body was left to rot outside Delhi and was then brought back by a Baniya from Mewat, so that he could have a decent burial. The past was
being mobilised in order to try to restore peaceful relations, and all this
shows how complex are the ties between the Meo and the Baniyas.
Nevertheless, as somebody explained to me, peaceful co-operation is a
thing of the past. The Arya Samaj's influence on the Hindu Baniyas
and the T.J.'s on the Meo have widened the distance between them and
brought to the fore their mutual opposition and conflict. In contrast, an
inverse movement occurred between the Meo and the neighbouring
Jats. But it is important to note, too, that the political and religious
relationships between the rural Jats and the urban Baniyas have been
growing more tense during the last ten years.

This latter observation shows how difficult it is to analyse present
circumstances simply in terms of Hindu-Muslim conflict, even if it is
part of the truth. The T.J. movement is not interested in Meo local
identity, because it wants them to become Muslims who will participate

fully in the Community of the Faithful. In a certain fashion and for opposite reasons, the Hindu nationalists are pushing the Meo in the same direction. As for the Meo themselves, they are experiencing an increasing sense of solidarity with other Indian Muslims, although they still want and try to keep their local identity and local relationships. The Meo are not just submitting to external events, and they try to react to them by mobilising the two forms of their identity—as a Rajput caste and a Muslim community—even if these imply conflicting values.

Another level of co-operation and confrontation between the Meo and local Hindus is also interesting. It concerns a particular Muslim saint, Lal Dass, considered by Hindus to be a renouncer. This saint lived three centuries ago. Two shrines are of particular significance here: one where his parents are buried and another where his personal tomb exists. Both places are important centres of worship and annual *melas* are or were held at them. Until 1943, Meo regularly visited the shrines where they held Muslim festivals and Hindus performed rituals for the renouncer Lal Dass. According to one legend, Lal Dass was worshipped during his life by both communities since he claimed to unite the two religions. When he died, both Meo and Hindus present at the funeral wanted to take the blanket covering his body. The dispute went on and when the blanket was removed, the body had disappeared. That is why, according to the legend, both communities can claim Lal Dass as their saint or renouncer. The situation changed in 1943 during the turmoil preceding independence. Hindus took complete control of the shrine where the parents of Lal Dass were buried and excluded the Muslims. A Brahman became the *pujari* or priest at this shrine. The Muslims kept control of the other shrine containing the tomb of Lal Dass, and a member of the fakir caste was the principal priest. However, the Hindus continued to visit the latter shrine. Following T.J. injunctions, the Meo stopped the annual *melas* they held for all regional saints, including Lal Dass. Nevertheless, individuals continued to make offerings to their saint. I was told that the Hindus want to take control of the second shrine with the help of the courts, claiming that the territory of the mausoleum is their property, not that of the Muslims. In 1993, some of my Meo informants considered that the local conflict over Lal Dass, which started several decades ago, was an indication of the more general religious problem between the two communities which ended in the Ayodhya events. One showed me the remnant of a mosque in the shrine controlled by the Hindus and added that the destruction of the Ayodhya mosque was not a new thing. It is important to note, however, that this conflict, which opposes religious communities irrespective of caste differentiation, continues to be regional. The Meo do not let other Muslims interfere in their problem and they try to find a local solution.

The Meo have lived through tension in the the 1930s and 1940s, and they are confronting it again today. The caste system and its kinship implications are being used here in both directions: as a medium for communal opposition between Hindu Baniyas and Muslim Meo, and as a way of reinforcing kinship and territorial solidarity between Hindu Jats and Muslim Meo. How long this tension can persist, and when and if the Meo will definitely have to take sides, nobody knows. Nevertheless, we might ask whether any solutions can be found for the problems of modern India without taking the social and cultural constraints of the caste and kinship system into account. That, anyway, is what the case of the Meo plainly suggests.

References

Aggarwal P. 1971. *Caste, religion and power, an Indian case study*. New Delhi: Shri Ram Centre for Industrial Relations and Human Resources.

Amir-Ali, H. 1970. *The Meo of Mewat: old neighbours of Delhi*. New Delhi: Oxford and IBH Publishing Co.

Jamous R. 1991. *La relation frère-soeur: parenté et rites chez les Meo de l'Inde du nord*. Paris: Ecole des Hautes Etudes en Sciences Sociales.

Marwah I.S. 1979. 'Tabligh movement among the Meos of Mewat'. In M.S.A. Rao (ed.), *Social movements in India 2: Sectarian, tribal and women's movements*. New Delhi: Manohar.

Mayaram S.K. n.d. 'Construction of the Meo movement in the Alwar state in the early twentieth century' Unpublished manuscript.

Parry, J.P. 1979. *Caste and kinship in Kangra*. London: Routledge and Kegan Paul.

Siddiqui M. 1986. 'History and society in a popular rebellion: Mewat 1920-1933.' *Comparative Studies in Society and History* 23:442-67.

Vatuk, S. 1975. 'Gifts and affines in north India.' *Contributions to Indian Sociology* (n.s.) 9:155-96.

Chapter 8

THE DISINVENTION OF CASTE AMONG TAMIL MUSLIMS

Frank S. Fanselow

This chapter is concerned with the question of whether Indian Muslims can be said to have caste. Madan (1981:61) and Lindholm (1986) have suggested that the answer to this question depends on whom one asks: the Muslims, the Hindus or the anthropologist. In this paper I shall examine the answers of all three using the example of the system of social stratification among Muslims in the Tirunelveli District of Tamilnadu, especially in the two towns Kayalpattnam and Kalakkadu.

The Muslim answer

Muslim society in Tamilnadu is the product of two different historical processes.[1] On the one hand, the old maritime trade between southern Arabia and south India brought into being the oldest Muslim communities in India. Through this Arab connection Muslim communities grew out of immigration, intermarriage and conversion. These all belong to the Shafi legal school that was dominant in southern Arabia at the time. On the other hand, there are those Muslim communities which are the result of political and military penetration from north India, particularly by the Mughal Empire and its successors during the eighteenth century when the area was ruled for a short period by the Nawab of Arcot. The Muslim communities which developed out of this process belong to the Hanafi legal school like the Persian, Turkish and Mughal rulers whom they served.

Each of these two historical processes brought forth different Muslim communities in the region. The Shafi groups in the two towns are the Maraikkayar of Kayalpattnam and the Tarakanar of Kalakkadu. The former see themselves as descendants of the original Arabs who settled in south India more than a thousand years ago. The latter are

[1] For more detailed accounts of the history of Muslims in Tamilnadu see Bayly (1989) and Fanselow (1989).

converts from local Hindu castes traditionally engaged in weaving and acting as middlemen in the textile trade for the Arab merchants on the coast, such as those in Kayalpattnam. The Hanafi groups in Kalakkadu are the Pattani, Urdu-speaking Muslims who claim descent from north Indian and ultimately, as their name suggests, from non-Indian Muslims, and the Rowther whose ancestors were local converts to Islam who served in the Nawab's army. Muslim society in Tamilnadu thus appears as a matrix in which ethnicity (Arab, Turkish, Indian), language (Urdu, Tamil) and sect (Shafi, Hanafi) are the distinguishing dimensions.

The two towns in which I conducted research[2] are located in the southern part of Tirunelveli District about 80 kilometres apart. Kayalpattnam is on the Coromandel coast and Kalakkadu at the foot of the Western Ghats. Because of their locations both have been historically frontier towns: Kayalpattnam was a major international entrepot in the pre-colonial Indian Ocean trade; Kalakkadu was the southernmost outpost of the Mughal Empire guarding the border with Travancore. Kayalpattnam's population is almost exclusively Muslim with a small Hindu minority, whereas Kalakkadu is a Hindu town with a Muslim minority of roughly 10 per cent of the population. Both towns are representative of a respective type. Kayalpattnam is typical of the big historical trading ports on the Coromandel coast, such as Nagapattinam, Nagore, Cuddalore and Kilakkarai. Kalakkadu is typical of inland towns throughout Tamilnadu with Muslim minorities working in the textile, leather, iron and grocery trades. The Muslims in both towns are therefore typical of the two historical processes which brought into existence Muslim society in Tamilnadu.

[2] This paper is based on fieldwork carried out in Tirunelveli District, Tamilnadu, for a total of seventeen months during various periods between 1981 and 1984 supported by the Wenner-Gren Foundation, the Central Research Fund of the University of London and a Tweedie Exploration Fellowship from Edinburgh University. Further fieldwork was conducted during the summers of 1991 and 1992 with the financial support of the Research and Conference Grant Committee of the American University in Cairo. I thank all these institutions for their support. I would also like to thank Dr. C.J. Fuller and Dr. M.A. Kalam for their critical and helpful comments on an earlier version of this paper.

Kayalpattnam: Maraikkayar

Today Kayalpattnam has only a small harbour for local fishermen located in a remote part of the District, but it has a long history of international trade and at one time Marco Polo described it as 'a great and noble city' (Yule 1875:313). Although geographically it has completely lost its central position in the Indian Ocean trade, its inhabitants still occupy strategic positions in international trade, particularly in the gem and gold trade. The contemporary remoteness of the town stands in sharp contrast to the cosmopolitanism of its population. Many of its men live or have lived most of their lives in Colombo, Bangkok or Hongkong, and have travelled widely to the centres of the international gem trade in Europe and America. During much of the year the inhabitants of the town are mainly women and children, as well as old men who have retired from their business careers. The centuries old pattern of male migration helps to explain the uxorilocal residence pattern of the town. Husbands reside in their wives' houses, in so far as they live in the town at all, and residential houses are inherited in the female line. Despite the wide dispersal of the male population of the town, Kayalpattnam remains the centre of their social and economic life. During annual Muslim feasts and life-cycle ceremonies large numbers of men return for visits to their families. Profits earned abroad are invested locally in agricultural land. Most of the land around Kayalpattnam as well as wetlands in the Tambraparni delta are owned by Kayalpattnam Muslims. Cultivation of the land is supervised by the old men living in the town and it is cultivated by local labourers and tenants belonging to Hindu agricultural castes.

But apart from being a wealthy and cosmopolitan community, the Muslims of Kayalpattnam also conceive of themselves as occupying a religiously exalted position among Tamil Muslims. Their account of their origin is an interwoven fabric of the history of the town and the history of Islam. It relates how their ancestors had to flee Egypt in the mid-ninth century because of their involvement in the famous *mutazila* theological controversy. The Mutazilites were a school of rationalist Muslim thinkers influenced by Greek philosophy, who argued among other things that the Quran was created rather than eternally existing.

Because of this they have been widely attacked throughout Muslim history as heretics, but in the mid-ninth century they gained the support of the Abbasid Khalifs for a brief period between A.D. 827 and 848. It was during the reign of the Khalif al-Wathik (A.D. 842-7) that the ancestors of the Kayalpattnam Muslims are believed to have been forced to flee because of their opposition to the Mutazilite heresy. They came from Egypt which was at the time a province of the Abbasid Empire. A popular local etymology of the name Kayalpattnam is that it derives from *kahira* (Arabic: Cairo) plus *pattinam* (Tamil: town). They left Egypt in five ships. One of these was lost at sea, and the others landed in Konkan, Calicut, Sumatra and Kayalpattnam respectively, to form the core of the Muslim communities in South and South-east Asia and to play a central role in the Islamisation of these areas.

In this interwoven fabric of local and world history, the relationship between centre and periphery is reversed. Those at the periphery—the small, marginal communities far from the heartland of Islam, implanted in or grafted on to foreign cultures—appear as the upholders of orthodoxy, refugees persecuted for their adherence to orthodox Islam and guardians of the true religion, at a time when both the political (Baghdad) and religious (Cairo) centres of Sunni Islam had fallen to heretics who persecuted the true believers and drove them into exile. At the margin those displaced from the centre in turn became the centre of a new Muslim society by spreading Islam through intermarriage and conversion. Instrumental in the conversion process in south India were Sufi saints, and one of the most important ones was Sadaqatulla (A.D. 1632-1703) whose descendants form a privileged lineage in Kayal-pattnam. He was a descendant of the Prophet and so are his descendants in the town, who rank as the elite of an elite community.

Kayalpattnam Muslims see themselves as the first Muslims in India and therefore as instrumental in the creation of Muslim society in south India. By implication other Muslims in the region owe their religion to them. Kayalpattnam Muslims continue to see themselves as custodians and transmitters of religious knowledge. Already Sadaqatullah's father had founded a *madrasa*. Later, Kayalpattnam Muslims developed an Arabised version of the Tamil language and the town became famous as

a centre for Muslim Tamil literature. It is still a centre of training for
imams throughout southern Tamilnadu. Most recently, the saint's
descendants continued this traditional role of custodians of knowledge
when, in 1972, they established the first Muslim college in the district
in the saint's name near Tirunelveli.

The town's social position within Tamil Muslim society is reflected
in its spatial structure. Kayalpattnam is an almost exclusively Muslim
town with only a small immigrant Hindu minority working in shops,
schools and government institutions. Its inhabitants see this spatial
separation and the consequent social segregation as crucial to the
preservation of its Muslim identity, in contrast with the surrounding
Muslim communities which exist as minorities within Hindu society, as
in Kalakkadu. This segregation between Muslims and Hindus is
paralleled by another between men and women. A unique feature of the
town lies in its architecture which segregates men and women.
Kayalpattnam is the only town in the area with the so-called 'zenat
lanes' which cross the entire town at right angles to its streets. These
lanes allow women to move about from one end of town to the other by
only crossing the streets between lanes, and thus they remain almost
unseen by men. The houses too were unique in that they had no front
but only side entrances, and all windows had wooden shutters making it
impossible to look into a house from the outside. At the individual
level, Kayalpattnam women are often said to wear full purdah, though
in fact this is less than total nowadays. The separation between
Muslims and Hindus and between men and women are two visible
indicators of the orthodoxy of the town's population.

Kayalpattnam Muslims thus have a clear sense of occupying a
unique position in Muslim society in south India. Other Tamil Muslims
are the recipients of their privileged knowledge, their disciples and their
students. The purity of descent and the purity of religious knowledge
and practice are inextricably intertwined. Other Muslims are Tamils
rather than Arabs, descendents of converts rather than original Muslims, latecomers to the faith in need of religious guidance and
instruction because their knowledge and practice of religion are still
corrupted by their Hindu origins and environment. Other Muslims not

only descended from Hindu converts to Islam, but live cheek by jowl with Hindus and are contaminated by Hindu practices. When I first came to the district to study a Muslim community I was told at Sadaqatullah Appa College not to study any of the interior towns, such as Kalakkadu, because there I would find only Muslims in name, whereas in Kayalpattnam alone would I find 'real' Muslims.

Yet this claim to Arab descent is a status claim within Muslim society only. In relation to wider Indian society, Kayalpattnam Muslims identify themselves as Indians. Precisely because of their claim to a non-Indian ethnic origin, they strongly identify themselves politically as Indians. During the Indo-Pakistan war, funds were raised by the town's population 'in support of the national defence effort' and its guest book proudly exhibits signatures from the visits of the former President R. Venkataraman and late Prime Minister Rajiv Gandhi.

Kalakkadu: Pattani

Like the Kayalpattnam Maraikkayar, the Pattani conceive of themselves as an elite community in Tamil Muslim society. Their most obvious distinguishing mark is language. In this part of Tamilnadu the name Pattani is a general category for all Urdu-speaking Muslims. Whereas the Maraikkayar identify themselves with an Arabised version of Tamil, the Pattani regard Urdu as their mother tongue, though they are equally familiar with Tamil and usually literate only in Tamil.

As their name indicates, the Pattani too claim to be of non-Tamil and even non-Indian origins. They are divided into endogamous subdivisions. Some groups of Pattani, such as those in Panagudi, claim to be Sayyids descended from the Prophet. Others loosely claim Turkish, Persian or Mughal descent, though generally this is expressed in terms of relations with Hyderabadi Muslims. For this reason, Pattani are also known as Dakni (i.e. from the Deccan). But categories such as Sayyid, Sheikh, Pathan and Mughal, which are familiar from north India, are only partially known and not systematically used.

In this part of southern Tamilnadu, Pattani are very thinly spread since Muslim rule was brief and tenuous. They usually form only small groups often made up of members of a single lineage. These are either

descendants of the military and administrative personnel of the Nawab
of Arcot, or they were granted land by the British after the East India
Company took over the territory in order to keep them from becoming a
destabilising element. They therefore see themselves as local zamindars. Although they often live near Rowther communities, Pattani
houses are often symbolically set apart, for example, by being located
near saint shrines. In some places, such as Kalakkadu and Pottalpudur,
the house of the main Pattani zamindar is still sometimes referred to as
'palace'. One of the biggest landlords in Kalakkadu is the Pattani
zamindar, but in many places they have ceased to be major landlords,
as land has been continually subdivided and sold. Since some of the
land they control is often *inam* land legally belonging to saint shrines
and formally under the control of the Tamilnadu Waqf Board, these
attempts to sell land by individuals have produced interminable legal
disputes within the lineages and with the Waqf Board. Owing to the
loss of major landholdings, many Pattani have migrated to cities, such
as Tirunelveli and Madras, where they have entered business or
government employment. This is another reason for the relatively small
number of Pattani in this area.

As already mentioned, part of the elite status of the Pattani derives
from their association with saint shrines (*darga*) and other religious
institutions, such as *madrasa*s and schools. Many saint shrines and the
land with which they are endowed are under the control of Pattani
trustees (*mutavali*) who often claim to be descendants of the saint and
who also act as ritual functionaries in these shrines. The major shrines
in the district, such as those in Pottalpudur and at Attankarai are
controlled by Pattani families, as is the much smaller and less important
one near Kalakkadu. The Pattani zamindar also donated land for the
establishment of a Muslim school in Kalakkadu in the 1930s.

There are clear parallels between the Kayalpattnam Maraikkayar
and the Pattani. Central to their claim to high status is non-Tamil
descent, Arab among the former and Turkish among the latter. Following from this are certain distinctive cultural practices, in particular
their association with Arabic and Urdu respectively. Equally important
is their association with Sufi saints and control of saint shrines. These

symbolise their role as transmitters and custodians of religious knowledge. The greater proximity to Islam, both in terms of space (geographical origin) and time (date of conversion), thus entitles them to a superior status in local Muslim society. Both communities are also largely endogamous and contain an internal hierarchy of endogamous subdivisions. Although intermarriages with Rowther and Tarakanar are not unheard of in the two communities, they are rare. The Maraikkayar of Kayalpattnam only marry among each other, or with Maraikkayar in the other major coastal cities, such as Kilakkarai or Nagapattinam. The Pattani, too, either enter into marriages with local Pattani or with members of their subdivision in distant places, even with those from other states who do not speak Tamil, rather than with Rowther nearby. Maraikkayar and Pattani claims to high status are anchored in economic and political realities which provide the foundation for their elite status in Tamil Muslim society. The Maraikkayar have been a wealthy commercial community for centuries and have invested part of their profits in agricultural land. The Pattani status as landlords is the result of the considerable political power which they wielded locally during the eighteenth century.

Despite these parallels between the two communities, there are hardly any relations between Maraikkayar and Pattani. Part of the reason for this is geographical: the Maraikkayar are concentrated in large towns along the coast, whereas the Pattani are dispersed in small numbers of local elite families in inland towns. Part of the reason is economic: each of the two communities occupies a different economic niche. The two have thus never been part of a system tying them together socially, politically or economically and the ideological question of relative rank between them did not really arise. Their respective rank was instead determined by their relations with other Muslim groups.

Kalakkadu: Rowther and Tarakanar

In contrast to the rich historical mythology of the Maraikkayar and Pattani, the Rowther and Tarakanar of Kalakkadu are people without history. They lack any conventional, collective, standardised account of their origins. All their statements about their origins and past remain vague and ambiguous. Their only definite history is that they are Tamils whose ancestors had converted from Hinduism. Everything else is uncertain. These ancestors might have converted thousands of years or maybe just a hundred years ago. They did not come from any particular caste, but from across the whole spectrum of castes, including Brahmans and Untouchables. Nobody knows why they should have converted and who converted them. They might have been converted by force, in an attempt to escape low-caste status, as a result of missionary activities by Sufi saints, or for all these reasons.

There is agreement, however, that they were converts from Hinduism and therefore their present-day descendants identify themselves as ethnic Tamils. Many Rowther and Tarakanar support the Dravidian nationalist political parties (the DMK and AIADMK) or the Congress Party rather than the Muslim League. This identification as Tamils with a Hindu past stands in sharp contrast to the Maraikkayar and Pattani, who identify themselves as non-Indian in origin and therefore without Hindu roots.

The Rowther and Tarakanar reacted with some incomprehension to my attempts to uncover their historical origins. In a cultural environment in which every group—Hindu, Muslim and Christian—has its own caste history, this total absence of an origin myth can only amount to the assertion that the past is irrelevant to their present identity as Muslims. The ambiguity, vagueness and conspicuous indifference towards their past stand in sharp contrast to the precision, detail and pride of the Maraikkayar and Pattani concerning their history. In place of the claim to prophetic and Arab descent, the Rowther and Tarakanar evince a casual indifference to historical origins, and vaguely claim to be descendants of both Brahmans and Untouchables. This apparent lack of interest in their origins is matched by a sceptical attitude towards the claims to foreign descent made by the other groups, which are met with cynicism and a certain amount of ridicule, and are denounced as an attempt by would-be Muslim Brahmans to recreate Hindu caste in an egalitarian Muslim society.

Rowther and Tarakanar have a similar kind of ambivalence towards the other status claims of the Maraikkayar and Pattani. In recent years, saint shrines have become the focus of increased criticism because of the syncretistic nature of their rituals. The annual festival of the local Rowther saint's shrine has lost much of its former grandeur, and it has been occasionally cancelled because of a dispute over its control. A mediator brought in to settle the dispute instead reproached the parties for arguing about an institution which was the centre of un-Islamic practices and should be abandoned rather than fought over. Saint shrines are often represented not as communal religious institutions, but as money-spinning enterprises by individual families.

Not only is the ritual performed in the saint shrines syncretistic, but its devotees often include Hindus as well. Some Muslim saint shrines seem to attract more Hindu than Muslim followers. Worse still from this point of view, some Muslims have actually participated in Hindu rituals in the past. In Kalakkadu the main Pattani zamindar's family was directly involved in the annual car festival of the town's Shiva temple, as sponsors of the second day's rituals. The family paid for the festival on this day and received temple honours in return, in the form of garlands and *prasada*. Indeed the the family house is located directly in front of the temple entrance, close to the head of the Brahman street. The practice of sponsorship was discontinued only in 1974, owing to pressure from both Hindus and Muslims. It is therefore not surprising that Pattani in particular are sometimes accused of styling themselves as quasi-Brahmans within Muslim society. This and other Muslim elite practices, such as the matrilocality of Maraikkayar—which is often associated with the matrilineality of the Nayar and ridiculed as requiring 'a man to eat in his wife's house'—provide easy ammunition for the Rowther and Tarakanar against the status claims of the Pattani and Maraikkayar.

I cannot overemphasise the different attitudes towards history in the two towns. In Kayalpattnam, I encountered constant reiteration of the historical, archaeological, cultural, social and most of all religious uniqueness of the town. I was reminded of its peculiarities which distinguish it from the rest of Muslim society in Tamilnadu and set it apart from and above the surrounding Muslim groups, so that the town

is in a class of its own and therefore worthy of study. I encountered a
keen sense of the town's historical identity and exclusiveness, and
because of this a clear sense, too, of the town as an object of research.
The neglect of archaeological remains, such as old mosques and
cemeteries, was bemourned and attempts were made to interest the
Archaeological Survey of India in them. Indeed one man, who had for
years been running the London operations of his family's international
gem-trading business, was a keen amateur historian, who had read
about the town's history in the libraries of the School of Oriental and
African Studies and the India Office, and kept notes with the intention
of publishing them one day.

Among the Rowther and Tarakanar of Kalakkadu, on the other hand,
I was frequently told that nothing distinguishes them from Muslims
anywhere else. Any specific characteristics or local pecularities were
dissolved within the great tradition of Islam. Such peculiarities were
immediately devalued as marginal, unimportant eccentricities, and
deviations from the proper, orthodox, great tradition of Islam. My
declared intention that I was there to study a Tamil Muslim community
was met with the assertion that Tamil Muslims were just like Muslims
everywhere; if in certain respects they were not, or particular individuals were not, then this was a deviation, an exception or an individual
eccentricity, not a characteristic of the community, and by definition it
was therefore not a worthwhile, legitimate subject of study.

The historical amnesia of the Rowther and Tarakanar about their
origins and their critical attitude towards the status claims of the
Maraikkayar and Pattani, must be seen against the background of their
historically inferior position relative to the latter two Muslim groups.
Both Rowther and Tarakanar started out as client communities of the
Maraikkayar and Pattani respectively. The term *tarakanar* means
'broker' in Tamil and the community was historically engaged in weaving and the textile trade as middlemen for rich merchants such as those
of Kayalpattnam or the Brahmans of Kallidaikuruchi in the Tambraparni valley (Pate 1917:216). The term *ravuttar* means horseman in
Tamil, and the Rowther are descendants of soldiers serving the Nawab,
who ruled the area for brief periods during the eighteenth century. They

were local converts to Islam, who served in the Nawab's army in positions subordinate to the Pattani officers and zamindars. Hence both Tarakanar and Rowther communities came into existence through conversion from local castes, which occupied dependent positions in relation to the Maraikkayar merchants and Pattani zamindars in the region. The relationships between the inferior and superior groups were, in the past, analogous to the hierarchical relationships between castes. There was residential segregation between the different groups of Muslims and each local community had its own mosque and cemeteries, and often also its own saint shrine. Intermarriage between the groups was rare and, if it occurred, it was hypergamous, so that the Maraikkayar and Pattani would take wives but not give their women in return. On the other hand, there is no evidence that entry into the mosque was ever forbidden to individuals from particular communities, or that there were any restrictions on commensality, although occasions for interdining might have been rare. This is consistent with the absence of an ideology of purity and pollution among Muslims on which virtually all ethnographies of Indian Muslim communities agree. Relationships were hierarchical, but hierarchy was not based on an ideology of purity and pollution, but on relationships of dependency stemming from differences in wealth and power.

In the past, the separate identities of the different groups of Muslims weighed heavier than their collective Muslim identity. The first contact between Shafis and Hanafis occurred through the early and sporadic Muslim invasions of south India under Malik Kafur and Khusrau Khan in the early fourteenth century. There was no sense of a shared Muslim identity; instead relations were marked by indifference or even hostility because the two groups found themselves on opposite sides in the political and military conflict. The north Indian Muslims seem to have thought of the south Indian ones as quasi-Hindus and vice versa. This pattern of separateness and indifference between the Hanafi and Shafi groups also obtained much later during the brief period of Muslim rule in the eighteenth century, and it was based on their occupying different niches in the economic and political landscape. There were few occasions for them to interact with each other and no reasons for them to unite socially and politically.

But the two groups' relations with each other began to change during the colonial period. When the Nawab's rule came to an end at the beginning of the nineteenth century and his administrative and military structures were dismantled, the Rowther were demobilised and ceased to be politically dependent on a Muslim administration. Most of them went into low-level government employment under the British, such as the army and police force, and petty trade. Similarly, with the decline of the local spinning and weaving industry, the Tarakanar ceased to be a community of weavers and middlemen for the Muslim merchants in the coastal towns. Many of them went into other kinds of trade, including the trade in industrially produced textiles, or followed the Maraikkayar through migration to Sri Lanka and South-east Asia. Both communities thus underwent a process in which the economic and political relationships which had placed them in an inferior position in relation to the other Muslim communities were untied.

At the same time colonial politics reinforced a collective identity of Tamil Muslims as opposed to non-Tamil Muslims. The colonial census conceived of north Indian Muslim society as parallel to Hindu society by distinguishing between high-ranking *ashraf* groups, which were believed to originate outside India, and low-ranking *ajlaf* groups, which consisted of descendants of converts. South Indian Muslim society was conceived in parallel terms, with Tamil-speaking Muslims classified as Lebbai, in contrast with Urdu-speaking Muslims who were classified in terms of north Indian categories such as Pattani, Sheikh and Mughal. In fact, the term Lebbai was originally the Tamil equivalent of imam. As imams serving in mosques all over Tamilnadu, the Lebbai are found in every Muslim community (*jamat*). They were generally among the poorest section of Muslims and depended on irregular payments by the community employing them or on small plots of land with which mosques are endowed for this purpose. In the late nineteenth century Muslims were the first community to be officially classified as 'backward' in Madras Presidency (Saraswati 1974:126). Later the category Lebbai was placed on the list of Backward Classes and most Tamil-speaking Muslims, including Rowther and Tarakanar, began returning themselves as Lebbai in the official census and even today they carry papers so identifying them. The category of Lebbai has thus become a new census-created category in Tamil Muslim society, which comprises all Tamil Muslims as opposed to Urdu-speaking ones.

This dissolution of hierarchical ties based on economic and political dependency between the Muslim groups effected a shift towards a collective Muslim identity among the Rowther and Tarakanar. Indeed, the very terms Tarakanar and Rowther are rarely used today and younger Muslims are often unfamiliar with them now. In the post-independence period, they seem to have been dropped from use as caste names, as evidenced, for example, in the marriage contracts in which the terms are no longer used.

The division between Rowther and Tarakanar has instead been redefined in terms of the Islamic distinction between Hanafi and Shafi legal schools. This is represented by minor and marginal differences between two interpretations of Islamic law—as, for example, in prayer times and posture during prayers—but it is without any social significance, such as rank or endogamy. The marriage records reveal that, since the beginning of the century, there has been a steady increase in intermarriages between Rowther and Tarakanar, slow in the first half of the century and much more rapid in the last twenty to thirty years. This has gone so far that it is sometimes no longer easy to decide whether an individual is a Hanafi (Rowther) or Shafi (Tarakanar), because intermarriage has taken place over two generations in the same family. An individual legally belongs to his father's group, but in practice his mother teaches him the rules of her group so that the two get mixed up, but this does not seem to concern anyone.

The submergence of separate Rowther and Tarakanar identities was accompanied by the development of a more egalitarian Islamic discourse basing itself on achieved rather than ascribed religiosity, contesting hierarchical institutions and practices, and denouncing them as un-Islamic and quasi-Hindu. The undoing of ties of political and economic dependency linking the Tarakanar to the Maraikkayar, and the Rowther to the Pattani, resulted in the elaboration of an egalitarian ideology emphasising unity and equality among Muslims. Anything which stands in the way of equality and unity of all Muslims is thus denounced as un-Islamic and quasi-Hindu. Indeed a violation of Hindu caste rules is tantamount to an affirmation of Muslim identity: for example, eating from large shared trays during funerals or marrying a parallel cousin.

No Rowther and Tarakanar today would deny that in the past these divisions were endogamous and 'like castes', but then according to this argument the past is irrelevant today. To admit that they had castes is the same as admitting that they were Hindus: nobody would dispute this. But according to them what matters nowadays is that they no longer have castes, that they are no longer ranked in some generally agreed order, and that they are no longer endogamous. Accordingly, the term caste (*jati*) is never used with reference to Muslims. The different divisions are called *piriva* (sect) or *inam* (division). Similarly, Muslims as a whole are never referred to as a caste but as *matam* (religion).

There can be little doubt that the vast majority of Indian Muslims, including the groups described here, are wholly or in part the descendants of converts from Hinduism, whether or not they claim Prophetic, Arab, Persian or Turkish descent. In the present case there is some circumstantial evidence in historical sources that the Rowther are in part related to Maravar converts, the Tarakanar to Iluvan converts, the Maraikkayar to Paravar converts and the Pattani to converts from Deccan castes. But their system of social stratification has been rethought and reconstructed in terms of Islamic sources of legitimation. The Pattani regard themselves as related to the Hyderabad Nizam and ultimately to Turkish groups, the Maraikkayar to Arabs, and the Rowther and Tarakanar see themselves as Hanafi and Shafi respectively. Each group has thus constructed for itself a new Islamic identity seeking to expurgate any signs of their Hindu origins.

Conversely, the attribution of Hindu beliefs and practices has become a standard device among Muslims for stigmatising other Muslims. Just as the Maraikkayar and Pattani attempt to disqualify the Tarakanar and Rowther as syncretists, so the Tamil Muslims counter the status claims of the other groups as attempts to re-erect Hindu hierarchical relationships and thereby to subvert the unity of Muslim society.

Tamil Muslims are thus engaged in a process of competitive Islamisation, as Mines (1975) has argued. According to him, the dynamics of this process of Islamisation derive from status competition within the Muslim community, and have nothing to do with relations between Hindus and Muslims, or competition between them as ethnic groups. Mines terms this new type of ethnicity 'congeneric' because it is based on intra-group rather than inter-group dynamics. Although Mines correctly identifies a process of competitive Islamisation in Tamil Muslim society, his concept of congeneric ethnicity fails to explain why status competition takes the form of Islamisation, rather than being pursued through other forms of symbolic capital, such as wealth, consumption or education. Viewed historically it becomes clear that this process of Islamisation must be understood in the context of Hindu-Muslim relations during the colonial period. McPherson (1969) has shown how starting with the Khilafat Movement in the 1920s, Tamil Muslims began 'a search for political unity and a definite political identity', during which 'the concept of themselves as a regional minority group had subsumed their previous tendency to think of themselves as members of a village or district quasi-caste'.

The Hindu answer

I therefore now turn to the Hindu perspective on the Muslim groups, or as Dumont (1970: 206) puts it 'the place which the Hindus made for the Muslims in their social hierarchy'. For this purpose, I administered a rank test including all communities in Kalakkadu.[3] Without hesitation, all respondents placed the Christians, the only other non-Hindu community in Kalakkadu, into the caste hierarchy. Their position is relatively clear because they are all hyphenated Christians (e.g. Christian-Harijan, Christian-Nadar) and their position in the hierarchy is determined by that of their original caste. There has obviously been no process of 'Christianisation' parallel to that of Islamisation outlined above.

[3] The test was given to two respondents from each of the 29 different communities in Kalakkadu. The respondents were presented with cards, which had the names of all communities written on them and were randomly shuffled, so that those of the Muslim and Christian communities were mixed up with those of the Hindu ones.

In the case of the Muslim groups about half the respondents excluded the Muslims from the single linear hierarchy and instead placed them in a separate hierarchy, arguing that they are not part of the caste system. The other half placed the Muslims into a single linear hierarchy, usually with Hindus in adjoining positions, so as to treat them both, in effect, as a single subdivided category. A few respondents treated each of the three types of Muslims as a separate group, irrespective of their common religion, and placed them separately in the hierarchy as if they were unconnected. Overall, the position of Muslims was determined by the status of the Rowther, who are numerically the majority community among the Muslims; they are also in closest contact with Hindus and are thus the most visible of the Muslim communities in Kalakkadu. Those respondents who placed Muslims into the caste hierarchy ranked them in the middle, among the higher non-vegetarian castes. They were most commonly placed near the Konar (Yadava) because Rowther and Konar live in adjoining streets and their houses are often mixed up in the side lanes. The two communities are traditionally linked by close neighbourhood and friendship ties among both men and women, and they therefore interdine. At both the collective and individual levels, their relations are generally seen as the closest that the Muslims have with any of the Hindu groups.

As for the ranking of the different Muslim groups in relation to each other, it has to be noted that many Hindus do not have a very clear idea of the internal divisions among the Muslims. Indeed, the terms Tarakanar and Rowther are not known to many Hindus and they distinguish them instead in terms of linguistic criteria: the Pattani are known as Urdu-speakers and the Tarakanar and Rowther are also distinguished as *wappa kuttam* and *appa kuttam* respectively, which pertains to a dialectical variation in the term for father used by the two groups. The Pattani ranked highest and sometimes—if the respondents did not rank the three Muslim groups consecutively—as high as the Naidu, a caste of Telugu warriors who ruled parts of Tamilnadu in the pre-colonial period. Their former political importance, their wealth as major landowners, and their ritually high status due to their control of saint shrines, all explain this superior status of the Pattani from a Hindu perspective. On the other hand, the Tarakanar are regarded as the lowest-ranking of the Muslim groups, and sometimes as low as the Iluvan, a local caste of weavers. Their low status in Hindu eyes is related to their traditional occupation of weaving, which ranks low on the Hindu scale. Like other communities of weavers, the Tarakanar live outside and downriver from the town, because they used to dye cloth and thus pollute the water. This also means that they live outside the social boundaries of the town in separate settlements like the Harijans and Nadar. In addition, the Tarakanar have also adopted certain egalitaran Muslim customs which are particularly polluting in Hindu eyes: for example, eating from large shared trays during life-cycle ceremonies. The Rowther rank in the middle between these two groups, since they neither occupy any privileged position economically, politically or ritually, nor carry any of the stigma of the Tarakanar which associate them with low-ranking Hindu castes.

There is thus a great deal of uncertainty and ambiguity among Hindus as to whether and how Muslims relate to the caste hierarchy. There seems to be no standard, generally accepted answer to such questions: are Muslims in Kalakaddu part of the caste hierarchy or not, and, if they are, do the different Muslim groups constitute one caste category with subdivisions or separate categories in the hierarchy? This ambiguity can be unravelled at several levels. At one level there is a recognition that in some ways Muslims can fit into the caste system by analogy (for example through their association with the Konar), but at other levels they clearly do not (for example, in relation to the ideology of purity and pollution).

Yet most significant in the present context is the fact that the Hindu claim that Muslims do indeed fit into the caste system is equivalent to the claim that Muslims in Kalakkadu are not 'real' Muslims, that 'our' Muslims are different from 'other' Muslims. Fitting into the same kind of discourse as one that argues that Muslims have caste and fit into the caste system is the general argument that—in the words of one Vellalar—'Kalakkadu Muslims are really Hindus'. Another Vellalar told me that if Mohammed Ali Jinnah had ever come to Kalakkadu, he would have abandoned the idea of Pakistan because he would have been shocked to see how similar were its Muslims and Hindus. In support of this argument, Hindus point to all the same cultural practices to which the Muslim groups point when they stigmatise each other as quasi-Hindus: the internal divisions of Muslim society, the ritual syncretism of the saint shrines, and the participation of the former Pattani zamindar in the annual temple car festival. Of course, on this occasion the signs are reversed: Hindus see these practices as an affirmation that Kalakkadu Muslims are different from other Muslims, that their local pecularities in relation to other Muslims show that they really fit into and are part of Hindu society.

Conversely, from a Hindu perspective, the argument that Muslims do not have caste, and thus do not fit into the caste system at all, is part of the wider argument that Muslims are fundamentally different from Hindus. Ultimately, therefore, they do not belong in Hindu society, and for a few extremists, they do not even belong to India. This view assimilates Muslims into an abstract, global society of Muslim—and particularly Arab—Others.

In this contradictory and inconsistent plurality of discourses on caste among Muslims, both by Muslims about themselves and by Hindus about Muslims, whom are we to believe? The Maraikkayar and Pattani, who accuse the Rowther and Tarakanar of being polluted by their Hindu origins and only Muslim in name? The Rowther and Tarakanar, who accuse the Maraikkayar and Pattani of perpetuating hierarchical values under a thin veneer of Muslim legitimacy? The Hindus who make the same kind of arguments but with reversed signs: moderate Hindus who argue that the local Muslims are sufficiently different from an abstract, external, global Muslim society to qualify them as quasi-Hindus and pseudo-Muslims? Or more extremist Hindus who see Muslim society as a monolithic entity with no place in Hindu and maybe even Indian society?

The question of caste among Muslims therefore cannot be separated from the question of identity. Underlying the opposing and contradictory interpretations of the place of Muslims in Indian society is the basic, logical equation that one cannot be a real Muslim and have caste, so that to have caste implies that one is not a true Muslim. Hence to ask whether Muslims have caste is equivalent to asking whether Muslims are Hindus; in reality this question no longer makes any sense to either Muslims or Hindus. If Muslims do have caste, then they are not real Muslims; if they are real Muslims, it makes no sense to ask whether they have caste. From the point of view of both Hindus and Muslims, the very question is based on false logic.

The anthropologists' answer

I now want to return to the initial question of whether there is caste among Muslims. As we have seen, the Muslim answer to this question is no, and the Hindu answer is both yes and no. Only for anthropologists is the answer generally yes.

Indeed, on this problem, the anthropological literature on Muslims in India contains an intriguing paradox. On the one hand, the ethnography makes it clear that Indian Muslims almost universally deny that their society exhibits any caste-like features at all. On the other hand, there seems to be a broad consensus among anthropologists—with a few exceptions such as Mines (1975) and Lindholm (1986)—which affirms the existence of caste or caste-like structures in Indian Muslim society. We thus have a bizarre picture in which anthropologists keep on insisting that Indian Muslims have caste, whereas Indian Muslims themselves strenuously deny any such thing (Mujahid 1989:109-10).

Ahmad (1973:xxvii), for example, mentions how in Calcutta 'the *existence* of an hierarchical order generally receives overt denial from the great traditional values of the Muslims'. Bhattacharya (1973:128) speaks of 'a sharp contrast between ideology and *practised* pattern' among Muslims in rural West Bengal. Aggarwal (1973:21) tells us how, in Rajasthan, the Meos 'deny the *existence* of caste, or caste-like divisions, in their society'. Examining Muslim social stratification in the Telengana region of Andhra Pradesh, Benson (1983:47) argues that '*objective* similarities between Hindu and Muslim culture are frequently denied by Muslims.... Muslim social stratification shows structural parallels with Hindu caste in terms of ranking, endogamy, and occupational specialisation. Local Muslim ideology, however, not only fails to support, but actively denies these caste parallels'.[4]

These examples conceptualise the situation as a contradiction between the facts of caste and an egalitarian ideology. But what are these 'facts' of caste? On closer inspection they turn out to be a matter of definition and depend on the specific facts selected by a particular anthropologist. In other words, it is the observer who decides that caste exists and not the actors. And once the observers have decided in favour of caste's existence, any rejection of this by Muslims can only be treated as a repression, rationalisation, or denial by actors who refuse to see the 'reality' as it is and continue to deceive themselves or the anthropologist.

Aggarwal (1973:22), for example, prefaces his discussion of whether Muslims have caste or not as follows: 'It is a matter of definition. Depending on our definition we may answer the question in the negative or the affirmative'. He then proceeds to answer it in the affirmative by defining caste 'as a ranked social division in which membership is determined by birth'. But according to this definition caste could also be said to exist in medieval European feudal society, the nineteenth-century American South, possibly in contemporary British society and probably in a fairly representative sample of complex societies throughout most of human history. Similarly, Ahmad (1973:xx) bases his definition of caste on Hutton (1946:49), adding to Aggarwal's definition occupational specialisation and a religio-ideological basis involving restrictions on social intercourse. The same defining criteria of caste are also used by most contributors to Ahmad's edited book (Ahmad 1973), as well as by others who have written on the subject, such as Mines (1972) and Benson (1983). Thus Hutton's classic definition of caste continues to be the basis on which Muslims in India are judged to have caste.

Theoretically more sophisticated is the conceptualisation of the problem of Muslim caste as a contradiction not between facts and values, but between two value systems or ideologies, namely Hindu hierarchical and Muslim egalitarian. But it turns out that one of these value systems is still judged to be somehow closer to the facts than the

[4] In each of the above quotations, italics have been added by the author.

other, for the facts are those that the observer judges the actors actually to believe, as opposed to what they say they believe. In this case, the problem of facts versus values is simply transposed to that of the actors' actual beliefs, as opposed to their claims to belief. Thus Dumont notes that 'underlying the ultimate or Islamic values are other values presupposed by *actual* behaviour' (1970:211). In similar terms, Ahmad distinguishes 'formal Islamic ideology' from '*actual* beliefs held by Muslims' (1973:xxvii-xxviii). The implication of the adjective 'actual' is presumably that Muslims do not really take Islamic values or ideology seriously. Caplan (1987) makes the psychological speculation implicit in this type of argument even clearer when he equates the 'formal Islamic ideology' with the conscious and the 'actual beliefs' with unconsciously held values.

Our examination of social stratification among Tamil Muslims has indeed revealed the existence of two opposed sets of values, one egalitarian and the other aristocratic, if not hierarchical. However, it has also shown that it would be completely misleading to equate the former with 'ultimate or Islamic values' and 'formal Islamic ideology' and the latter with 'the other values presupposed by actual behaviour' or 'actual beliefs'. The difference between the two sets of values is not a matter of ideology versus praxis, or of actual beliefs versus self-deceptive rationalisations, or of unconscious versus conscious values. It is rather a matter of two competing interpretations and strategies for behaviour, which are employed to make sense of changing economic and political realities, and therefore have to be understood in the context of these realities.

The problem with functionalist and structuralist formulations of the problem of caste among Muslims is that their ahistorical approach makes them unable to deal with a situation in which two fundamentally different value systems confront each other (Lindholm 1986). With reference to an essentially ahistorical and decontextualised view of both Muslim and Hindu values, Islam is equated with egalitarianism, so that any deviation from the latter or any evidence of inequality is treated as contrary to Islamic values; thus it must be a survival or diffusion of Hindu values into Muslim culture. This represents not only a simplistic view of Muslim societies and their history, but also a reductionist, essentialist and ahistorical theoretical approach.

By contrast, some recent work has focused on the historical character of caste. Dirks (1987; 1989), for example, speaks of the 'colonial invention of caste', and I would argue that we must understand Muslim social stratification in similar historical terms. During the colonial and post-colonial periods, it underwent transformations because of changed economic and political realities, and new forms of ideological representation, which drew on exclusively Islamic sources, began to emerge.

Moreover, I would also argue that, to some extent, the invention of caste and the invention of Muslim stratification are related. In so far as caste was developed into a 'gate-keeping' concept of Hindu civilisation, it kept Muslims out, rather than in.[5] As caste became the central symbol of Hindu society, to admit to the existence of caste structures among Muslims would be to negate Muslim identity. Thus in so far as caste or caste-like structures and values existed among Muslims they had to be disinvented. The universal denial of caste among Muslims is a logical necessity for their identity as Muslims in a modern world, in which the boundaries between being Muslim and being Hindu can no longer be left undefined. When caste became a gate-keeping concept, it thus also became an ethnic boundary marker to distinguish Hindus from non-Hindus. Hence, alongside the invention or redefinition of caste, Muslims invented or redefined a universalist and explicitly Muslim system of stratification drawing on exclusively Islamic sources of legitimation.

The transformation of the Muslim stratification system should therefore be placed in the context of Islamisation and Muslim ethnicity. The argument by Dumont (1970) and others that Muslims in India share in the culture of caste simply because they live in an Indian social and cultural environment and are of Hindu origin, is ultimately based on the assumption that our understanding of inequality in contemporary Indian Muslim society can be advanced by analysing it as a diffusion or

---

[5] The 'gate-keeping' concept was coined by Anjan Ghosh in his paper for the 'Caste Today' workshop.

survival of caste practices and values among Muslims. This reflects a misconception of how ethnicity works by creating boundaries and oppositions precisely between those who are closest, so that the 'others' are then assimilated to those who are distant.

References

Aggarwal, P.C. 1973. 'The Meos of Rajasthan and Haryana.' In I. Ahmad (ed.), *Caste and social stratification among the Muslims* New Delhi: Manohar.

Ahmad, I. 1973. 'Introduction.' In I. Ahmad (ed.), *Caste and social stratification among the Muslims*. New Delhi: Manohar.

Ahmad, I. (ed.) 1973. *Caste and social stratification among Muslims* New Delhi: Manohar.

Bayly, S. 1989. *Saints, goddesses and kings.* Cambridge: Cambridge University Press.

Benson, J. 1983. 'Politics and Muslim ethnicity in south India.' *Journal of Anthropological Research* 39:42-60.

Bhattacharya, R.K. 1973. 'The concept and ideology of caste among the Muslims of rural West Bengal.' In I. Ahmad (ed.), *Caste and social stratification among Muslims*. New Delhi: Manohar.

Caplan, L. 1987. 'Caste and castelessness among south Indian Christians.' In L. Caplan (ed.), *Studies in religious fundamentalism.* London: Macmillan.

Dirks, N.B. 1987. *The hollow crown: ethnohistory of an Indian kingdom.* Cambridge: Cambridge University Press.

___. 1989. 'The original caste: power, history and hierarchy in South Asia.' In M. Marriott (ed.), *India through Hindu categories.* New Delhi: Sage.

Dumont, L. 1970. *Homo hierarchicus: the caste system and its implications.* London: Weidenfeld and Nicolson.

Fanselow, F.S. 1989. 'Muslim society in Tamilnadu: an historical perspective.' *Journal of the Institute of Muslim Minority Affairs* 10:264-89.

Hutton, J.H. 1946. *Caste in India.* Cambridge: Cambridge University Press.

Lindholm, C. 1986. 'Caste in Islam and the problem of deviant systems: a critique of recent theory.' *Contributions to Indian Sociology* (n.s.) 20:61-73.

McPherson, K. 1969. 'The social background and politics of the Muslims of Tamil Nad, 1901-1937.' *Indian Economic and Social History Review* 6:381-402.

Madan, T.N. 1981. 'Religious ideology and social structure: the Muslims and Hindus of Kashmir.' In I. Ahmad (ed.), *Ritual and religion among Muslims in India.* New Delhi: Manohar.

Mines, M. 1972. 'Muslim social stratification in India: the basis for variation.' *Southwestern Journal of Anthropology* 28:333-49.

——. 1973. 'Social stratification among Muslim Tamils in Tamil Nadu, south India.' In I. Ahmad (ed.), *Caste and social stratification among the Muslims.* New Delhi:Manohar.

——. 1975. 'Islamisation and Muslim ethnicity in south India.' *Man* (n.s.) 10:404-17.

Mujahid, A.M. 1989. *Conversion to Islam: untouchables' strategy for protest in India.* Chambersburg: Anima Books.

Pate, H.R. 1917. *Madras District Gazetteers: Tinnevelly,* vol.1. Government Press..

Saraswati, S. 1974. *Minorities in Madras State.* Delhi: Impex.

Yule, H. 1875. *The book of Ser Marco Polo.* London: John Murray.

Chapter 9

IDENTITY AND DIFFERENCE OR EQUALITY AND INEQUALITY IN SOUTH ASIAN MUSLIM SOCIETY[1]

Sylvia Vatuk

There has been much ink spilled in debates among anthropologists of South Asia over the question of whether or not Muslims in the region are organised according to a system of 'castes'. No observer denies the presence of social differentiation within the Muslim population of the subcontinent and most agree that, generally speaking, named sub-groups in a given locality are ranked, at least loosely, in a prestige hierarchy, both among themselves and in relation to those Hindu castes with which they are in regular contact. A tendency for the members of such groups to marry endogamously has also been widely observed. Furthermore, some Muslim groups at least have been described as playing functionally interdependent roles within the larger rural social system of which they are a part that are hardly distinguishable from those performed by Hindu occupational and ritual specialists.

In all of these respects patterns of social stratification among South Asian Muslims display obvious similarities to those that prevail among Hindus, even representing, in the words of Dumont, 'a kind of replica

[1] Research for this paper was supported by NEH Grant No.RO-21894-89 and by grants from the Social Science Research Council, Wenner-Gren Foundation for Anthropological Research, Rockefeller Foundation Bellagio Study Centre, American Institute of Indian Studies, and the University of Illinois at Chicago Office of Social Science Research and Campus Research Board. Too many people have contributed to my research for me to be able to list them all here, much as I would like to do so. I must, however, express my deep gratitude to Dr. Zakira Ghouse and her sisters, Miss A.W. Shakira and Dr. A.M. Nasira, as well as to Mrs. Rahat Anwar, for the many hours they have spent helping me to learn about their *khandan.* Moiz Uddin, Yasmin Zaim, Omar Nasib and Amjad Shafiq provided invaluable assistance at the University of Illinois at Chicago with the transcription and translation of tapes and handwritten Urdu materials. I am grateful to all of the participants in the workshop at which it was first presented, and especially to Katy Gardner and Chris Fuller, for their comments and suggestions for improvement of the original version of this paper.

of the Hindu system' (1970:206). Most scholars explain this as the result of influences from the surrounding society upon those Muslims who came to South Asia from elsewhere, the 'survival' of Hindu ways among local converts to Islam being another important factor.

Under the circumstances it is not surprising that references to 'Muslim castes' should be common, not only in the older ethnographic survey and gazetteer literature, but also in more recent anthropological works on South Asian social organisation. Indeed, the first serious scholarly attempt to examine analytically the nature of social stratification among South Asian Muslims contains this phrase in its title (Ansari 1959). However, particularly since the publication of Imtiaz Ahmad's edited volume on social stratification among Muslims in India (1973b), there has been considerable dispute about the appropriateness of using the term 'caste' to label South Asian Muslim social groups (see, for example, Barth 1960; Dumont 1970; S. Ahmad 1971; Alavi 1972; Bhattacharya 1973; Goodfriend 1983; Gaborieau 1977; Das 1984; Lindholm 1986; Werbner 1989).

Critics argue, on the one hand, that while there are superficial resemblances between Hindu and Muslim patterns of social stratification, there are a number of respects in which the latter do not conform to the sociologist's definition of 'caste' systems. Thus, in a prototypical system of this kind group membership is irrevocably ascribed by birth. However, the boundaries of Muslim social groupings have often been observed to be relatively permeable, providing some scope for individual (as well as group) mobility. Furthermore, whereas strict group endogamy is generally understood to constitute one of the defining features of 'caste societies', intermarriage between members of different Muslim social groups is reportedly not uncommon (see, for example, I. Ahmad 1973a). It is further pointed out that the Hindu caste system is embedded in a comprehensive and integrated Hindu worldview. Rank and hierarchy, as fundamental concepts linked to relative degrees of ritual purity, underpin the social order. Since Muslims 'disavow the basic premises for stratification and affirm instead the basic equality of all believers', they cannot be said to partake truly in the caste system (Lindholm 1986:68). For many of those who have studied Muslim communities in South Asia a larger question is how to reconcile analytically the contradiction arising out of 'the juxtaposition of the Islamic doctrine of the equality of all men and the existence of social hierarchy' in Indian Muslim society (Prindle 1988:260).

A related question is to what extent Muslims themselves are aware of the contradiction, and how they deal with it. The problem is not peculiar to South Asia. In Muslim societies everywhere competition for social prestige, rank, and individual and group honour is a central and absorbing activity, despite 'scriptural' Islam's profession of equality. As Levy, among others, has shown, the contradiction has produced active controversy and conflict throughout the Muslim world for centuries (1965:53-90). Ethnographers of South Asia have tended to frame the analytical question as one of ideology versus 'practice'. They suggest that those Muslims who are aware of the disparity, and who are committed to Islamic orthopraxy, handle it cognitively by such means as denial, rationalisation, or the selective, context-specific use of alternate 'discourses' of status (Bhattacharya 1973; Prindle 1988).

Rather than attempt to enter into these debates about Muslim 'caste', I would suggest that the questions that underlie them need to be reframed. There has been an unfortunate tendency in the literature to use an idealised and essentialised concept of Hindu 'caste' as a model against which to measure observed Muslim social patterns and modes of thought. In so doing, insufficient recognition is given to the diversity and variability over space and time of 'caste' as it operates among, and is rationalised by, Hindus themselves. Secondly, and more important for the present discussion, attention is diverted from the task of analysing patterns of Muslim social stratification in their own terms. And scholars may even be hindered in their descriptive enterprise, inasmuch as they are influenced to attend chiefly to those aspects of social organisation and ideology that have already been identified as central to 'the Hindu caste system', possibly neglecting others having special salience for Muslims.

What is needed is to try to come to a better understanding of how South Asian Muslims themselves think about identity and difference, equality and inequality. We need to find out how they categorise themselves in relation to all others inhabiting their social universe, and how they act upon these conceptualisations and draw upon them in designing and enacting their daily lives. Further, we need to take an historical perspective, asking to what extent and in what way Muslims in South Asia today approach the issue of social inequality differently from the way they did in the past. Such an approach is consistent with Béteille's suggestion, at the workshop for which this paper was originally prepared, that rather than looking narrowly at the phenomenon of 'caste' in the contemporary world of South Asia, we ought to be looking much more broadly at 'fields of inequality', whatever particular forms these may display.

It is obviously not sufficient to rely upon the words of Islamic religious texts for insight into the 'ideology' aspect of these matters. Here I do not mean to become embroiled in the other controversy that has dominated academic discourse on South Asian Muslims, namely the question of the relationship between scriptural Islam and the everyday life of Muslims in the subcontinent (Robinson 1983; 1986; Das 1984; Minault 1984). Clearly, Muslim scripture and law cannot be disregarded in this enterprise, but our starting point has to be the local context in which they 'are elaborated, understood and...reproduced' (Eickelman 1982:1).

A *Nawwayat* khandan *of Hyderabad and Madras*

It is hardly necessary to emphasise here the great cultural and social heterogeneity of those who fall under the general rubric of 'South Asian Muslim'. Given this diversity, there cannot be a single set of answers to the questions I have posed. My own research has been carried out in southern India—specifically in Madras and Hyderabad cities—among a people calling themselves Naiti or (in the plural) Nawwayat. It was in Hyderabad in 1984 that I first encountered members of one large Nawwayat *khandan* (or 'family', as they say when they speak in English). Later I met others in Madras, where their immediate forebears have resided for many generations.[2]

[2] In a survey of households conducted in 1984, I identified a total of 666 persons in Madras and Hyderabad who regard themselves as affiliated to this *khandan*, either through one or both parents or through marriage. I also have

Frequently when I was introduced to someone new the conversation would turn to matters of family history, to an enumeration of the particular characteristics and qualities of the Nawwayats and of this *khandan* in particular, and to the accomplishments of its most notable figures, living and dead. Certain themes kept recurring in these people's recitals of their family lore that I later found reiterated when I read essays and books that they or their ancestors had written. Their mode of presenting themselves as members of a very special group seemed to encapsulate many shared understandings about who they were, and to implicitly communicate something about where they perceived themselves to be situated in relation to other Muslims and to Indian society at large (see Vatuk 1990).

Men and women of this *khandan* almost always began by telling me about the Nawwayat *qaum*, a people who came to India from Arabia by sea, many centuries ago, to trade and spread the Islamic faith.[3] Initially these people settled on the west coast of southern India, but gradually they dispersed throughout the region. This *khandan*'s own ancestors were renowned Islamic religious scholars (*'ulama*) and legal specialists, some of whom rose to prominence as *qazi*s ('judges') in the service of the Sultans of Bijapur. This family tradition has continued up to the present day, the post of Chief Qazi of Tamilnadu having been occupied for many generations by a member of their family.

A prominent ancestor (whom I will call by the pseudonym Ghulam

---

knowledge of another 500-600 members of the *khandan* currently living in Pakistan and elsewhere in the world. A manuscript biographical register of the *khandan* includes listings for over 2,500 individuals (at least half of them deceased), who either trace descent from the *khandan*'s apical ancestor or are married to one of his descendants (Majid 1984).

[3] Urdu-speaking Nawwayats (and others) usually employ the word *qaum* to refer to a people, ethnic group, community, (Hindu) caste or *jati*. The word derives from Arabic where it is loosely applied to 'any group defined by a concept of common ancestry—"tribe", "caste", "lineage", "family"' (Lelyveld 1978:143; see also Platts 1977:796). In the late nineteenth century it began to be used for Indian Muslims as a quasi-ethnic group made up of those who share a common Islamic religious identity. Lelyveld (1978:143) credits Sayyid Ahmad Khan with major responsibility for this shift in meaning. In contexts other than the one I am discussing here, the Nawwayats also use the word *qaum* in this latter, expanded sense.

Mahmud)[4] had once been Diwan to the Nawwab of the Carnatic. A son
had succeeded him, remaining in office until Nawwabi rule *(hukumat)*
was abolished and the country taken over by the British. Their *khandan*
is widely known for their devotion to scholarship and their deep love of
books. In family libraries and homes they have preserved important and
valuable collections of old scholarly manuscripts and printed volumes,
many official records of the Arcot Nawwabi, and quantities of books,
manuscripts, and other materials written by members of their own
family.[5]

It is, they say, a particular feature *(khususiyat, makhsus)* of their
khandan that for many hundreds of years they have neither taken
women from nor given them to other *khandan*s, but have married exclusively among themselves. Thus they have preserved the purity of their
blood for generations. The result of this can be seen in certain unique
physical traits, especially pale skin, long necks, distinctive eye shape
and facial features, that make members of the *khandan* recognisable
wherever they go, not only in India but anywhere in the world.

In this almost formulaic self-presentation certain central themes—
ancestral origins in Arabia, close kinship connectedness through
common descent and intermarriage, a long tradition of religious
devotion and scholarship, and prominent connections with the erstwhile
Carnatic Nawwabi—emerge very clearly. They are not only indications
of the family's distinctiveness, but sources of pride for its individual
members. It is worth noting, however, that this description includes no
direct reference to where the members of the *khandan* place
themselves—or the Nawwayats generally—vis-à-vis other Muslim (or
non-Muslim) *qaum*s in their social universe. Their discourse is not an
explicit one of relative rank or social hierarchy. However, in so far as
many of the characteristics that they associate with themselves are
known to be highly valued in Indian Muslim culture, it is not difficult

---

[4] I use this name in order to protect the privacy of living members of the
khandan, some of whom prefer that the family not be easily identifiable in what
I write about them.

[5] These records and writings by family historians have made it possible
greatly to supplement my ethnographic observations and provide historical
depth. See especially Ahmad-ul Madini 1871; Mazhar 1949; Hashmi 1963;
Ghouse 1973; Iqbal 1973; Majid 1984.

to detect in their self-presentation some implicit clues to the way they perceive their own social standing. For example, Arab origins, illustrious ancestry, fair skin colour, scholarly accomplishments, and close association with the former ruling powers frequently serve as bases for claims to social precedence, not only in India but in the Muslim world generally. Furthermore, the emphasis they place upon a longstanding practice of *khandan* endogamy suggests the practice of a kind of social exclusivity that tends to be associated with high status not only in this but in all societies.

It is not easy to say, from an outsider perspective, precisely what kind of a social unit the Nawwayat *qaum* constitutes. The category 'Nawwayat' itself is somewhat elusive: British and Western-trained Indian writers differ from Nawwayat writers in their perceptions of what Nawwayat identity entails, as well as in their interpretation of the historical record, such as it is. The name itself appears in a variety of forms (including Nait, Naiti, Navayat, Nevayet) in Arabic, Persian, Urdu, Portuguese and English sources dating from at least the fourteenth century. An even earlier occurrence is reported from an eleventh-century Goan inscription (D'Souza 1955:185-6). The numerous modern historical accounts based upon these sources and upon Nawwayat oral traditions (see Wala 1976:35-55; Pais 1919:41-6; Murtuza 1942; D'Souza 1955:1-59; Hashmi 1963:4-15; Kokan 1963:21-6; Ghouse 1973:32-9; Iqbal 1973), agree that the ancestors of the Nawwayats were among the many groups of Arab seafarers who began to settle on the western coast of India even before the advent of Islam in the seventh century (see Bouchon 1986; Murtuza 1942; Bayly 1989:73-86).

The nineteenth-century British gazetteer and caste-and-tribe literature suggests that the name Nawwayat was used to label several distinct populations, separate from one another geographically and differing in language and culture as well as in their particular origins. An Indian sociologist, in a 1955 ethnographic account of a group he calls 'the Navayats of Kanara', says that 'at least three different communities are known by the generic name of Navayat', each of them being 'strictly endogamous' (D'Souza 1955:23, 25). What all three have in common is their claim to descent from Arab mariners, hence their name, deriving (in D'Souza's view) from an Arabic word for 'sailor'.[6] D'Souza believes that they do not all have a single origin but represent the descendants of several groups of migrants, hailing from different Arab 'tribes', who came to India at different times. The Nawwayats to whom his own ethnographic monograph is devoted live around the town of Bhatkal in South Kanara district, Karnataka. The Konkani Muslim community of the Bombay area is also said to have been formerly known by the names 'Naitia' or 'Nawait' (Edwardes 1909:147-8, 254-5). Finally, D'Souza identifies those he terms 'the Navayats of the Deccan' (1955:24-5). The Nawwayats of Ghulam Mahmud's *khandan* belong to this group.

In 1904 a Hyderabad Naiti of Madras and Bijapur ancestry published a book-length historical and ethnographic account of his people, entitled *Tarikh-un Nawwayat* ('History of the Nawwayats') (Wala 1976).[7] He speaks of 'the Nawwayat people' (*qaum-i Nait*) as divided into three 'branches' or descent lines (*shakh*). Two of these lines are collateral to that of the Prophet Muhammad, and a third traces its descent directly from him. All three *shakh* are said to have left Madina for Baghdad in the late seventh century A.D. because of political differences between their leader and the local governor. Persecuted in Baghdad by the local Shi'a ruler for refusing to abandon their Sunni faith, they later migrated as a body to Basra. In the fourteenth century, again fleeing oppression, they sailed for India (Wala 1976:40-55).

Wala and other Nawwayat writers thus also speak of a three-fold division of their *qaum*, but the divisions they describe are genealogical segments, not associated in any way with the three 'communities'

---

[6] The question of the derivation of the name is a matter of heated controversy among Nawwayat writers, many of them being in strong disagreement with D'Souza on this point. See, for example, Ghouse 1973:34-8.

[7] The writer is also a Dakhani Nawwayat and his family is distantly related to the *khandan* of Ghulam Mahmud. All references to this work are to a later edition of the narrative portion which was reissued in 1976 by the author's grandson, Dr. Hasanuddin Ahmad. Some information about Wala and his ancestors may be found in the Introduction to this edition. A published biography of Dr. Ahmad's father, Deen Yar Jung, also contains information about the family (Mudiraj 1964).

identified by D'Souza. Nor do they attempt to identify the three *shakh* with particular localised communities of Nawwayats in India today. Wala also refers to the existence within the *qaum* of large numbers of 'surname groups' that are associated with different modes of livelihood, places of origin, and so on. However, he makes no attempt to map out these different groups on to the Indian landscape or explore the nature of the on-going social relationships, if any, that exist among them today. He and other Nawwayat writers are more interested in exploring the Nawwayat *qaum*'s presumed common origin and heritage, for it is this particular history that validates and legitimises their perception of themselves as a unique and special people. For them the important questions to be asked are where the ancestors of the Nawwayats came from and when, what their genealogical connections are with the Prophet of Islam, and what special physical and cultural characteristics and habits have been passed on through the generations to continue to distinguish them from others as a separate and identifiable 'people'. Like most contemporary Nawwayats with whom I have become acquainted, these writers tend to think in terms of a wider Nawwayat identity and do not find very convincing the notion that several fundamentally 'different' groups of people in various parts of south India may have simply somehow come to share the same name.

The Nawwayats and South Indian Muslim society

Muslim society in the part of India where these people live presents a complicated picture, with its population of diverse origins, languages and sectarian affiliations, among other differences (see DuPuis 1960:80-96, 215-45; McPherson 1969; 1975; Mines 1972b; 1973; 1975; Bayly 1989:71-103; More 1993). A broad division can be made along linguistic lines, between those who speak Urdu (or its local dialect, Dakhani) as a mother-tongue, and those who speak one of the Dravidian languages. Those who have historically spoken Urdu are concentrated mainly in the northern part of the region (called in English the Deccan), which experienced centuries of Muslim domination before the coming of the British. Most descend from north Indians who came with or in the wake of the Mughal penetration of the region in the seventeenth century. In Hyderabad a stream of north Indian migrants continued to arrive through the early part of the present century, in conjunction with the Nizam's recruitment of British-educated men for his modernising administration.

Other long-time Urdu-speakers trace their origins to soldiers and officials who were in the service of Muslim rulers of the Deccan even before the Mughal incursions. Hence the name *'Dakhani'* (or Deccani), meaning 'southerners', although many of them also trace their ultimate origins back to north India, to Persia, or elsewhere. The Urdu-speakers, for the most part, are divided along lines familiar from the literature on northern India (see, for example, Mujeeb 1985; I. Ahmad 1972; 1973c). Most belong to the majority Sunni sect, although there is also a sizeable Shi'i group among them, especially in Hyderabad. They tend to claim 'foreign' origins, tracing their ancestry to the various waves of Muslim invaders and other immigrants who first came to northern India from outside of the subcontinent. Thus they are often referred to as 'Ashraf' ('noble, respectable'), in contrast to the so-called 'Ajlaf' descendants of more recent north Indian converts. The former are further divided into the familiar categories of Sayyid, Shaikh, Mughal and Pathan, commonly ranked in declining order of social precedence. The latter often bear names indicating their occupation or the Hindu caste from which their ancestors came.

Finally, a much smaller number of Urdu-speaking Muslims claim descent from Arabs who came at an early date directly to southern India by sea. The Nawwayats with whom I am concerned here fall into this category. Their ancestors, in the course of their long and close associations with the Bijapur and other Deccan courts, adopted the language as well as certain other features of Dakhani culture. However, they continue to regard themselves as a group entirely distinct and apart from the Dakhani Muslims as well as from Urdu-speaking Muslims of more recent north Indian origin, whom they generally refer to as 'Hindustanis'.

Muslim speakers of Dravidian languages include the Mappilai of Kerala (see Dale 1980), various Tamil Muslim groups concentrated in southern Tamilnadu (see Mines 1972a; 1972b; 1973; 1975; More 1993;

McPherson 1969), and Telugu-speaking Muslims in Andhra Pradesh (see Benson 1983), among others. Like the Nawwayats, some of these also trace their origins to early Arab maritime traders. But conversion, especially through the activities of Sufi saints and devotional cults at Muslim shrines, has been a major factor as well in the formation of the Muslim community in this region, just as it was in the north (Eaton 1978; Bayly 1989).

In Madras city, where the larger part of this *khandan* resides, both Urdu- and Tamil-speaking Muslims are found in large numbers, although the census does not provide a firm basis for estimating their relative proportions in the populations. Many of the ancestors of the former were relatives, officials, soldiers, servants, and other followers of the Nawwabs of the Carnatic who came to Madras in the eighteenth or early nineteenth centuries. The latter are a largely mercantile community, with some engaged in manufacturing occupations where they monopolise the leather and tobacco industries (see DuPuis 1960:215-45). Among them the Labbai are the principal sub-group. They are said to be the descendants of unions between early Arab settlers and local Hindu women. Another, much smaller, sub-group is the elite and exclusive Maraikkayar, claiming pure Arab ancestry. Their major settlements are in the port towns of the Coromandel coast where they have engaged for centuries in overseas trade (cf. Fanselow, ch.8, this volume). There are also in Madras numerous groups of avowedly convert origin.

The Tamil Muslims generally are said to 'identify the bulk of their cultural traditions with those of the Tamil population' (Mines 1975:405), rather than with the Mughal ruling and courtly traditions that provide so strong a point of orientation for most Urdu-speaking Muslims, here and elsewhere in India. However, for at least a century there has been a marked religious, cultural and political tension within the community between the strength of their Tamil ethnic identification and both internal and external pressures for greater orientation toward orthoprax Islam and more active ties with fellow Muslims in India and in the outside world (see Mines 1975; McPherson 1975; More 1993).

In Hyderabad the Muslim population is much larger (both absolutely and proportionately) and probably also more diverse than in Madras. Here Urdu-speaking Muslims of north Indian or Dakhani origin predominate. There are in addition large numbers of descendants of Telugu-speaking local converts, as well as many Muslims whose ancestors came at various times in the past both from other parts of India and from foreign countries, attracted by opportunities at the Nizam's court. In neither Hyderabad nor Madras are Nawwayats found in any significant numbers. They represent only a tiny group relative to the total size of the Muslim population. In fact, there were never very many Nawwayats in these two cities, even when they constituted a much more prominent, influential, and well-to-do group than they do today.[8] Their small numbers have implications for their position within their local society and for the extent to which they interact with other Muslims and with the Hindus, who constitute a majority in both cities (especially Madras). In their work and social life (and in Hyderabad in their home neighbourhoods as well) very few of the people they come into contact with belong to their own *qaum*. Thus they tend to have a heterogeneous circle of acquaintances and friends, including Hindus and people of other religions. This is especially so for the men of the *khandan* and for educated and employed women. On the other hand, many of the older women and those who are not western-educated still lead quite secluded lives, restricting themselves largely to their own homes and those of close relatives.

Many of those who have written about Muslim social structure in these two cities have alluded to the presence of a consciousness of differences in rank or social status among the various groups that

[8] In only a few early Census reports for the Madras Presidency are the Nawwayats listed separately. In 1891 just under 4,000 persons were so returned (listed under 'Traders' in the 'Castes, Tribes, and Races' tables). In the Tamil and Telugu Divisions of the Presidency (those that mainly concern me here), there was a total of 1,651 Nawwayats, 472 of them in Madras City itself. But in 1901 there were only 203 Nawwayats in the city, out of a total Muslim population of more than 57,000 (Stuart 1893; Francis 1902). This decline is consistent with a long-term trend that had begun in the 1860s when, after the dissolution of the Carnatic Nawwabi, many of those formerly associated with the court left Madras for Hyderabad and other places in search of employment. In 1901, members of Ghulam Mahmud's *khandan* must have accounted for most of the Nawwayat population still in the city.

inhabit them. However, none has attempted a systematic analysis of Muslim social stratification in either place. Mines, from the perspective of rural and small-town Tamilnadu, describes a division of Tamil Muslims into a number of distinct named groups that he claims are merely *differentiated* from one another, not ranked in a prestige hierarchy. He notes that these groups tend also to be separated territorially, except in urban settings. In his view, this, together with a preference for close kin marriage, largely explains why, in the absence of any 'rule' prescribing group endogamy, most marriages take place within the group (1973:65-6).

Mines observes that differences in status are indeed recognised on an individual level, but are based upon such 'achieved' criteria as age, wealth, and religiosity, rather than group affiliation (ibid.:62-4). In this respect he notes a contrast between southern Tamilnadu and the Deccan, where, he asserts, it is higher rank that is associated with 'foreign' origins, just as in northern India (ibid.:68). Mines does not address the question of status differences between Dakhani and Tamil Muslims in those settings where the two come into contact. Bayly, however, maintains that Urdu-speaking Muslims generally claim 'to be superior to other Muslims in the region' (1989:96). But she implies that such an hierarchical ordering may lack consensus, because there are in southern India two distinct 'definitions of elite Muslim rank'. The older one is based upon pride 'in assertions of pure Arab descent..., [combining] an ideal of high Islamic purity with a tradition of service and honours derived from non-Muslim kings', while a newer one, brought from the north by migrants to the Deccan, is based instead on claims of 'ancestral connections to the Persianate courts of the Mughals or the Deccani sultans' (ibid.:101). Bayly and others have said that pride in their Arab origins is especially marked in the case of the Maraikkayar and the Nawwayats. The former 'have long stigmatised all these other Muslims [such as the Labbais] as being "mere converts"... and therefore of lower social standing'. Their own Arab origins and affiliation with the Shafi'i *mazhab* are taken 'as proof of their separate and superior status and identity' (ibid.:80). Various eighteenth- and nineteenth-century British sources likewise remark that the Nawwayats look down upon Tamil Muslims because of their allegedly 'lowly' or 'mixed' origins (see, for example, Cox 1881:305).

People calling themselves Nawwayats were prominent at least from the fifteenth century in the service of various Muslim rulers of the Deccan. When the latter regimes were overcome by the Mughals, many Nawwayats went into imperial service. At the beginning of the eighteenth century much of present-day Tamilnadu became a province of the Mughal empire, subject to the over-arching authority of the Nizam of Hyderabad. A Nawwayat who had formerly been in military service under the Sultan of Bijapur was appointed to administer the territory. Sa'adatullah Khan established his capital at the town of Arcot and he and his descendants ruled the area until the middle of the eighteenth century. Then, after a period of dynastic struggle, his heirs were replaced by a close military retainer of the Nizam, a native of north India named Anwaruddin Khan.

This appointment was resisted by members of the deposed dynasty and their Nawwayat supporters and armed conflict continued. The British and French became actively involved, supporting opposing aspirants for control of the Carnatic in a struggle that ended in the 1750s with the defeat of the Nawwayat contender and the assumption of the title of Nawwab by the British-backed son of Anwaruddin Khan. Muhammad Ali Walajah remained in office for almost half a century, and his descendants continued the dynasty until 1855. However, after 1801, when the entire territory of the Carnatic was annexed by the British, they were rulers in name only, receiving a fixed revenue share as well as various honours and entitlements, but exercising no independent political authority (see Ramaswami 1984; Bayly 1989; Burhan Ibn Hassan 1934; 1939; Nazir 1950).

Although the period of Nawwayat rule in the region was relatively short and had effectively ended by 1744, and although in the early years at least the Walajah dynasty had good reason to be unsure of the loyalty of the former Nawwab's people, many Nawwayats continued in office through the changes in regime and others were able to regain posts of influence at court after the passage of time. Several ancestors and collaterals of the family with which I am concerned here were among them.

In 1801 a middle-aged religious scholar (*'alim*) Ghulam Mahmud, whose father was superintendent of the Nawwab's law court at Arcot, was presented with an unexpected opportunity for career advancement. The British had found the legitimate heir to the Nawwabi unwilling to cooperate with their intentions for annexation of the Carnatic and offered the title instead to one of his cousins. Years before, when Ghulam Mahmud had been attached to the royal household as a tutor, this young man had been his pupil. The unpopular new Nawwab, regarded as an upstart and traitor by most of his relatives and other members of his late uncle's court, needed advisers whom he could trust and hence asked Ghulam Mahmud to become his Diwan. Ultimately, as a consequence of his rise to a position of such prestige and power, Ghulam Mahmud came to occupy a focal position for his descendants as their *khandan* 'founder', their *jadd* or *bare buzurg* (lit. 'great ancestor').

Exclusivity in marriage and khandan *identity*

From the outset it was quite clear to me that exclusivity in marriage plays a central role in maintaining this *khandan*'s sense of group-belonging and boundedness. In speaking about their marriage practices they typically use such expressions as 'we marry among ourselves' (*apas me*) or 'within our own family' (*apne khandan me*). A potential mate from within the *khandan* is referred to as 'one of our own' (*zati*) girls (or boys). Someone who is not of the *khandan* but comes from a more 'distantly' related family—perhaps one with whom there have been marital ties several generations back—is referred to as of *ba'id* or *dur khandan*. An unrelated Nawwayat is usually called simply *ahl-i Nawwayat*, literally 'a Nawwayat person'. Anyone not a member of their own *khandan* is said to be of *ghair khandan*. This term is usually employed when referring to someone not of the Nawwayat *qaum*. While all of these expressions imply a structure of bounded and nested social groups, in fact, except perhaps at the level of the *qaum*, firm boundaries are absent by virtue of the fact that descent is traced cognatically, rather than exclusively in the male line. The facts that the *khandan* has no name and its members bear no common surname contribute to a certain vagueness about who is meant to be included when expressions such as 'among ourselves', 'within the family' (*khandan me, 'ashirah me*), or 'our own' are used.

As these expressions indicate, the kinship universe for these people is ordered conceptually in terms of degrees of closeness, with no distinction made between links through women and through men. This is in spite of the presence of a patrilineal ideology that manifests itself in certain contexts, for example in the way in which family historians present their ancestral genealogies. Such a structure is typical of bilateral systems and corresponds closely to what has been described by ethnographers of a number of Muslim societies in the Middle East, North Africa and Afghanistan (for one example, see Geertz 1979). The prohibited degrees for marriage in Muslim law are likewise bilaterally applied and very limited. The only consanguineally related women forbidden to an unmarried man are his sister, mother (or other female ascendant), daughter (or other female descendant), the sister of a parent, and the daughter of a sibling.[9] Any other unmarried female relative of the appropriate age is considered marriageable and, indeed, preferred for marriage over any unrelated woman.

Among Muslims generally it is the groom's family that takes the initiative in mate selection, and it is usual to begin the search among one's close relatives (*qarabat, 'aziz, rishtedar*). Especially suitable candidates (from the perspective of the prospective groom's parents) are the daughters of one's siblings or first cousins. People often mention that a match with the father's brother's daughter is the most desirable of all, but such a preference is neither strongly nor consistently expressed. While such unions are common, they do not predominate over all other kinds of cousin marriages. A large proportion of intra-*khandan* unions, especially in the past, resulted from

---

[9] The wife's sister is also forbidden to a man who is already married. The female relatives listed are together classed as *mahram*, from the Arabic *haram*, 'forbidden' or 'sacred'. Reference is to the women's space within the home, from which any man with whom sexual relations would not be incestuous (*namahram*) is barred entry (Platts 1977:1008). A wife becomes *mahram* to her husband after her marriage, as does a husband to his wife.

agreements between pairs of siblings (of same or opposite sex) to marry their children (or their grandchildren) to one another. Often these agreements were made when the potential bride was still a baby or a very young child. If no match was possible within this circle of first cousins or first cousins once removed, a match would be sought from among those who shared descent through both parents from an apical ancestor (Ghulam Mahmud or one of his sons or daughters). Such people are sometimes referred to, especially in the written sources, as *najib-ut tarfain*, 'noble from both directions', to distinguish them from relatives who have some outside ancestry.

In some of the written sources, the term *kufu* or *kuf* is used in the context of discussions of matchmaking. For example, it is said in one biography that a man was married 'outside' the *khandan* 'because no mature girl of the same *kuf* was available' (Mazhar n.d.). Wala uses the same term in his discussion of Nawwayat endogamy:

adherence to the principle of equality in marriage (*kufu ki pabandi*) is this *qaum's* chief characteristic...the way in which the Nait *qaum* adheres to [this principle] is not seen in any other *qaum* in Hindustan... However wealthy or however noble the ancestry of the other party, if they are not of the Nait *qaum*, then they will neither be given daughters nor will daughters be given to them. This has the fortunate consequence of maintaining the pedigree (*nasab*) of the *qaum*. (1976:58-59)

Note that Wala speaks as if the entire Nawwayat *qaum* constituted the relevant endogamous unit, although in fact most marriages (in his own family as well as in Ghulam Mahmud's) were confined to a very much smaller circle of close kin. Only rarely would a Nawwayat consider marrying his daughter, or even a son, to an unrelated Nawwayat. From this point of view, adherence to the principle of *kufu* actually meant marrying within the immediate kindred, defined in terms of the concept of *najib-ut tarfain*. Simply marrying some other Nawwayat would not meet this qualification.

Scholars who have discussed social stratification among South Asian Muslims have often drawn attention to Islam's 'egalitarian' ideology, while failing to note the emphasis placed by Islamic law on status equality in marriage. In Arabic this is known as *al kafa'a fi zowaj*

(literally, 'equality—or similarity—of the couple'). The doctrine pre-
scribes that a woman be married to a man of social status equal to or
higher than her own. According to the Shafi'i school of law, the
principal criteria of *kafa'a* are descent, freedom (a free woman should
not be married to a slave), and religion (a Muslim woman should not be
married to a non-Muslim or to one whose family was converted to
Islam more recently than hers). The occupations of groom and bride's
father are also to be considered in judging whether the pair are
'similar'. These are not simply preferences, but can serve as grounds
for invalidating a marriage if it is later discovered that the parties were
not *kufu* ('of equivalent status') at the time they wed (see Ziadeh 1957;
Spectorsky 1993:14-16; Ali 1976:326-31).

The doctrine of equality of the couple is found not only in esoteric
legal texts and in scholarly works like Wala's history of the Nawwayats, but also in treatises on proper Islamic practice intended for
ordinary readers. For example, Ashraf 'Ali Thanawi's well-known
reformist tract, *Bihishti Zewar,* written around 1906 especially for
women readers, devotes space to this matter in Book 7, on marriage
(1962; 1973).[10] Instead of the terms *kafa'a* and *kufu*, which would
doubtless have been unfamiliar to his readers, he uses the more colloquial *barabari* ('equality'), explaining that, when selecting a son-in-
law, care should be taken to find a man 'of equal status' to the bride
(*barabar darjah ka).*[11]

Nawwayats commonly employ the related concepts of blood purity
and purity of pedigree to justify their endogamous preferences and

[10] Metcalf's 1991 translation of selected portions of this work does not
include the section on marriage.

[11] Thanawi's discussion of this doctrine proceeds from the perspective of
Hanafi law, as applied in India, which, in this respect, does not diverge
materially from the Shafi'i law followed by Nawwayats. The criteria of
'equality' he lists are: pedigree (*nasab*), the number of generations elapsed
since conversion to Islam, religiosity, wealth, 'occupation' (his examples
suggest that he means traditional 'caste' occupation), and mental capacity (that
is, an insane man is not a suitable mate for a mentally sound woman)
(1962:267-8; 1973:409-11). Thanawi defines *nasab* within the framework of
the four strata of Ashraf Muslims, and states specifically that it is descent in the
male line that matters, the natal origins of the mother being irrelevant. The
people of Ghulam Mahmud's *khandan* would, of course, strongly dispute this
latter qualification.

practices. 'Marrying among ourselves' is said to be desirable specifically because it enables the family to 'maintain the blood' (*khun baqi
rakhna, qaim rakhna*) as well as 'preserve the pedigree' (*nasab ko
mahfuz rahna*). The word *khalis* ('pure, unmixed') is also used to characterise the lineage or blood in this connection.

With the blood are said to be transmitted 'qualities' (*khassiat,
khisal*) that can be lost or diluted through admixture. Among the many
good qualities possessed by the lineage are 'moral' ones (such as
honesty, simplicity, religiosity and self-respect), abilities (such as
intellectual prowess), and physical traits (such as fair skin). Thus it is
said by those who favour close kin marriage that the practice should be
continued 'lest the colour become inferior' (*ghalat rang na hona, rang
kam na hona*).

The issue of the transmission of qualities through the 'blood' has
become a somewhat sensitive one in recent decades. At a time when
many social forces have been propelling a move toward a more
extensive network of marital alliances, 'scientific knowledge' about the
presumed deleterious effects of close-kin marriage has also been
spreading. A genetic study of the *khandan* conducted by a local
university team in Hyderabad in the 1960s contributed to feelings of
unease about the consequences of *khandan* endogamy. The question, of
course, usually arises not in the abstract but in connection with
discussions about the advisability of particular matches. Some use
'genetic' arguments to support their opinion that the *khandan* should
abandon close kin marriage. Others hotly contest this. They deny, on
the one hand, that their traditional practice could lead (or has led) to
genetic defects. But, on the other hand, they also point out that if
genetic principles do operate in the way that they are said to do, then it
is better to keep on marrying endogamously so as to continue to
replicate the *khandan*'s good traits. If this also means that some
hereditary defects will be passed on, it is better that these be the
relatively mild defects that are already known to be carried within the
family (such as poor eyesight). It is risky to begin engaging in marital
exchange with *khandan*s of whose bad qualities one may be unaware.

Ghulam Mahmud's *khandan* possesses genealogical records (*shajre*) through which their ancestry can be traced back to the fourteenth century. In the late nineteenth century much of this information was consolidated by a grandson of the founder in a Persian manuscript entitled *Tarikh-i Ahmadi* (Ahmad-ul Madini 1871). Another genealogical source is a 'biographical register' of the *khandan*, compiled by a female descendant of Ghulam Mahmud and kept up-to-date until shortly before her death at an advanced age in 1984 (Majid 1984). In these two documents there is sufficient information to enable the reconstruction of marital alliance patterns back to the late eighteenth century.

The record shows that before the first quarter of the nineteenth century, the marriage network in which the *khandan*'s ancestors were involved encompassed a fairly wide group of related families. The author of *Tarikh-i Ahmadi* presents genealogies for nine conceptually distinct Nawwayat patrilines (*shakh*). All are closely interconnected through marriage and descent. Included are the author's own ancestral patriline, several lines collateral to it, and the ancestral patrilines of Ghulam Mahmud's wives and children's spouses. One of the latter is a Sayyid lineage. The *sadat*, by virtue of their claim to be direct descendants of the Prophet, occupy in Muslim societies everywhere a position of social precedence. In north India they are said to be largely endogamous, occasionally taking non-Sayyid women in hypergamous unions, but rarely if ever giving daughters in return. Thus, according to Mujeeb,

The Sayyids...could practise any profession, they could be rich or poor, but it would be considered unfortunate if a Sayyid girl married someone who was not a Sayyid. (1985:211).

According to Madini's genealogies, however, the Nawwayat *sadat* have long engaged in marital exchange with other Nawwayats. Indeed, for nine ascending generations in the ancestral line of Ghulam Mahmud's son-in-law a majority of all recorded unions involved a non-Sayyid spouse. Especially common were marriages of a man to his matrilateral cross-cousin or to the daughter of his male matrilateral cross-cousin. Ghulam Mahmud's ancestors repeatedly gave women in this way to their Sayyid kinsmen. Furthermore, many Sayyid women were given in

marriage to non-*sadat*. However, the fact that overall more women
were taken in as brides than were given out in marriage to non-*sadat*,
suggests some degree of conformity to the notion of Sayyid social
superiority.

Ghulam Mahmud married off his two young daughters shortly
before he became Diwan, during a period when his employment
prospects were unpromising. He was related to both sons-in-law
through the marriages of female relatives—his wife's sister in one case,
his own sister and father's sister in the other. Furthermore, the fathers
of both sons-in-law were successful and influential men, who would
have been in a position to help his career, although this ultimately
proved unnecessary.

Twenty years or so later, when Ghulam Mahmud was well-
established at the Nawwab's court, he married both of his sons to
relatives of their mother. By 1855, when the last Nawwab died without
issue, these two sons occupied the two key offices of Diwan and Chief
Qazi and one of their nephews was Bakshi ('treasurer'). Eleven other
grandsons of Ghulam Mahmud were also on the Nawwabi payroll,
several in posts that were considered by the British of sufficiently high
rank as to entitle their holders to lifetime pensions, in contrast to the
severance pay or simple dismissal accorded the vast majority of the
Nawwab's 3,500 or so employees (see *Madras Political Consultations*,
22 January 1856, 24 March 1857, 31 March 1857). In marrying off
their children the men and women of this second generation confined
their choices to a much more limited circle of kin. Almost all of
Ghulam Mahmud's thirty grandchildren married first cousins or first
cousins once removed.

It seems reasonable to interpret this *khandan*'s increasing marital
exclusivity as arising out of their newly enhanced status in the social
order of the Nawwabi. The family appears to have been regarded as a
solidary and powerful group, and was, as a consequence, viewed by
some with jealousy and suspicion.[12] When they were at the height of

[12] For example, in 1856 a group of the Nawwab's soldiers sent a protest to
the Government Agent asking for an inquiry into alleged 'irregularities' by the
Diwan, accusing him of favouring his own kinsmen in implementing a British-
ordered reduction in pay for the former Nawwab's employees. It reads, in part,

their power and influence, there were a considerable number of other Nawwayat *khandan*s in Madras whose men moved in the same scholarly-religious circles (see Kokan 1974, Wasif 1982). At least one other Nawwayat family was even represented among the chief officers of the Nawwab. Thus the *khandan*'s increased tendency toward endogamy cannot be accounted for by the non-availability of other Nawwayats of similar social standing in their immediate vicinity. By declining to look beyond their immediate kindred for the purpose of marriage, even though it would have been easy to do so, the family made a statement about where they perceived themselves to be positioned vis-à-vis other Nawwayats of their acquaintance, including those with whom their ancestors had had affinal ties in the past.

The dissolution of the Nawwabi brought major dislocations for the *khandan*. Without a secure economic base, most of its members were dependent on British pensions and had been forced to vacate their homes in the former royal compound. For decades their elders had been leading Muslim resistance to the onslaught of western education and the English language, which they correctly perceived as a threat to Islamic systems of knowledge and to their own position of moral and intellectual authority over their co-religionists. Therefore, none were qualified to offer their talents to the new rulers, even if they had been so inclined. Two documents were produced in the post-Nawwabi period that indirectly suggest attempts to consolidate and redefine the boundaries of their 'in-group' by means other than the direct one of marriage alliance. One of these documents was Madini's family history. The other was a formal agreement, drafted in 1863, that sets forth new guidelines for the celebration of weddings in the *khandan* (Mazhar 1930-1). Whereas the 'History' sets out an official version of who the people of the *khandan* are and where they came from, the 'Regulations for the Celebration of Marriages' (*Zabitah-i Rasum-i Nikah*) attempts to define for them a new active role as religious and social reformers. Explicitly aimed at bringing their ritual practices in line with what they

---

'It is also well known to the Government that when the Newayath caste people become favourites of any King, Rajah and Nawob, they however ruin them as Meerasaduc did ruin the Tippoo Sultan, and Nawob Siddie Ally Khan ruined the Rajah of Nagpore' (*Madras Political Consultations*, 22 January 1856).

saw as the true dictates of the *shari'at*, the 'Regulations' were framed in the context of a widespread, all-India movement for the 'reform' of Islamic marriage and other life-crisis ritual that had been going on for many decades (see Metcalf 1991). But its timing in terms of the *khandan*'s own history suggests that it was meant to serve as a manifesto, a statement to an audience of their fellow Muslims, that, although they no longer held the legitimate authority adhering to their former Nawwabi offices, they still intended to claim a leadership role in the local religious arena.

With the signing of this agreement the *khandan*'s marriage circle contracted further, inasmuch as the 'reformist' authors refused to make any match unless the other party agreed to dispense with the elaborate traditional wedding rites. These rites were considered by most Muslims to be indispensable, inasmuch as they made a union socially, in addition to simply legally, valid. Because many *khandan* members were in the beginning strongly opposed to the changes, the reformers had little choice but to marry most of their children to one another. Debates over the issue raged within the *khandan* for over thirty years, creating an incipient cleavage that might eventually have divided it into two distinct marriage circles. However, the reformers gradually won over the rest, and marital relations among them resumed. The original signatories' expressed wish to influence other Madras Muslims to follow their example was apparently not realised, however, on any significant scale.

While parentally arranged marriages followed the patterns I have described, there were always occasional unions in which adult *khandan* men, acting on their own initiative, took 'outsider' (*ghair khandan*) women in marriage. Such unions were quite prevalent prior to the beginning of this century, although there are a number of more recent examples as well. The men involved were usually widowers whose previous wife or wives had been *khandani* women. Only very rarely did a man take a *ghair khandan* woman while his first wife was still alive. Polygamy was in any case extremely rare among these people and there is not a single case of two *khandani* women being married simultaneously to the same man.

There is little information in the record about the background of these women. Some were Hindus, often reputedly of low caste, perhaps servants or entertainers, converted to Islam for the purpose of the marriage. These are usually described in the biographical register as *naumuslim* ('new Muslim'). Some were slaves or *haram*, freed and married by their owners. Often Muslim women of other *qaum*s were properly given by their parents in marriage to men of this *khandan*, but since they were considered by his kin to be of insufficiently 'good' family they were not welcomed into the fold as a *khandani* bride would be. Their nuptials (*nikah*) sometimes took place without the knowledge of the man's family. Or even if the latter were aware in advance of the upcoming wedding they might withhold their approval by failing to attend the ceremony and neglecting to perform all of the subsidiary rituals (in which women are central players) that normally accompany a full Muslim wedding (*shadi*).

Ghair khandan women married in this way are usually referred to in the *khandan* register as *mankuhah*; in conversation they may be called *nikahi* or *nikahati bibi*. These terms can best be glossed 'legally married wife', and imply a woman married *only* in the eyes of the law. Their children were sometimes called, accordingly, *nikahi bacce*.[13] While in Islamic law performance of the simple nuptial ceremony is in fact all that is required to make a marriage valid, a wedding in whose arrangement and celebration the man's (or woman's) family has not participated is considered socially incomplete. The status of the woman is affected accordingly.[14]

[13] Wala mentions a term *dogle* or *dogli*, which he says is used by Nawwayats for those whose mother and father are of different *qaum*s. He remarks that he had always assumed this to be simply a derogatory term, until he met a Nawwayat in Gujarat 'who frankly introduced himself as "Zia-ud Din Dogle", explaining that while his father was a Qureshi, his mother was an Ahir' (1976:226). I have never heard this term used, nor does it appear in any of the *khandan*'s written materials that I have seen.

[14] This helps to explain some of the strong opposition within the *khandan* to the 'reformers'' proposal to curtail elaborate wedding ceremonial. Although the reforms did not actually go so far as to reduce the observances to the bare reading of the *nikah*, a family historian reports the use by some opponents of the epithets *nikahi bibi* for those women married in accordance with the new guidelines, and *nikahi bacce* for their children (Mazhar 1930-1:n.p.). Wala also notes this mode of denigrating the children of women married in the reformed

Khandan biographies shed further light on the way these unions, and the women involved in them, were regarded. A man who had a *mankuhah* almost invariably set up a separate household for her, away from the home of his other family members and certainly apart from that of his *khandani* wife, in the rare instances that he had one.[15] *Ghair khandan* wives were rarely welcome in the women's quarters of *khandan* households. For example, in separate biographies of two of his prominent nineteenth-century female ancestors, Mazhar notes how discriminating they were about the women they associated with. Of one he says that she would only socialise 'with women of her own *khandan* or other *khandans* with which [approved] marital alliances had already taken place' (Mazhar n.d.).

Elsewhere the same writer reports his grandmother's unwillingness to appear in front of the 'outsider' wife of her half-brother. The man is commended by his biographer for never allowing his elder half-sister's aloofness to diminish his regard for her. He continued to behave toward her with the greatest respect and affection, for he understood that it was wrong of his wife to even presume that she was worthy to enter his *khandani* kinswoman's presence (Mazhar 1930). This is only one example of the role women assumed in symbolically maintaining the boundaries of *khandan* exclusivity, even while their menfolk were actively engaged in breaching them in practice.

Family records do not suppress the existence of these irregular unions, and the offspring they produced are usually listed in the register as well. However, information about subsequent generations is often

manner in his discussion of this movement among the Nawwayats (1976:85).

[15] In the first part of the nineteenth century large 'joint' households do not appear to have been the rule. Adult, employed men usually set up independent households some time after marriage, sometimes accommodating a widowed female relative or orphaned minor siblings. However, their residences tended to be close by, first along the seashore in the neighbourhood of the Nawwab's palace, and later on a large plot of land further inland which took the form of a 'family compound'. When members of the family began to move to Hyderabad in the late nineteenth century, households became larger and more complex, as several related couples and single men would join together in rented accommodation and later in large houses purchased by the more well-to-do men of the family. Since India's independence, nuclear and small extended family households have again come to predominate, both in Madras and in Hyderabad (see Vatuk 1989).

meagre or nonexistent. Nowhere is it explicitly stated (either in the written record or orally) that the offspring of such unions are considered ineligible to marry the offspring of *khandani* women. In fact, when I raised this question in the abstract I was usually told that such marriages could and did take place. However, with only one exception that I have been able to find, the genealogical data show otherwise.

Typically mates were found for the children of *mankuhah* either outside the *khandan* altogether (sometimes among their mother's relatives) or, occasionally, with the so-called *nikahi* children of other *khandan* men. Their children also married outsiders and, as a consequence, contact with their descendants could easily be lost after one or two generations. By excluding (in practice, if not through the operation of a stated 'rule') the offspring of these 'irregular' unions from marriage within the *khandan*, the family was in fact able to ensure the purity of their 'blood' and 'pedigree', while at the same time providing an avenue whereby that minority of men who wished to establish unsanctioned unions with outsider women could do so.

After the turn of the century, by which time a branch of the *khandan* had settled in Hyderabad, a new kind of *ghair khandan* marriage began to take place. These unions were arranged by the couples' parents, and involved taking women in marriage from other 'respectable' (*sharif*) Muslim families. This trend is also noted by Wala, who notes that some people of the *qaum* have 'now' (that is, in the early twentieth century) begun to act contrary to the principle of *kufu ki pabandi* 'by establishing marriage relations (*nisbat*) with other *qaums*'. However, he also notes, such people are still 'the exceptions that prove the rule' (1976:59). These marriages were viewed quite differently from the unsanctioned, 'irregular' *ghair khandan* unions discussed above, but they were not free of controversy. In the beginning not all *khandan* members were prepared to lend their approval to this new trend, but in time such matches became commonplace. Those men who first looked outside the *khandan* for daughters-in-law were among the more successful in the family, economically and occupationally. Their sons were of the first generation in the *khandan* to have some western education. Their brides were from families of 'good' ancestry and similar economic and class standing. One of the early outsider brides, for example, was the daughter of a man belonging to the prominent north Indian *'ulama* family of Farangi Mahall, a branch of which had been in Madras since the late eighteenth century and had been closely associated there with the *khandan*'s ancestors (see Robinson 1987).

After some delay *khandan* girls also began to be given in marriage outside the close kindred. A marriage between a *khandan* girl and a Nawwayat man of a distantly-related family is often cited as one of the first examples of this kind. The marriage was not very successful, however, and is sometimes mentioned in support of arguments against giving daughters 'outside'. Some years later a young woman of the Madras branch of the *khandan* was married to a man who is identified in family records as a Labbai.[16] The groom's father was a prominent local political leader and close associate of the bride's father. The bride was better educated than most *khandan* young women in Madras at the time; she is now a medical doctor. This match is still considered to have been a rather odd one, especially because of the language difference between the husband and wife. Furthermore, the husband's skin colour is distinctly darker than the wife's. The two reported to me a (now) humorous incident early in their marriage when the police stopped them as they walked on the Madras beach, suspecting that the man was trying to abduct unwillingly 'a girl of good family'.

Like the offspring of earlier *ghair khandan* unions, the offspring of these arranged *ghair khandan* marriages rarely marry a *najib-ut tarfain* descendant of the *khandan* ancestor. They are not especially likely to marry even within the Nawwayat *qaum* (unless, of course, their 'outsider' parent was also a Nawwayat). Either they marry a close relative of their *ghair khandan* parent or a 'suitable' (*munasib*) match is found elsewhere within the Muslim community. The reasons for this

[16] He, however, identified himself in an interview as a Rowthar. This inconsistency may be an indication of a vagueness on the part of Nawwayats in labelling other Muslims with whom they are in casual, but not close and regular contact. Note that the compiler of the biographical register was a woman who had led a life of strict seclusion in Hyderabad, where in any case neither Labbais nor Rowthars are found in significant numbers. It may also be that in actual usage 'Labbai' and 'Rowthar' as semantic categories are not absolutely mutually exclusive, but overlap to some degree.

marriage pattern are more complicated and not as clearly related as
before to traditional *qaum* and *khandan* status considerations. What
seems to be happening is that there is increasing emphasis placed upon
the class and economic position of the families involved in a marriage
alliance. In addition, the individual characteristics and qualifications of
the bride and groom (especially in terms of education and employment)
are taking priority in the matchmaking process. No longer is it the case
that *khandan* families will refuse to consider a match with a person of
partial or full *ghair khandan* ancestry, but the chances that such an
opportunity will present itself are relatively small, given the small size
of the *khandan* and the very large field of choice that now presents
itself to those of their class who are seeking to make a match.
Increasingly, for people of this *khandan* as for other Muslims, the key
criteria for 'equality in marriage' have become socio-economic in
nature, rather than being attached primarily to concepts of blood purity
and respectability of pedigree. This does not mean that the latter are no
longer important. *Shajre* are still routinely examined by prospective in-
laws when the family with whom a match is being considered is not
known. Even published material in books by research scholars has been
known to be referred to in such situations, placing a heavy
responsibility upon scholars like myself to be discreet while at the same
time respecting the historical record.

Dowry considerations loom large today as well. In this *khandan* it
has never been the custom to give a dowry. Today, when bringing in a
ghair khandan bride, it is still almost unheard-of for a *khandan* family
to ask for such a payment. Some say that outsiders therefore find the
young men of this *khandan* especially attractive, if they have obtained
the kind of modern qualifications that make them suitable for girls from
western-educated, upwardly mobile Muslim families. On the other
hand, the dowry system creates special difficulties for *khandan* parents
who wish to find a *ghair khandan* husband for their daughter, since the
making of substantial 'demands' has become routine among Muslims
in India and Pakistan. This may be one reason why some *khandan*
families continue to resist the trend toward abandonment of their
former endogamous practices (see also Vatuk 1993).

The figures show that before 1920 first marriages arranged outside of the *khandan* were extremely rare. By the decade of the 1940s, however, over one-third of all first marriages (of women as well as of men of the *khandan*) were with *ghair khandan* spouses. And in the 1970s half of the marriages reported in the *khandan* register involved a *ghair khandan* spouse (see Vatuk 1994:155). This finding is, however, less dramatic than it seems, because the great majority of those marrying 'out' (especially of women marrying 'out') are themselves the offspring or grandchildren of 'mixed' couples. Furthermore, a high proportion of out-marriages have taken place in Pakistan, where a large branch of the *khandan* has been settled since the late 1940s. There is still a large 'core' group of 'full' *khandan* members in Madras and Hyderabad who, until recently, clearly preferred leaving their daughters and many of their sons unmarried rather than marry them to outsiders. This is reflected today in high proportions of the never-married in the 30-65 age group (Vatuk 1989, 1994). But by the 1990s even this core group's reluctance to give women outside of the *khandan* has eroded significantly. If this trend continues, in another generation the *khandan's* distinctive identity as an exclusive and self-sufficient marriage circle may almost disappear.

Conclusion

I began this discussion by proposing to discover how one particular group of South Asian Muslims think about social difference, to what extent their ideas are expressed in an idiom of rank and inequality, and how these ideas are translated into practice as they interact with other Muslims. I have shown that these people conceptualise their society as made up of many distinct, named social groups, or *qaums*. They regard each *qaum* as a group of people who marry largely among themselves and consequently transmit their shared blood, with its particular moral and physical qualities, from one generation to another. They identify themselves with the geographically widely dispersed, but locally very sparsely represented, Nawwayat *qaum*. They take pride in the knowledge that Nawwayats have historically occupied positions of power and social prestige in the part of south India where they and their ancestors have lived, because of their association with Muslim rulers, their role as religious authorities, and their literary and scholarly accomplishments. There is historical evidence that in the past the Nawwayats considered themselves, and were considered by others, to constitute an exclusive social elite within the very diverse Muslim population of the region. Their claims to high rank were based not only upon the prominent positions many of them occupied in the higher strata of Deccani Muslim court society, but also upon their tradition of pure Arab ancestry. Thus they could draw upon both of the definitions of elite status that Bayly refers to as prevailing among south Indian Muslims in this period (1989:101).

At the present time, however, few of the Nawwayats with whom I am acquainted would formulate a statement about the place of their *qaum* relative to the generality of Indian Muslims in precisely this way. In discussions of such matters, I found that they typically reject altogether the notion of a hierarchical ordering of social groups within Muslim society, citing the well-known Islamic principle that all believers are equal before God, and should be so regarded and treated by one another. They see themselves as ever striving to be 'good' Muslims; well-versed in the Muslim scriptural tradition as most of them are, social egalitarianism is one of the Islamic values that they most sincerely espouse. They tend also, again fairly self-consciously as 'modern', educated citizens of a democratic Indian state, to share a liberal social conscience that further contributes to their reluctance to make explicit claims of superiority over others, especially claims based on birth or other ascriptive criteria. Furthermore, the matter of claiming 'foreign' origins as a mark of distinction is also today an extremely touchy one for Muslims generally, as members of a threatened minority community whose 'loyalty' to India is constantly being called into question by political demagogues of the Hindu right. All in all, the topic of social inequality among Muslims is one that few seem to feel comfortable discussing at any length, beyond denials that they are disposed to think in such terms at all.

I became particularly aware of the sensitivity of this whole issue from reactions to a passage in an earlier paper, wherein I referred to the

Nawwayats' Arab origins and observed that, within the wider context of South Asian Muslim systems of social ranking, their ancestry gives them 'a particularly effective claim for superiority within the category of "foreigners" to Indian soil' (1990:120). A highly-educated woman of this *khandan*, whose reactions to the paper I had solicited, pointed out that her family is indeed proud of their Arab descent, but only because it signifies their closeness to the birthplace of Islam, not because it means that they are of 'foreign' origin. Furthermore, saying that they are proud of their ancestry is not at all the same as saying that they feel superior to other Muslims because of it.

There is clearly considerable ambivalence underlying the *khandan*'s discourse on these matters. There is also considerable ambivalence in the Islamic scriptural tradition itself. I have pointed out that the stereotyped notion that Islam provides believers with a completely egalitarian model of the social order is oversimplistic. True enough, all Muslims are brothers before God, yet to go no further than this fails to take account of the way that inequality among men (and women) is in fact institutionalised in the *shari'at* itself. This is, of course, largely manifested in relation to marriage, rather than in other domains of social and religious life. And in this *khandan* too, it was largely in the context of marriage alliance that we have seen how notions of blood purity and pedigree translated into a consciousness of elite social position and into behaviour that reflected a desire to maintain social exclusivity. It may be worth pointing out, however, that the meaning of the concept of *kufu* is itself open to ambiguity. It can be rendered *either* as 'equality' *or* 'similarity', and when taken in the latter sense is not necessarily inconsistent with a denial of social hierarchy.

I have also tried to show here how important it is to examine this issue within an historical context, rather than focusing only on the ideas expressed by informants at a single, contemporary point in time. As this example shows, ideas and behaviours relating to group identity and difference have changed considerably over the past two centuries, in response to external social and political conditions and to the various circumstances in which the people of this *khandan* have found themselves. Though the themes of 'pedigree' and 'suitable' matches between equals have survived in this family for at least two hundred years, the extent to which these have been acted upon has declined. Particularly in the modern period, as the young people of the *khandan* have come to resemble other educated middle-class young men and women, and as their families have become oriented toward seeing that their children achieve success within the modern Indian secular context, the value of investing everything in one's pride of illustrious ancestry has begun to be questioned. This is reflected in an increasing tendency to be willing to marry outside of the family and to be fully accepting of those who do so, and of their offspring, in a way that was not the case even a century ago.

Clearly these people are today more comfortable with a discourse of *difference* than they are with one of *inequality*. Viewing their diverse society from this perspective, each *qaum* can be seen to have its own history, its own qualities, and its own peculiarities, just as does every *khandan* within the *qaum*, as its special characteristics, passed down from one generation to the next, become ever more concentrated and refined. Members of this family have little difficulty identifying the special qualities that they share—as Nawwayats and as people of this particular *khandan*. They are explicit also about the fact that most of these qualities are ones that they and other Muslims value highly and that are therefore worth exerting efforts to preserve. In the opinion of some, such efforts ought to include continuation of the marriage patterns that have kept them separate from others for so long. However, this recognition of difference does not immediately translate into a readiness to place themselves, as Nawwayats, or as members of this particular family, in a hierarchical rank order relative to other Muslims in south India or in the world at large.

References

Ahmad, I. 1972. 'The Ashraf-Ajlaf dichotomy in Muslim social structure in India.' *Indian Economic and Social History Review* 12:48-61.

———. 1973a. 'Endogamy and status mobility among the Siddiqui Sheikhs of Allahabad, Uttar Pradesh.' In I. Ahmad (ed.), *Caste and social stratification among the Muslims*. New Delhi: Manohar.

———, (ed.) 1973b. *Caste and social stratification among the Muslims*. New Delhi: Manohar.

———. 1973c. 'Introduction'. In *Caste and social stratification among the Muslims*. New Delhi: Manohar.

Ahmad, S. 1971. 'Social stratification in a Punjabi village' *Contributions to Indian Sociology* (n.s.) 4:105-25.

Ahmad-ul Madini. 1871. *Tarikh-i Ahmadi* [Persian]. Unpublished manuscript.

Alavi, H. 1972. 'Kinship in West Punjabi villages.' *Contributions to Indian Sociology* (n.s.) 6:1-27.

Ali, A. 1976. *Mahommedan law*, vol.2 (7th ed.). Lahore.

Ansari, G. 1959. *Muslim caste in Uttar Pradesh: a study in culture contact*. Lucknow: The Ethnographic and Folk Culture Society.

Barth, F. 1960. 'The system of social stratification in Swat, North Pakistan.' In E.R. Leach (ed.), *Aspects of caste in India, Ceylon, and North-West Pakistan*. Cambridge: Cambridge University Press.

Bayly, S. 1989. *Saints, goddesses and kings: Muslims and Christians in south Indian society, 1700-1900*. Cambridge: Cambridge University Press.

Benson, J.E. 1983. 'Politics and Muslim ethnicity in south India.' *Journal of Anthropological Research* 39:42-59.

Bhattacharya, R.S. 1973. 'The concept and ideology of caste among the Muslims of rural West Bengal.' In I. Ahmad (ed.), *Caste and social stratification among the Muslims*. New Delhi: Manohar.

Bouchon, G. 1986. 'Quelques aspects de l'Islamisation des régions maritimes de l'Inde à l'époque médiévale (XIIe-XVIe s.)'. *Purusartha* 9: 29-36.

Burhan Ibn Hassan. 1934. *Tuzuk-i Walajahi: sources of the history of the Nawwabs of the Carnatic*, Part 1 (edited and translated by S.M.H. Nainar). (Madras University Islamic Series no.1.) Madras: Madras University.

———. 1939. *Tuzuk-i Walajahi: sources of the history of the Nawwabs of the Carnatic*, Part 2 (edited and translated by S. M. H. Nainar). (Madras University Islamic Series no.4.) Madras: Madras University.

Cox, A.F. 1881. *A manual of the North Arcot District in the Presidency of Madras*. Madras: Government Press.

Dale, S.F. 1980. *Islamic society on the South Asian frontier: the Mappilas of Malabar*. New York: Oxford University Press.

Das, V. 1984. 'For a folk-theology and theological anthropology of Islam.' *Contributions to Indian Sociology* (n.s.) 18:293-300.

D'Souza, V.S. 1955. *The Navayats of Kanara*. Dharwar: Kannada Research Institute.

Dumont, L. 1970. *Homo hierarchicus*. Chicago: University of Chicago Press.

DuPuis, J. 1960. *Madras et le nord du Coromandel.* Paris: Librairie d'Amerique et d'Orient Adrien-Maisonneuve.

Eaton, R. 1978. *Sufis of Bijapur, 1300-1700.* Princeton: Princeton University Press.

Edwardes, S.M. 1909. *The Gazetteer of Bombay City and Island,* vol.1. Bombay: Times Press.

Eickelman, D.F. 1982. 'The study of Islam in local contexts.' *Contributions to Asian Studies* 17:1-16.

Francis, W. 1902. *Census of India, 1901.* vol. XV-A Madras, Part 2 (Imperial Tables). Madras: Government Press.

Gaborieau, M. 1977. *Minorités musulmanes dans le royaume Hindou du Nepal.* Nanterre: Laboratoire d'Ethnologie.

Geertz, H. 1979. 'The meaning of family ties.' In C. Geertz, H. Geertz and L. Rosen, *Meaning and order in Moroccan society.* Cambridge: Cambridge University Press.

Ghouse, Z. 1973. 'Baquir Agah's contribution to Arabic, Persian, and Urdu literature.' Unpublished M.Litt. dissertation, Madras University.

Goodfriend, D. 1983.'Changing concepts of caste and status among Old Delhi Muslims.' In I. Ahmad (ed.), *Modernization and social change among Muslims in India,.* New Delhi: Manohar.

Hashmi, Nasiruddin. 1963. *Maulvi 'Abdul Qadar* [Urdu]. Hyderabad: Aijaz Machine Press.

Iqbal, Muhammad Afzaluddin. 1973. *Tazkirah-i Sa'id* [Urdu]. Hyderabad: Sayeedia Library and Research Institute.

Kokan, Muhammad Yusuf. 1963. *Khanwadah-i Qazi Badar-ud Daulah* [Urdu]. Madras: Dar-ul Tasnif.

———. 1974. *Arabic and Persian in Carnatic 1710-1960.* Madras: Ameera and Co.

Lelyveld, D. 1978. *Aligarh's first generation: Muslim solidarity in British India.* Princeton: Princeton University Press.

Levy, R. 1965 (1957). *The social structure of Islam.* Cambridge: Cambridge University Press.

Lindholm, C. 1986. 'Caste in India and the problem of deviant systems: a critique of recent theory.' *Contributions to Indian Sociology* (n.s.) 20:61-96.

Madras Political Consultations, 1856-1857. India Office Library and Records.

Majid, Amat-ul. 1984. 'Biographical register of the *khandan* of Ghulam Mahmud'. Unpublished manuscript.

Mazhar, Muhammad. (n.d). 'Aisha Bibi Mahall-i Sharf-ul Mulk Awwal' [Urdu]. *Mushir-un Niswan* (unpublished manuscript serial).

———.1930. 'Sarguzasht-i Khandan-i Mufti Sahab: 'Abul Mukaram Haji Hakim Isma'il Marhum' [Urdu]. *Bazm-i-Adab* (unpublished manuscript serial).

———. 1930-31. 'Tazkirah-i Tahrik-i Islah-i Rasum' [Urdu]. *Bazm-i Adab* (unpublished manuscript serial).

———. 1949. 'Maulana Muhammad Murtuza ki Halat' [Urdu]. Special Issue, *Ruh-i Taraqqi* 9.

McPherson, K. 1969. 'The social background and politics of the Muslims of Tamilnad 1901-1937.' *Indian Economic and Social History Review* 6:381-402.

———. 1975. 'The Muslims of Madras and Calcutta: agitational politics in the early 1920s.' *South Asia* 5:32-47

Metcalf, B. 1991. *Perfecting women: Maulana Ashraf 'Ali Thanawi's Bihishti Zewar.* Berkeley: University of California Press.

Mines, M. 1972a. *Muslim merchants: the economic behaviour of an Indian Muslim community.* New Delhi: Shri Ram Centre for Industrial Relations and Human Resources.

———. 1972b. 'Muslim social stratification in India: the basis for variation.' *Southwestern Journal of Anthropology* 28:333-49.

———. 1973. 'Social stratification among Muslims in Tamilnadu, south India.' In I. Ahmad (ed.), *Caste and social stratification among the Muslims.* New Delhi: Manohar.

———. 1975. 'Islamization and Muslim identity in south India.' *Man* (n.s.) 10:404-19.

More, J.B. 1991. 'The Marakkayar Muslims of Karikal, south India.' *Journal of Islamic Studies* 2:25-44.

———. 1993. 'Tamil Muslims and Non-Brahmin atheists, 1925-1940.' *Contributions to Indian Sociology* (n.s.) 27:83-104.

Mudiraj, K. K. 1964. *Life of Nawab Deen Yar Jung Bahadur.* Hyderabad: the author.

Mujeeb, M. 1985 (1967). *The Indian Muslims.* New Delhi: Munshilal Manoharlal.

Murtuza, M. 1942. 'Suwahil-i Hindustan par Musulmanon ka Tuwattan.' [Urdu]. *Mujallad-i Talesanin* 6:18-52.

Nazir, Ghulam 'Abdu'l Qadir. 1950. *Bahar-i 'Azam Jahi: sources of the history of the Nawwabs of the Carnatic,* Part 5 (edited and translated by S.M.H. Nainar). (Madras University Islamic Series, no. 11.) Madras: University of Madras.

Pais, A.A. 1919. 'The Navayats: an account of their history and their customs.' *Quarterly Journal of the Mythic Society* 10:41-58.

Platts, J.T. 1977 (1884). *A Dictionary of Urdu, classical Hindi and English.* New Delhi: Oriental Books Reprint Corporation.

Prindle, C. 1988. 'Occupation and orthopraxy in Bengali Muslim rank.' In K.P. Ewing (ed.), *Shari'at and ambiguity in South Asian Islam.* Berkeley: University of California Press.

Ramaswami, N.S. 1984. *Political history of Carnatic under the Nawabs.* New Delhi: Abhinav Publications.

Robinson, F. 1983. 'Islam and Muslim society in South Asia.' *Contributions to Indian Sociology* (n.s.) 17:185-203.

———. 1986. 'Islam and Muslim Society in South Asia: a reply to Das and Minault.' *Contributions to Indian Sociology* (n.s.) 20:97-104.

———. 1987. 'Problems in the history of the Farangi Mahall family of learned and holy men.' In N.J. Allen *et al.,* (eds.), *Oxford University Papers on India.* vol. 1, part 2. Delhi: Oxford University Press.

Spectorsky, S.A. 1993. *Chapters on marriage and divorce: responses of Ibn Hanbal and Ibn Rahwayh.* Austin: University of Texas Press.

Stuart, H. A. 1893. *Census of India, 1891,* vol. XIII (*Madras*): *the report on the Census.* Madras: Government Press.

Thanawi, Muhammad Ashraf 'Ali. 1962 (1906). *Bihishti Zewar* [Urdu]. Delhi: New Taj Office.

——. 1973. *Bahishti Zewar (Requisites of Islam)* (translated by Rahm Ali Al-Hasmi, and edited by Syed Ashtarul Islam). Delhi: Dini Book Depot.

Vatuk, S. 1989. 'Household form and formation: variability and social change among South Indian Muslims.' In J.N. Gray and D.J. Mearns (eds.), *Society from the inside out: anthropological perspectives on the South Asian household.* New Delhi: Sage Publications.

——. 1990. 'The cultural construction of shared identity: a south Indian Muslim family history.' In P. Werbner (ed.), *Person, myth and society in South Asian Islam. Social Analysis* 28:114-31.

——. 1993. 'Women, property, and marriage transactions among Indian Muslims.' Unpublished paper presented to the Annual Meeting of the Association for Asian Studies, Los Angeles, California.

——. 1994. 'Schooling for what? The cultural and social context of women's education in a south Indian Muslim family.' In C.C. Mukhopadhyaya and S. Seymour (eds.), *Women, education, and family structure in India.* Boulder: Westview Press.

Wala, Aziz Jang. 1976 (1904). *Tarikh-un Nawwayat* [Urdu] (2nd rev. ed.). Hyderabad: Wala Akaidami.

Wasif, Muhammad Mahdi. 1982 (1854-5). *Hadiqat-ul Maram: 'Ulama-i Madras* [Urdu] (translated by S. Mirza). Karachi: Anjuman-i Taraqqi-i Urdu.

Werbner, P. 1989. 'The ranking of brotherhoods: the dialectics of Muslim caste among overseas Pakistanis.' *Contributions to Indian Sociology* (n.s.) 23:286-315.

Ziadeh, F. J. 1957. 'Equality (*Kafa'ah*) in the Muslim law of marriage.' *American Journal of Comparative Law* 6:503-17.

Chapter 10

RECASTING TAMIL SOCIETY: THE POLITICS OF CASTE AND RACE IN CONTEMPORARY SOUTHERN INDIA[1]

Nicholas B. Dirks

Caste and anthropology

If under colonialism caste became the foundational basis of Indian society, it became so in part as a form of civil society which could be used both to explain how Indian civilisation survived its history of despotisms and political failures and to justify British colonial rule. When caste became the central trope for India, it was understood as a unitary social form that could be recognised as fundamentally religious rather than political. However, caste was read not as autonomous from but opposed to the 'state'; religiosity has always been seen in the Indian case as a threat to politics, in the pre-modern period to the potential power of kingship, and in the modern to the eventual development of representative political institutions (Dirks 1992). When in 1909—just after the swadeshi movement had introduced the possibility of mass agitational politics as well as the spectre of communal violence into Bengal—H.H. Risley contemplated the political implications of the caste system, he was clear that caste opposed nationality and would hinder the growth of nationalist politics.

Now that colonial history has metamorphosed into post-colonial politics, caste has become central to new forms of contradiction, reworking colonial legacies with new difficulties and dangers. Caste continues to be seen as one of the major impediments to modernity, even as it is thought by many to survive as the sedimented marker of traditional privilege and oppression. The debate over the report of the Mandal Commission and its intended uses by V.P. Singh highlighted

[1] I am grateful to Val Daniel, David Ludden and Sumathi Ramaswamy for their suggestions and encouragement while drafting this paper in Madras during the summer of 1993; I would also like to acknowledge the helpful feedback I received from the participants of the 'Caste Today' workshop, as well as more directly the comments of Chris Fuller.

some of the contradictions in the contemporary politics of caste, creating conditions that made it possible—and frighteningly compelling —for BJP party ideologues to assert that a newly defined notion of Hinduism might be less divisive than caste as a focus for national politics. Caste has now been turned into a symbol of traditional decadence, to be replaced by other forms of tradition—chief among which seem now to be the equation of 'Hindu-ness' with Indian nationality and the celebration of Hinduism's extraordinary history of tolerance and incorporation. These new forms will counter the mischievous use of caste by Congress and other pseudo-secularists who have, so the charge goes, said one thing and done another.

If contemporary political discourse seems thus to echo many of the key features of colonial sociology and history, it is important to recognise that any attempt today simply to wish caste away inevitably finds itself in ideological alliance with forces of communalism that appear to make the myriad problems of the politicisation of caste a relatively minor evil. Anthropology, and the allied study of the history of colonial sociology and social transformation, is once again in a position where it must address the politics of the study of caste, even as it attempts sagely to evaluate the politics of caste itself.

In this chapter, I will engage with this double articulation of the politics of caste through a focus on southern India, tracing the history of Dravidianist discourses about caste and race, and also evaluating the anthropological repercussions of the anti-Brahman movement in Tamilnadu, which I shall call the communalisation and racialisation of caste. In framing a paper about Tamil cultural politics by a discussion of a political crisis that has not yet emerged in any direct form in Madras, I am specifically attempting to link questions and perspectives that are usually kept rigidly apart; while the politics of Madras may indeed be very different from the rest of India, I argue here that even extreme difference has been formulated in relation to all-India processes and developments. Before turning to the southern case, however, it might be useful to recall the anthropological debate between Risley and Ghurye, in the related context of the rise of an anti-Brahman movement in Maharashtra in the early decades of the twentieth century. This debate not only brings into focus some of the anthropological issues that attend any analytical debate about the fundamental nature of caste, it also highlights the complex set of relations between European ideas of race, anthropological analyses of caste and the politics of social mobilisation in modern India.

Risley[2] had justified the emphasis he put on anthropometry as central to the ethnographic survey of India on the grounds that:

anthropometry yields peculiarly good results in India by reason of the caste system which prevails among Hindus, and of the divisions, often closely resembling castes, which are recognised by Muhammadans. Marriage takes place only within a limited circle; the disturbing element of crossing is to a great extent excluded; and the differences of physical type, which measurement is intended to establish, are more marked and more persistent than anywhere else in the world.

However, Risley went even further, seeking to demonstrate the racial basis of caste endogamy throughout the Indian social system, predicating his entire theory of caste on his belief that the mutual aversion of Aryans and non-Aryans led to prohibitions concerning free inter-marriage. Caste, he wrote, was animated by 'the antipathy of the higher race for the lower, of the fair-skinned Aryan for the black Dravidian'. Characteristically, he saw this view confirmed by the elitist character of the demands for representative political institutions made by the Aryan leaders of the nationalist movement, in total disregard of the needs and concerns of the lower, non-Aryan castes.

Perhaps the first explicit treatment of the anthropological politics of British colonial sociology in India can be found in the work of the eminent sociologist G.S. Ghurye. In his *Caste and Race in India*, first published in 1932, Ghurye took up Risley's theory of race, as well as his use of anthropometric methods and data. Ghurye was very critical of both the data and their uses, and ultimately determined that only in the Punjab and parts of the United Provinces was there a possible correlation between race and caste, in which Brahmans betrayed physiognomic indications of their hereditary connection to the 'Aryan'

[2] Quoted by the Secretary to the Governor of India: Government Order No.647, Madras Public Department, 26 June 1901.

invaders of the subcontinent. Everywhere else, and for all other groups, general miscegenation had eroded any racial distinctiveness in caste. Ghurye emphasised the mixing of castes particularly in Maharashtra and Madras, where he also felt that caste, in the form of anti-Brahman movements, had become dangerously (and with a racial justification erroneously) politicised.

Ghurye was also directly critical of Risley's role in politicising caste, especially in relation to the census. Although Risley was not the first to use the decennial census for collecting and presenting material about caste, Ghurye noted that 'This procedure reached its culmination in the Census of 1901 under the guidance of Sir Herbert Risley of ethnographic fame' (1950:157). Risley had assumed that an intelligible picture of social groupings in India could be gained only by using a classification of 'social precedence as recognised by the native public opinion'. Ghurye complained that Risley adopted this procedure despite 'his own clear admission that even in this caste-ridden society a person, when questioned about his caste, may offer a bewildering variety of replies', according to whether he chooses to emphasise his sect, sub-caste, exogamous section, titular designation, occupation or region. Ghurye lamented the growth of caste *sabhas* (associations) organised expressly around the attempt to press forward claims of higher status in the census. He quoted with approval the remarks of a Mr. Middleton, one of the two Census Superintendents in 1921, to the effect that the so-called occupational castes, 'have been largely manufactured and almost entirely preserved as separate castes by the British Government', and that 'Government's passion for labels and pigeon-holes has led to a crystallisation of the caste system, which, except amongst the aristocratic castes, was really very fluid under indigenous rule' (ibid.:160).

Ghurye also felt that various decisions by government had encouraged the anti-Brahman movement, and he criticised in particular the use of quotas to restrict government employment for Brahmans in Maharashtra and Madras. Ghurye saw this as part of a general strategy on the part of the British to use caste for the purposes of 'divide and rule'. He quoted as evidence the 1865 statement of James Kerr, Princi-

pal of the Hindu College at Calcutta, that 'It may be doubted if the
existence of caste is on the whole unfavourable to the permanence of
our rule. It may even be considered favourable to it, provided we act
with prudence and forbearance. Its spirit is opposed to national union'
(ibid.:164). Ghurye's critique of the role of the British in dividing and
ruling India sustained his critique of non-Brahman politics in Maharashtra and Madras, where he argued against reservations and communal awards. Concerned about national unity, he asserted that 'Where it
is a question of engendering a feeling of unity the people must be made
to cooperate irrespective of caste' (ibid.:290). Ghurye further wrote that
the anti-Brahman agitation had not only divided Indians at a time of
pressing nationalist concern, but also produced few concrete results. In
any case, he suggested, 'Whatever liberalising of the Brahmin attitude
in this respect has taken place during the last forty years is mainly due
to education and social reform campaign and not to the very recent
reserved or communal representation' (ibid.:290). Only in the case of
untouchables, owing to the cruel and exploitative treatment they had
received from caste Hindus, did Ghurye accept the need for reservation
and positive discrimination, although he disapproved of Ambedkar's
attempt to politicise caste around an untouchable movement. So even
though Ghurye lamented the decline of the 'priesthood', and was
particularly worried about the rise of prejudice against Brahmans, he
clearly was critical of caste, particularly of the politicisation of caste
under British rule. But this was a political critique, for Ghurye was
clear that the British were largely responsible for caste's alleged
antipathy to nationalist ideals.

In a subsequent edition of his book (1950), Ghurye wryly noted the
disapproval and neglect of his political analysis within the official
circles of British anthropology. He observed that in the review of the
first edition of his book in *Man*, the reviewer concluded by writing:
'The last two chapters have rather a political or semi-political, trend,
and so need not be discussed here' (ibid.:337). Ghurye went on to note
that 'Even the highly appreciative reviewer of the book concluded his
script in the *Literary Supplement* of the *Times* London (November
1932) prefacing his final laudatory remark with "Politics apart"'

(ibid.:338). Only after India's independence in 1947, Ghurye discovered, did *Man* accept an article dealing with the effects on Indian social
systems of recent political change (the article was by Kathleen Gough).

Although Ghurye accepted many more colonial assumptions in his
anthropology than he rejected, his critique of Risley and the census
anticipates recent critical concern about the role of colonial governance
in simultaneously changing and reifying caste in India in ways that
have had serious political repercussions. However, it is not without
significance that Ghurye's concerns had a politics of their own, deeply
worried as he was about the rise of caste politics in Maharashtra around
the anti-Brahmanism of the 1920s and 1930s. As an active exponent of
a view of India that stressed inter-caste harmony and gave no quarter to
arguments about essential biological difference, Ghurye was clearly
situated in a sociology of knowledge of his own, however much his
work demonstrates more than his own particular caste positioning, and,
more generally, the possibility of nationalist resistance within
professional discourse. But writing this paper in 1994, I cannot help but
think of Ghurye in connection with the ways in which professional
discourses around caste have been caught up in the post-colonial
politics of caste, both in relation to the agitation over Mandal in 1989
and, especially in southern India, to the perception that Brahman
identity entails a set of particular interests that seek to depoliticise the
study of caste for reasons linked to its own concern with the maintenance of caste privilege. I will now shift to a consideration of anthropological politics in Madras, raising questions about the contemporary
state of caste politics, and what they have done to the field of caste
relations in everyday life, as well as in political and academic
discourses.

Caste in the Tamil country

Anthropologists have long commented on the peculiarity of the 'caste
system' in the south of India, where the absence of representative
Kshatriya and Vaishya castes makes for a two- (or three-) tiered
system, with Brahmans, Shudras and Adi-Dravidas. Deference to the
salience of the *varna* template for caste structure has had an ironic

effect, since the Dravidianist claim that non-Brahmans constitute a relatively homogeneous caste group has been accordingly bolstered by reference to 'Brahmanic' models. Partly because of this and partly because of the lack until recently of serious work in historical anthropology, anthropologists have generally paid little attention to the rise of the anti-Brahman movement in relation to the fundamental structures of caste society. Throughout the south, the growing ethnicisation of caste—as well as the steady urbanisation and 'modernisation' of Tamil society—has generally led to a widening of marriage circles and a reduced emphasis on a variety of intermediate endogamous structures (such as residential streets, village identities, temple affiliations), even though the units of exogamy have been increasingly redefined in specifically kinship—or even biological—terms (for example, as lineages). These changes have both shaped and been shaped by the reorganisation of land systems, the rise of cities, the demise of old kingdoms, the expansion of colonially controlled forms of commercialisation and market economy, the establishment of British colonial administration and the heavy recruitment of Brahmans into that administration; the changes have also worked to naturalise the assertions of the anti-Brahman movement. In part, therefore, much social scientific writing about southern India has taken for granted the putatively wide gulf between Brahmans and non-Brahmans, and has made very little reference to the consolidation of local power and dominance among 'non-Brahmans' and between non-Brahmans and Adi-Dravidas.

In Anil Seal's study of the emergence of nationalist activity in India, he observed that: 'In much of south India the gulfs between Brahmins and the rest of the community were so wide, and the natural antipathies so bitter, that society here was divided at least as effectively by caste as elsewhere it was divided by religion' (1968:112). Most subsequent studies of the rise of the anti-Brahman movement in southern India have similarly shared this view, averring that the traditional divide between Brahmans and non-Brahmans has been at least partly responsible for the political and cultural antipathy between these 'communities'.

Eugene Irschick has written that: 'Above and beyond all these points of difference between south India and north India was a peculiarly social one: the extraordinarily high position of the Brahmans in the social hierarchy, particularly in the Tamil and Malayalam areas' (1969:5). Lloyd and Susanne Rudolph have echoed these conclusions:

Brahmans in the south have tended to be more separated from the rest of the population than Brahmans in the north...The wide ritual gulf between the tiny Madras Brahman elite and other castes contributed to and was compounded by their domination of modern political, administrative, and professional life. (1967:76-7)

Robert Hardgrave put it more directly:

The Brahmin of South India often socially and psychologically aloof, has retained an exclusiveness of caste orthodoxy. Often combining economic power derived from land ownership with religious authority, the Brahmin further separated himself from the lower castes and increased his control over them.... The position of the Brahmin engendered suspicion, if not hatred, in the mind of the non-Brahmin. (1965:11)

These statements all reflect what Seal's statement expresses most directly: the kind of communalist discourse and politics that in much of the rest of India has been seen to surround the social identities of 'Hindu' and 'Muslim' has been inscribed in south India in the identities of Brahman and non-Brahman. Although Seal's pronouncements about nationalism have long been criticised and to a large extent discounted, many scholars of nationalist history (such as Partha Chatterjee or Ranajit Guha) either continue to accept his view of the south, or ignore the region altogether. This is so despite the fact that recent scholarship has made it abundantly clear that the foundations for these general assumptions about south India emerge not out of primordial tradition but rather from nineteenth-century sources. Irschick was one of the first to demonstrate how the general conviction underlying much Dravidian radicalism—that the subjection of non-Brahman Dravidian peoples and cultures was based on the Aryan conquest of the Dravidian south—was in large part an invention of evangelical Christian missionaries, resentful of the role of Brahmans in frustrating their efforts to proselytise. Nevertheless, current scholarship—from nationalist history to general anthropology—continues to accept that Brahmans and non-Brahmans occupied fundamentally different cultural spheres, and that the roots of the anti-Brahman movement can be found in the social facts of south Indian adherence, in the absence of extensive Islamic influence, to primordial forms of Hindu hierarchy and social structure.

The conviction of primordiality, the sense that there are some fundamental institutions and beliefs that are simultaneously (as it were) pre-modern and transcendent of historical process and origins, is perhaps one of the most basic signs of modernity. Recent scholarship has frequently undertaken the task of historical unmasking, arguing that what was once thought to be primordial not only has a specific history but one rooted in relatively recent historical transformations. But these scholarly interventions rarely work to reshape political and phenomenological commitments, even as it is now clear that one form of unmasking can be seen in other contexts as another form of masking.[3] What I seek to understand in this chapter—partly by tracing historical genealogies and partly by excavating contemporary cultural politics and discursive formations—is how caste has been strengthened and re-shaped in southern India. In particular, caste now refers to macro categories of social classification—especially around the distinction between Brahmans and non-Brahmans—in ways that can be explained by the historical process and can also be seen to shape the very character of politics and history. But to attend to the historicity of caste, and to assert (as I do) that caste identities and antipathies have been dramatically transformed by colonial rule and modern history, makes it likely that, in some of the contexts in which we write, such assertions will be understood as apologies for privilege.

Colonialism and Tamil cultural discourses

The emergence of Tamil identity as non-Aryan and non-Brahman, like so many other 'natural' assumptions in Indian society, owed a great deal to the forces of colonial history. The categories of 'Brahman' and

[3] See Dirks (1995) for my argument about the lack of epistemological reflexivity in some of the work associated with the 'invention of tradition'.

'non-Brahman' were first constituted as essential categories—based on the philological and racial categories of Aryan and Dravidian—by the Scottish missionary, Robert Caldwell, in the mid-nineteenth century. Caldwell's first major publication was an ethnographic work on the Shanar toddy-tapper caste living in the southern portion of the Tamil country; this caste became one of the principal objects of Caldwell's proselytising efforts. His book, *The Tinnevelly Shanars* (1849), provoked a largely negative reaction from educated members of the Shanar caste, who were particularly upset by Caldwell's assertion that the Shanars were non-Aryan. The book was actually withdrawn from publication after a series of riots against it in 1869. But Caldwell did not abandon his central thesis, instead generalising it to apply to all Tamil non-Brahmans. In his *A comparative grammar of the Dravidian or South-Indian family of languages*, first published in 1856, Caldwell wrote that the Dravidians had occupied the southern portion of the Indian subcontinent sometime before the Aryan invasion. It was only well after the invasion that they were subdued by the Aryans, 'not as conquerors, but as colonists and instructors'. Caldwell argued that 'The Brahmans, who came in "peaceably, and obtained the kingdom by flatteries", may probably have persuaded the Dravidians that in calling them Sudras they were conferring upon them a title of honour' (1875:109). But in fact, Caldwell continued, the Brahmans, as representatives of the Aryan race, made the Dravidian groups accept an appellation reserved in the north for the servile castes. Dravidians, Caldwell maintained, had even accepted the falsehood that Tamil was inferior to and dependent on Sanskrit, the language of the Aryan race and Brahmans in particular.

Caldwell's articulation of the racial and historical basis of the Aryan-Dravidian divide was perhaps the first European valorisation of the Dravidian category cast specifically in racial terms, although he was following conventional wisdom in his uncritical acceptance of an Aryan theory of race, in which Dravidians were seen as the pre-Aryan inhabitants of India.[4] Where Caldwell differed from others was in his

[4] In terms of his grammatical theory, Caldwell followed and built on the earlier suggestions of Francis Ellis, who had noted the non-Sanskritic origin of

unusual suspicion of Aryans and his celebration of Dravidian culture and civilisation; for the most part, British writers used racial theory to justify a view of Dravidians as markedly inferior to Aryans. In the 1860s and 1870s, Henry Maine and Meadows Taylor emphasised the barbarity and superstition of the early Dravidians who 'had infected ancient Hindu society and destroyed its pure Aryan features' (Leopold 1970:281). James Fergusson and R.H. Patterson took this argument one step further, arguing (in anticipation of Risley) that the caste system— with its inbuilt racial suspicion and endogamous taboos—made upper-caste Hindus more ambitious and progressive than they might otherwise have been, because it discouraged intermarriage between Aryans and non-Aryans.

The Aryan theory of race, based on William Jones's well-known 'discovery' of the Indo-Aryan family of languages and developed by German comparative philologists in the 1840s and 1850s, maintained that the speakers of Indo-European languages in India, Persia and Europe were of the same culture and race. While most western writers on this subject ignored the racial equality which this theory afforded to Asian subjects of British colonial rule, Max Müller praised their common descent, although he lamented the demise of Indian civilisational genius in the medieval period. By the time of Müller, however, most English observers had become extremely critical of Indian civilisation and denied any connection between India and Britain, biologically or culturally.[5] A number of Indian intellectuals, on the other hand, used both Müller's praise and the general theory of 'Aryanism' to claim equality and unity between Britons and Indians. Chief among these in the nineteenth century were Debendranath Tagore and Keshab Chandra Sen. As the nineteenth century yielded to the twentieth, most Indian nationalist leaders underplayed the racial connection, either because they were less interested in Indo-European solidarity than in Indian self-esteem, or because they were aware that an Aryan theory of race would necessarily be seen as divisive within

---

Telugu and Tamil as early as 1816. For a discussion of Ellis, see Trautmann (n.d.).

[5] See the wonderful discussion of the transition from 'indomania' to 'indophobia' in Trautmann's important work (n.d.).

the Indian political community. Bal Gangadhar Tilak was an exception
in this regard, though he was widely criticised for antagonising non-
Brahmans in Maharashtra. Other nationalist leaders used 'Aryan' less
as a racial term than as a gloss for ancient Indian religious tradition.
Dayananda Saraswati, Vivekananda, Ranade and Annie Besant all
variously urged that the Aryan faith, which had united north and south
in ancient times, be used to bring India together again.

But in the Tamil country the theories of Aryanism, whether they
linked or separated language and race, mostly worked in precisely the
opposite direction. Aryan was opposed to Dravidian, in linguistic, racial
and cultural contexts. Caldwell's grammatical writings played a
particularly crucial role here, because he wrote in a spirit of praise and
respect for both the Tamil language and the southern cultural
inheritance; it is small wonder that in the south Caldwell's work stood
out against the wider scorn for non- or pre-Aryan cultural achievements
among British writers. Caldwell's influence has had an extraordinary
career in Madras, exceeding in many ways the influence of any other
European ideological formulation in the history of British colonial
knowledge in the subcontinent. This was partly because of the
emphasis on language, which subsequently became appropriated and
inscribed in the deification of Tamil through the cult of Tamil Tay (the
mother goddess of Tamil), as excellently discussed by Ramaswamy
(1992). But partly too, it was because Caldwell used the developing
discourse pertaining to the character and significance of civilisation
itself to build an argument about the dynamics and mechanisms of
cultural imperialism, set within the context of southern concern about
exclusion from the promise (and the perils) of Aryanism as the basis for
cultural pride and civilisational glory.

Like the earliest propositions about the Aryan theory of race,
Caldwell's principal arguments were philological, and were made in the
context of an extremely learned grammatical treatise. Caldwell
proclaimed not only the antiquity and autonomy of Dravidian culture,
but also that the Tamil language, the 'most highly cultivated *ab intra* of
all Dravidian idioms, can dispense with its Sanskrit, if need be, and not
only stand alone, but flourish, without its aid' (1856:49). He further

held that Brahmans had brought Sanskrit with them when they moved to the south, along with a strain of Hinduism that emphasised idol worship. As he wrote: 'Through the predominant influence of the religion of the Brahmans, the majority of the words expressive of religious ideas in actual use in modern Tamil are of Sanskrit origin' (ibid.:51). The missionary's concerns are perhaps nowhere more obvious than in this condemnation of Brahmanical religious influence, for in asserting the Tamils' independence, he also seemed to claim their souls for Christian conversion. Moreover, the move from a concentration on language to the formulation of a counter-discourse to Aryan theories of culture and civilisation was first made in arguments of this kind.

Caldwell's historical and philological praise for Dravidian—read non-Brahman—culture in the south was more than matched by the zeal of certain British officials to dislodge the disproportionate reliance on Brahmans and 'Brahmanical culture' in other domains as well. This reflected the growing reaction to Brahman dominance in defining the fundamental features of Indian civilisation as the nineteenth century progressed. (It also reflected the internal struggles for influence among Orientalists distributed across the subcontinent in different regions with competency in different languages.) Burnell, Brown and Ellis had all been critical of Brahmanical domination in social and literary arenas, as well as in the practice of Hindu law. The most vocal opposition to Brahmanical law was heard from J.H. Nelson, an English judge and civil servant, who failed to be promoted to the Madras High Court, partly because of his strenuous Orientalist exertions and particularly because of his vigorous condemnation of Brahmanical influence. Nelson's central argument is summarised by Derrett:

a fantastic situation had developed in which the law of certain Sanskrit law books was being applied, as if it were their law and custom, to millions of people who had never been governed by any of their contents before, who were not in sympathy with their terror, and who were entitled to have their own customs applied to them. (Derrett 1961:365)

Nelson saw the effect of British rule as not only reifying Brahmanical law in a general sense, but also extending it to sectors of society which were totally unfamiliar with it.

Criticisms of Brahmanism were also characteristic of much early anthropological writing, in which Caldwell's earlier depiction of the simple, sometimes barbaric, but relatively harmless nature of Dravidian religion was always contrasted with the enlightened malevolence of Brahmanical beliefs. W.T. Elmore, for example, supplies the following list:

The debauchery of many of their [Brahman] festivals, the shameless-ness of many places of pilgrimage, the attachment of dancing girls to the temples with all which that implies, the lives of many of the relig-ious mendicants, the unmentionable things in connexion with the worship of the lingam, the proceedings in temples which women visit to pray for offspring. (1925:157)

All these Brahmanical features provide a target for much more serious condemnation than the morally neutral instrumentalism of Dravidian ritual practice.

Not all British writers, however, even those who identified with the south, allied themselves so directly with the anti-Brahman cause, and residual prejudices about Dravidian inferiority continued to inform official understandings of Tamil popular culture, social structure and political aspiration. Colonial writings about Tamil religion invoked perhaps the most extreme version of racial and cultural division between Aryan and Dravidian traditions. Thus Elmore wrote that Drav-idian religion was connected with no literary tradition and no philo-sophical corpus: 'The Dravidians are not a literary people, and their religion has no literature. There are no Vedas or other writings telling of their gods. Their history is contained in the somewhat confused legends recited by wandering singers who attend the festivals and assist in the worship' (ibid:.ix). In the hands of other writers, these judgments became increasingly negative. Official opinion cast non-Brahman religious practices as barbarous and crude, with particular reference to 'pre-Aryan' and 'Dravidian' rites such as hook-swinging, fire-walking and vow-taking for offspring in goddess cults. Edgar Thurston inscribed official opinion within anthropological wisdom; his *Ethno-graphic notes on southern India* (1906) drew material directly from official debates about such matters as the possible suppression of barbarous rituals. As I have explained elsewhere (Dirks n.d.), Thurston neglected to mention that the process of constructing colonial interpretations of popular cultural practices was the result of a complex negotiation between British concerns to regulate local cultural life and—after the great rebellion of 1857—the official policy of not interfering in 'native religious practice'. This negotiation was conducted through an official reliance on Brahmanical opinion and advice, solicited through the development of a discourse on values and civilisation which built on the escalating interdependency of British and Brahman sensibilities about governmental responsibility and, more generally, the moral authority of the governing classes. These long conversations contributed to the production of new orthodoxies about the nature of Hinduism, Brahman hegemony over a wide variety of everyday matters of life, and the shared values of secular Brahmans and enlightened colonials (in which, for example, the Theosophical Society in Madras played an incalculably important role). In these conversations, however, Tamil was ignored and Dravidianism was reified, denigrated and relegated as illiterate superstition and native, non-Brahmanical popular culture.

During the late nineteenth and early twentieth centuries, an assumption of absolute racial difference between Aryan and Dravidian was grafted on to this discursive fabric of cultural assumption and civilisational prejudice, whatever the character of the actual judgment. Elmore, whose book on Dravidian religion actually documents a wide variety of syncretic religious customs and traditions, anchors his historical argument in racial assumptions. Thus he begins his analysis of religion by pointing out that 'when the Aryan invaders came to India they found another race in possession of the land—a race which they gradually subjugated, and to some extent assimilated. In South India, the Aryans are now represented almost exclusively by the Brahmans' (1925:2). This certainty was one of the axioms of colonial sociology in India.

The denigration of Dravidian religion—and the fact that it tended naturally to tarnish a wide range of assumptions about Dravidian culture, philosophy and literature—provoked a number of reactions. These reactions frequently grew directly out of the discursive formation of a dominant Aryan-Brahmanical civilisational complex in the Indian subcontinent even though they were in specific opposition to it. Indeed, neo-Shaivism, a generalised intellectual and religious movement in the late nineteenth and twentieth centuries that reconstituted Shaivism as the pre-Aryan religion of the south, cannot be understood apart from the history of Aryanism itself. Without in any way detracting from the impressive originality of the neo-Shaivite movement, it is impossible to understand it in isolation from a recognition of the extraordinary strength and power of the British and Indian Orientalist formations that made Brahmans, Sanskrit, Vedic sacrifice and Upanishadic speculation, and Aryans and Aryanism, synonymous with the sphere of India's own civilisational genius and accomplishment. In many ways, neo-Shaivism constituted a direct substitute for the Brahmanical sophistication and self-consciousness that colonial opinion had declared to be no part of Dravidian religion.

The Dravidian renaissance entailed a multitude of intellectual, religious, cultural and political activities from the late nineteenth century onwards. While Caldwell made philology a privileged domain for scholarly investigations into the glories and autonomous history of Tamil, U.V. Swaminatha Iyer's 'discovery' of Sangam poetic texts gave the Tamil country a classical literature of its own, which could claim the antiquity, density and poesy of any great civilisation. Characteristically, the most dramatic activities in the 'Dravidianist' movement located issues of language, and specifically Tamil, at their core. Sumathi Ramaswamy has recently argued that the importance of Tamil, and language politics more generally, to the history of Tamil cultural nationalism hinged on the capacity of language to be central in a wide variety of cultural and political movements, at the same time that it could be used to unite a wide variety of potentially divisive identities and groupings. As Ramaswamy makes clear, however, the salience of Tamil also fed into the steady marginalisation of Brahmans and Aryanism from the core features of the Dravidian renaissance and its associated political movements. As, for example, central figures such as Swaminatha Iyer and Subramania Bharati illustrate, Brahmans played an impressive role in the Dravidian movement. Moreover, as

Ramaswamy shows, there was an extraordinary rapprochement between certain areas of southern nationalist activity and the key preoccupations of Dravidianism, including its stress on Tamil literature and language, its claim to a distinguished and autonomous Dravidian civilisation, and its assertion of a distinct role for the south in India's nationalist career. Despite all this, Brahmans nevertheless became increasingly inscribed as the internal other, the 'Muslims' of the south.

Nationalism and Tamil cultural politics

In E.V. Ramasamy Naicker, the nationalist movement directly spawned Brahmanism's most outspoken and dramatic critic. Naicker, or E.V.R. as he was normally called, first achieved prominence when he led a *satyagraha* campaign in 1924 to secure the admission of untouchables into temples in Vaikom, in the old Travancore princely state. Although E.V.R. seemed well on his way to becoming Gandhi's principal ally in the south Indian movement, he soon became disillusioned by what he felt were Brahmanical double standards. The immediate issues that led to his resignation from Congress in 1927 were the separate dining of Brahmans in a Congress-sponsored school, Congress resistance to communal representation, and Gandhi's ideological adherence to the principles of *varnashramadharma* which seemed to E.V.R. to perpetuate caste, rather than, as Gandhi maintained, to transform it. E.V.R. went on to establish the Self-Respect Movement—a social reform association that stressed inter-caste marriages, Brahman-free rituals, the uplift of women and so on—and later the Dravida Kazhagam (Dravidian Association).

E.V.R. was one of the initial leaders of the anti-Hindi movement in Tamilnadu, and became a dogmatic exponent of the philosophy of 'rationalism'. In one of his diatribes against religion, he wrote: 'The Self-Respecters contended that the Vellalas' eyes were partially opened to their cultural grandeur by the English Missionary Dr. Robert Caldwell, but still they remained under the spell of Smartaism, which could only be dispelled by the magic wand of the Self-Respect movement' (quoted in Visswanathan 1983:357). In his conviction that Brahmans and north India constituted the greatest threat to the south, he abandoned the nationalist struggle entirely, writing at one point: 'If 97 per cent of the people become alive to their rights and realise the absurdity of the claims of the so-called superior caste and that is called "communalism", I wish that we may always have that communalism as the cardinal principle of life' (quoted in ibid.:238). E.V.R. continued to play an important role in post-independence Tamil politics, although from the early 1950s this was chiefly through his alienated disciples, most of whom only succeeded in politics after breaking with him: notably C.N. Annadurai (the first DMK chief minister of Madras) and M. Karunanidhi (the present leader of the DMK, whose last term as chief minister of Tamilnadu ended in January 1991).

E.V.R. is perhaps best remembered for leading processions to protest against the role of temples and priests in south Indian society, dramatically humiliating idols and Brahmans by beating them with his slippers. In retrospect, his early enthusiasm for nationalism reveals certain deep continuities in his life, despite the usual charges about his quixotic impulsiveness. Remember that his first and most conspicuous political act had been to lead a *satyagraha* against the exclusion of untouchables from a Brahmanical temple. During this early campaign, he wrote:

They argue that pollution would result if we untouchables passed through the streets leading to the temple. I ask them whether the Lord of Vaikkom or the so-called orthodox Brahmans would be polluted by the presence of untouchables. If they say that the presiding deity at the Vaikkom temple would be polluted, then that could not be God, but a mere stone fit only to wash dirty linen with'. (quoted in ibid.:43)

The rhetoric of this statement is directly reminiscent of much earlier *bhakti* critiques of Brahmanical ritualism in its emphasis on the contradictions of pollution concepts. But E.V.R. did not follow the path of *bhakti* and instead embarked on a secularist political struggle which, unlike the sometimes linked but always constitutionally-oriented Justice Party, elevated religion as the chief source of oppression. Yet E.V.R.'s preoccupation with matters of religion, as well as the careful deployment of religious symbols and practices in his movement, suggest a very specific kind of secularism. And, as I have argued elsewhere (Dirks n.d.), E.V.R.'s particular concentration on Brahmanic religion was specifically enabled by nineteenth-century colonial refigurations of ritual identities and meanings.

E.V.R. was an impressive, complex figure, a kind of Rabelaisian Tamil alter ego for Gandhi; he rivalled Gandhi in his capacity to manipulate political symbols and gestures, and he reviled Gandhi by proclaiming his massive and carnivorous diet, his prowess in matters sexual, his interest in the things money could buy. Also like Gandhi, he wrote and spoke prolifically, and often seemed to contradict himself in his continual engagement with a world of political strategy and contingency. He was particularly slippery on the subject of Brahmans. At times he seemed to call upon his fellow non-Brahmans to go out and murder Brahmans (although they should be prepared to accept the legal consequences; given the numerical disparity between the two communities, however, enough eyes for eyes would have dramatically greater demographic impact on Brahmans than on non-Brahmans).[6] At other times, E.V.R. made clear his friendship with individual Brahmans, most conspicuously C. Rajagopalachari, and specified that his concern was not about Brahmans but Brahmanism. Throughout his political career, however, he played with the referential borders between the two allied terms, frequently blaming all the problems in the south on the Brahman Raj.

The rhetorical politics of the Dravidian movement depended upon a number of fundamental assumptions and classificatory logics. Brahmans and Brahmanism were synonymous with Aryans and Aryanism; Aryans were northern invaders and so were Brahmans. Elaborate historical anthropologies were constructed and unleashed to support these syllogisms and to sustain the view that Dravidians once had a great non-Brahman polity and civilisation, which had been destroyed

[6] Even when the government imprisoned him for directly calling for the murder of Brahmans, E.V.R's supporters protested, using the police transcript of the speech, that he had only said 'if the Brahmans did not mend their ways then the Dravida Kazhagamites would have to resort to killing the Brahmans'. E.V.R's agent went on to note: 'But the speeches were misreported by the Press. A rumour was afloat in the North that the leader of the Dravida Kazhagam incited his followers to resort to murder of Brahmins', Government Order no.893, Public (Confidential), 18.3.1958, Tamil Nadu Archives.

by Aryan conquests and Brahman hegemony. C.N. Annadurai was one
of the most effective propagandists of this view. In his book entitled
The history of Eelam (1953), he wrote:

It was by saying that India is a single country that it was possible for
the Aryans to make the land from the Himalayas to Cape Comorin their
happy hunting ground and to be masters in the sphere of politics,
teachers in the sphere of education, priests in the sphere of religion,
lords of the earth in society and in the economic sphere to be people
leading a pleasant time without toiling; and consequently a situation
arose in which the people belonging to other races had to toil hard as
servants and workers and became physical wrecks and languish. The
best way of removing this tyranny is to divide the country so that a
region may be assigned to each race.

Some authors were even more explicit about the racial basis of the
difference. M. Annalthango, in his *Mummurtigal unmai teriyuma?*,
wrote that:

Brahmans and Tamilians are different in dress, habits, ideas, general
outlook and culture and cannot be regarded as belonging to the same
race; the Tamilians should admit this fearlessly and draw a separate
scheme for the advancement of their race and serve the Tamil race, the
Tamil language, and the Tamil State.

He went even further, arguing explicitly that there had been no mixing
of the blood of Tamilians and Brahmans, even though they share a
mother tongue. He blamed Brahmans for keeping their women from
non-Brahman men, despite his claim that Brahman women are
notoriously 'loose'.

The rhetorical fury of the Dravidian movement deployed a wide
range of anthropological, historical, philological and political arguments in denouncing Brahmans, north Indians, Aryans and the
Congress Party, among others. Race was one but by no means the only
predicate of the Dravidianist critique. Nevertheless, the scientific
certainty that Brahmans were Aryans and that Dravidians and Aryans
were racially distinct underwrote most of the anthropological politics of
the movement.[7] Race was so important because, after the middle of the

---

[7] It is beyond the scope of this paper to speculate further about the

nineteenth century, it made the ultimate argument about difference, inscribing into political discourse biological metatruths which blended the legitimating apparatus of western science with Indian beliefs about blood and being (see Barnett 1970 and Daniel 1983).

So powerful was the separatist argument that many Tamil Brahmans have sought to refute their difference at the risk of their own ritual and social ontologies of identity.[8] After Caldwell, philological scholarship became one of the principal terrains for arguing about Brahman identity, with a number of authors vigorously contesting Caldwell's view that Tamil and Sanskrit are unrelated.[9] Historical scholarship has often concerned itself with the character of Dravidian society before the Aryan invasion, the nature of Aryan influence and the rise of a *varna* caste system, as well as with a set of questions about whether Tamil Brahmans came from the north or were recruited and converted within the south. Anthropological debate, as we saw clearly in Ghurye's writing, also evaluated the anthropometric evidence about caste distinctness in the light of the politics of identity: Aryan versus non-Aryan, Brahman versus non-Brahman.

The power of race was that it naturalised a variety of claims about history, society, language and identity. At one level, race seems to have eclipsed caste. But despite the diminution in the significance of certain caste categories, and the powerful critiques of caste that E.V.R. and the DMK introduced to the Tamil scene, the power of race was also that it was grafted on to caste. In the south Indian case, the caste structure was

admixture of concepts of race and biology in the cultural constructions of Brahmans and non-Brahmans in southern India in the twentieth century.

[8] I mean here that these questions are fraught with consequences and difficulties; Brahmans must rethink their identities to acknowledge both differences from other groups and differences within the Brahman community, which have often been valorised in terms of claims about origins and ritual-biological purity.

[9] See, for example, R. Swaminatha Aiyar, *Dravidian theories* (1975), who argued against 'the current theory which assigns a remote antiquity to the development of the Dravidian languages and regards their structure as unaffected by contact with Aryan idioms'. The preface, by P.N. Appusamy, averred that 'His labours should help promote national integration, by showing how, over two or three millenia ago, people living in different parts of India lived in linguistic amity taking free from neighbouring languages and thereby enriching their own'.

particularly vulnerable to racial grafting, partly because of the specific history of colonial discourses on caste. The Orientalist insistence on *varna* as the all-India scale for natural caste identity made it possible on the one hand to argue that caste was exogenous, and on the other to sustain the racial identification of Dravidian with Shudra and Aryan with Brahman. At the same time that Dravidianist political ideology ostensibly argued against *varna* as a meaningful category for the south, the Tamil deviation from the *varna* system strengthened caste by opening it to a form of racial thinking that, with caste, dominates political discourse to this day.

Colonial transformations and nationalist contradictions

I have elsewhere argued (Dirks 1987) that the view from Pudukkottai—a marginal region of the Tamil country that remained under royal rule through the eighteenth century, before it was 'frozen' under the colonial theatrics of indirect control as a princely state—provides important perspectives for understanding both the nature of caste relations in the pre-colonial period and the dynamics of colonial transformation during the last two centuries. Without rehearsing my entire argument here, let me relate a story I was told when I recently returned to Pudukkottai for a short visit. A man I had known for many years as the driver of the Pudukkottai royal family had a son who was a gifted athlete. He would play volley-ball on the palace sporting grounds, and through his access to the court he got to know and then fell in love with a young Brahman girl, also a gifted volley-baller. When the couple announced their intention to marry, the palace crowd assumed that the girl's family would protest and probably prevent the alliance from occurring. But after various pleas and representations, the Brahman family capitulated, saying that they would adjust. However, the father of the palace driver—a Maravar from Kulamankalam village in southern Pudukkottai state—steadfastly refused to consider the marriage. 'What?' he said, 'marry outside our Thevar community? Impossible.' When mutual friends from the palace intervened and told him that he should relax, particularly since the girl was clearly from a superior caste, he closed the subject, asserting that he was a Thevar and could consider an alliance only with another Thevar family, no matter what anyone else might think. Indeed, he said he would be thrown out of local Thevar society if he allowed the marriage to take place. So much for Brahman superiority.

Returning to Pudukkottai, I once again saw visible evidence of a very different kind of society from that apparent in contemporary writings and political discourses centred in and on Madras. The forms of caste power and deference continue to inscribe the king—now in the guise of his various representatives and replacements—as the dominant figure of the social system, while the Brahman is a figure of parody and fun, necessary for ritual life, fundamental to kingly society, but still and ultimately yet another retainer of the court.

I had earlier observed that the assumptions of Sanskritisation, even modified to Vellala-isation, seemed not to apply in Pudukkottai, in marked contrast to the area around Tanjore just fifty kilometres to the north. Whereas in Tanjore the old Tamil saying about caste change— that Kallars, Maravars, Agamudaiyars, little by little become Vella-lars—seemed to reveal the fundamental truth of M.N. Srinivas's assertion about the cultural dynamics of social mobility, the saying was conspicuously absent in Pudukkottai. Why would a member of a royal community become a mere Vellalar, I was told over and over again. Vellalars of course sustained the major burden of Sanskritisation in the southern country, by changing their diet, Brahmanising their customs and securing cultural hegemony through a specific kind of alliance with Brahmans. But this process seemed not only limited in provenance, but specific to historical conjunctures that clearly intensified in the late medieval period, a time when colonial transformation was already anticipated by the changing political economy of Vijayanagara and the patrimonial ambition of the Mysore sultanate. It was only in the nineteenth and twentieth centuries, under British colonial rule, that Brahmans attained the particular significance now assumed to be 'traditional', and Sanskritisation—as a 'natural' social process of replication and mobility—could attain the cultural force that sustained the theorising of Srinivas and also occasioned the kind of systematic resentment that has contributed to the development of strong anti-

Brahman sentiment throughout the south (and in Maharashtra). Puduk-kottai is thus useful not only to think about the pre-colonial character of kingly (feudal) society in the southern country, but also to de-familiarise and de-naturalise the contemporary certainties associated with the cultural politics of both Sanskritisation and anti-Brahmanism.

Nevertheless, when I returned to Madras, Pudukkottai seemed a very long way away and even more irrelevant than the court Brahmans of that diminutive kingdom. Madras, of course, is the world to which the Brahmans of Pudukkottai had come in such large numbers during the nineteenth and twentieth centuries, selling off *brahmadeyam* lands granted in earlier centuries by kings, and investing steadily and successfully in English education and employment in the new Company Raj. The growing domination of Brahmans in the government of Madras, as well as their prominence in print capitalism and nationalist politics, have been widely reported and carefully documented. But the Brahmans' political and economic position alone does not explain the rise of either Dravidianism or anti-Brahmanism, as is widely claimed. Rather, the cultural politics of Madras in the twentieth century must be understood in relation to a complex history of displacement, status anxiety and cultural hegemony, in which the contradictions of modernism and the curious collaboration of Brahmans in the basic cultural institutions of British colonialism require new forms of critical attention and analysis. An adequate understanding also entails recognition of the extent to which Madras now defines the cultural, social and economic aspirations of Tamils in the twentieth century.

In this paper, I cannot elaborate the above claim in detail, but a couple of examples will suggest the starting point for analysis. In my earlier discussion of Dravidian religion, I discussed some of the ways in which Orientalist scholarship worked to constitute the taxonomies of opposition and difference that oriented the scholarly study and revivalist construction of non-Aryan, genuinely Dravidian domains of religious custom and practice. One arena in which these different constructions came into play in particularly virulent colonial form was British concern to abolish the practice of hook-swinging, when devotees would string themselves up on hooks attached to poles mounted on temple cars and be paraded around the streets of a temple town at annual festivals for the goddess Mariyamman. Some British administrators, lobbied and harassed by missionaries who were outraged at governmental countenance of these barbarous practices, attempted during the early 1890s to suppress the practice by administrative decree. The problem was that the colonial government, in response to the great rebellion of 1857, had declared its intention not to interfere in native religious practice, and thus it could only prohibit the practice of hook-swinging if it could determine that it caused grievous bodily harm, under the provisions of Section 144 of the Indian Penal Code. Thus the government instituted an inquiry into hook-swinging, consulting leading citizens as well as scholars about its religious nature, and about the possible repercussions of its prohibition.

The files generated by this inquiry reveal the extent to which Brahmans and upper-caste Vellalars actively participated in the construction of a new understanding of Hinduism, which affiliated itself with Sanskritic, Aryan and Brahmanical terms of reference and justification. This new understanding was increasingly opposed to growing scholarly certainties about a pre-Aryan sedimentation of Dravidian practices and beliefs that could hardly, so the files said, be considered Hindu. As Lata Mani (1989) has demonstrated in a different context for the debate on *sati*, arguments about Hinduism ultimately referred to textual sources and canonical understandings about what was true, scripturally mandated and authoritative. Thus the absence of any scriptural (Shastric) justification for hook-swinging was seen as the possible basis for outlawing the practice on the grounds not simply of avoiding any interference in native religious practice, but also of rendering it more authentic and more genuinely 'Hindu'. Many Brahman commentators who were consulted by the government probably suppressed any reference to their own multiple affiliations to local tutelary cults and deities in the countryside, in favour of a more Sanskritic self-fashioning in relation to the moral imperatives of colonial discourse and state regulation. Not only, therefore, were the conditions for Sanskritisation as a social process of cultural transformation set in motion by colonial histories such as this one, but both Brahmans and Hinduism were in fact fashioned anew in relation to colonial orthodoxies about religion and the state.

Indeed, the history of the establishment of the Hindu Religious and Charitable Endowments Board in Madras Presidency is full of examples of forced Sanskritisation, always justified by a rhetoric of non-interference (Appadurai 1981; Presler 1987). In constituting religion as a domain that was to be separated from politics, myriad and powerful forms of political intervention were justified and deployed. The state took power by ceding its apparent authority to a newly-constituted 'church', a unified religious authority and establishment that was encouraged and incited to speak for religion in a new world in which the state was committed to the protection of religious freedom and autonomy. Significantly, Brahman and non-Brahman bureaucrats alike pushed forward this new, secular, colonial state agenda, leading to the creation of a very different set of understandings and institutional practices around religion. In Pudukkottai, for example, the princely state's local version of the HR&CE Board abolished the customary practice of widow remarriage by a particular caste in its own caste temples, on the grounds that temples had to be protected from overt social influence by communities controlling their managerial rights. It is small wonder that these administrative interventions were seen as part of a new conspiracy on the part of the colonial state and a Brahmanical power elite to use the modern state apparatus to provide the basis for a new form of Brahman hegemony, but what got missed in the outrage accompanying specific protests was any realisation of how new the cultural basis of this colonial form of Brahmanical self-consciousness actually was.

If there was concern in the countryside about the way Brahmans, having frequently left their rural *agraharams* and sold off their benefices, returned with a vengeance made possible by their dominance in the institutions of the colonial state, this concern fed directly into a growing recognition of the extent to which Brahmans were able to take advantage of new opportunities in education and employment in Madras, as well as in the district capitals of the Presidency. As Madras became the centre for the articulation and administration of colonial policy and law, and ultimately nationalist politics, the cultural politics surrounding the role of Brahmans—on both sides of the colonial divide—intensified exponentially.

Nevertheless, there were profound contradictions within colonial discourses in southern India. On the one hand, the British used Brahmans as their chief informants about the nature and structure of south Indian society, and as their principal administrative assistants in the bureaucratic and political project of ruling south India. The early propositions about the Aryans were predicated on collaboration with and admiration for a Brahmanical view of the Indic world. On the other hand, the British saw Brahmans as a 'wily' and self-interested caste, as the source of high Hinduism that impeded missionisation, and, from the late nineteenth century, as the main source of nationalist aspiration and activity in the south. But within the fault lines of this contradictory colonial relationship, Brahmans became unwitting agents in the writing of an anti-Brahman discourse—incited as they were to participate in the colonial project of enunciating a systematic series of religious and textual measures for authentic Hinduism, as well as in their general commitment to an Aryan theory of Indian civilisation. This is a complex story, involving a thick history of colonial interventions designed to control, codify, civilise and contain India, made up of simultaneous attempts to assimilate and accentuate cultural difference. The point here is simply to note that the 'Sanskritisation' of south Indian society by colonial discursive and administrative rule, as part of the more general process, transformed a Brahmanical dream into a colonial nightmare.

Caste and the post-colonial condition

There seems little doubt today that the long history of political dissent over issues of caste—including perhaps the most coherent and sustained opposition to caste society anywhere in India in the writings and political activities of E.V.R.—has left a legacy in which caste has scarcely been abolished as a focus for political identity, affiliation and mobilisation. If anything, modern forces and understandings of ethnicity, race and communalism have worked, even in dissent, to inscribe themselves inside caste. At the same time, any attempt to criticise the focus on caste runs the risk, as I stated above, of underplaying the extraordinary history of social consciousness around caste issues in the Tamil country, of undermining the ways in which caste, for better or worse, has provided a discursive vehicle for the mobilisation of what at times have clearly been progressive political and social forces, and finally of underwriting new rhetorics of Indian nationalism, which oppose caste to nation and rewrite the latter with the unifying claims of a reborn Hinduism.

Despite these risks, I wish to conclude this chapter with two observations about the social and cultural discourse of caste in the Tamil country today. First, in an interview given in June 1993 by the founder of a relatively new progressive political party, the Pattali Makkal Katchi (PMK), based in the low-caste Vanniya community of northern Tamilnadu, certain striking continuities in the place of caste and race in contemporary political discourse in southern India can be seen. The founder, a man called Ramdoss, had set up an extraordinary challenge to the Dravidian movement's claim to provide the only basis for subaltern representation in the politics of Tamilnadu. When the PMK burst upon the scene a few years ago, it promised to revive discussion about issues of caste privilege and exclusion which, particularly under the mystificatory populism of the M.G.R. years, had gradually disappeared from the normalised politics of an established, centrist 'Dravidian' party. But two things emerged in this interview which seemed to recapitulate and even reify the limits set by the position of caste in contemporary political discourse in the south. First, a new populist movement seemed to require, and was then totally conditioned by, a particular—albeit genuinely subaltern—caste- rather than class-based constituency and rhetoric. Secondly, Ramdoss ritually repeated the caste orthodoxies of the earlier Dravidian movement in asserting the need to keep the Brahman threat alive. In making this second point, Ramdoss noted that Brahmans were racial outsiders to the Dravidian political, social and cultural inheritance, being members, as he said, of the Aryan *inam* ('species'). That such a claim was made in 1993 by a progressive subaltern political leader underscores the continuing power and centrality of early Dravidianist preoccupations with caste and race as the ideological conditions of a popular movement. It also suggests the extent to which the threat of the internal other, the Brahman, must be maintained even when, by the objective criteria that were established much earlier in the twentieth century, the character and significance of Brahman dominance has diminished so greatly.

My second observation concerns political discourse among intellectuals in Tamilnadu today. In recent years, there has been a resurgence of writing by these intellectuals about contemporary politics in ways that simultaneously seek to address and respond to intellectual currents and movements outside the south itself. This writing reflects an extraordinary vitality, but it also exposes a particular kind of post-colonial vulnerability. While the larger national issues of the Mandal Commission report and the Ayodhya mosque seem far removed from Madras, they are used to translate and justify local concerns which, like those reiterated by Ramdoss, reveal the strikingly involuted character of Tamil political discourse. Within the south, Mandal is frequently seen as an attempt by Delhi to catch up with the progressive history of Tamilnadu or, alternatively, as an attempt to do to Brahmans everywhere what has already been done to them in Tamilnadu, where affirmative action began with the Justice Party's agitation in the early 1920s. At the same time, however, Mandal is also seen as a direct index of caste positionality, for one's opinion on Mandal will be directly determined by, and also an absolute test of, one's fundamental social commitment and identity. Moreover, it is widely held in Madras that non-Brahmans are opposed to the BJP position on fundamentalist Hinduism and that Brahmans are uniquely susceptible to and often outspoken advocates of the BJP line. More generally, however, there is considerable frustration about the fact that all-India political issues are formulated in ways that exclude the principal concerns of the south, marginalising it by establishing its relevance only through issues like Mandal and Ayodhya.

Indeed, although the use of the Madras case by authors such as André Béteille—who argued (1990) against Mandal by reference to the experience of the south—seems to make the south relevant (though as a negative example), many Madras intellectuals continue to feel marginalised even as they tend to read all-India politics in terms of the immediate caste concerns of southern debates. More particularly, there is concern that the representation of the south is controlled by groups of Brahmans now holding positions of prominence in Delhi, who either fled the anti-Brahman movement in Madras, or are simply more cosmopolitan and less committed to provincial life in the south than most other Tamils. At the same time, there is general frustration that the Dravidian movement has not only been misrepresented by powerful, frequently Brahman, interests throughout India, but even more critically sold down the river by the cumulative impact of the appropriation of Tamil political discourse by M.G.R. and then Jayalalitha. Jayalalitha's extraordinary political popularity during the early 1990s has been taken as a particular blow; not only is she a Brahman, she has inaugurated a massive temple renovation fund, established state funds for institutions of Vedic learning, fashioned herself as a modern-day image of Draupadi following her alleged abuse by men of the DMK, and made a number of gestures of support for the BJP party. Small wonder that among many intellectuals and critics in Tamilnadu, Jayalalitha's avowal that she is in a direct line from E.V.R. and Annadurai has been viewed as sacrilege. However, Jayalalitha's prestige has also been seen as emblematic of the wider return of Brahman hegemony, a much more dubious proposition. In a number of recent essays, published in both Tamil and English journals, the return of Brahman hegemony in Madras has been widely reported and thoroughly condemned. Despite a theoretical fluency which includes Marxist forms of argument, subalternist modes of historiography, feminist frames of reinterpretation and post-structuralist languages of critique, caste—and specifically the divide between Brahmans and non-Brahmans—therefore always seems to be the rhetorical point of over-determination.

Most recent writing about post-colonialism assumes that cultural hegemony is both constituted and contested in relation to a fractured but still powerful history of European colonialism, in which the anxieties of ambivalence and the myriad traumas of mimetic impoverishment inform our theoretical understanding of the contradictions of life after (yet with) colonialism. Cultural hegemony is thought to be harder to see than economic neo-imperialism, and even more persistent and evasive than the political strategies adopted to mystify and mask the continuation of colonial forms of dependency and domination in the post-colonial period. But in most explorations of the predicament of (cultural) post-colonialism, there is a clear understanding that the absent presence for its definition is Europe. Europe, as we have seen, is historically deeply implicated in the production of the particular forms of argumentation and assumption about the dominant forces of hegemony in Tamil society, just as the forces of colonialism have dominated India's modern history in virtually every domain of life. Yet in the Tamil south, the post-colonial picture is complicated by the double presence of the displaced colonial other, figured most directly and conspicuously in the Brahman (and by implication or association the north Indian and the Aryan). In a history that begins with the language of Caldwell in casting the Aryan as a colonial figure, we confront a post-colonial condition with a difference. And thus both colonialism and post-colonialism move offstage, to be replaced by a colonial theatre of double mimesis, in which the Brahman plays the role—not quite, but well enough—of the British colonial ruler, and in which colonialism might be said to have ended not in 1947, but only in 1967, with the ascension to political power of the DMK.

So it is that by looking at caste in southern India we engage the larger national politics of caste at a peculiar angle, refracted both by the specificities of Tamil history and the way in which that history has oppositionally engaged both British colonialism and Indian national-ism. The history of caste in Tamil India has underscored colonial determinations even as it has made clear why the reification of caste affiliations and identities has been linked not only to the convenience of colonial power, but also to the articulation of political resistance to what have become represented as traditional and modern forms of class domination. The strange career of Tamil caste thus provides a variety of potent ways to tell the story of the myriad contradictions surrounding caste more generally, in colonial history, anthropology and India's post-colonial predicament.

Coda: towards an anthropology of audience

If my argument and approach hold good, even to a limited extent, we can appreciate in new ways the difficulty of writing about what we call caste, as also the different ways in which criticism can veer out of control once we begin to engage multiple audiences. I have recently discovered that *The Hollow Crown* (1987), in which I explore the colonial role in the construction of modern forms of caste and social identity in India, can be (though I would resolutely insist that it need not be) read as an apology for Brahmanism, since I argue there, as here, that the spectre of Brahmanism—as presented to the anti-Brahman movement of Madras—was only genuinely produced in the colonial period. A critique of one form of colonialism is the object of critique by another version of colonialism. The anthropology of caste becomes transnationalised and denationalised, animated and then debunked, in this new hermeneutical field of sceptical historicising. Where do we write? Why do we write? And to whom? I close this discussion by referring back to my earlier question, about how the anthropological debate over the politics of caste has itself entered into the debate, so that we ignore only at great risk the multiple political implications and contradictions which circulate around the scholarly objective of understanding changing caste in contemporary south Asia. Even as anthropology has historically helped to document as well as to constitute the changing character of social relations in colonial India, it has now become a critical player in the politics of identity and privilege in India today. The stakes have never been higher, and the lessons we might learn—not just about caste itself, but also about the politics of anthropological knowledge in general—have never been plainer.

References

Annadurai, C.N. 1953. *The history of Eelam*. Madras.
Appadurai, A. 1981. *Worship and conflict under colonial rule: a south Indian case*. Cambridge: Cambridge University Press.
Barnett, S. 1970. 'The structural position of a south Indian caste.' Unpublished Ph.D. thesis, University of Chicago.

Béteille, A. 1990. 'Caste and reservations'. *Hindu*, 20 October 1990.
Caldwell, R. 1849. *The Tinnevelly Shanars*. Madras: Christian Knowledge Society's Press.
——. 1875 (1856). *A comparative grammar of the Dravidian or South-Indian family of languages*. London: Trubner and Co.
Daniel, E. V. 1983. *Fluid signs: being a person the Tamil way*. Berkeley: University of California Press.
Derrett, J.D.M. 1961. 'J.H. Nelson, the forgotten administrator-historian of south India.' In C.H. Phillips (ed.), *Historians of India, Pakistan and Ceylon*. London: Oxford University Press.
Dirks, N.B. 1987. *The hollow crown: ethnohistory of an Indian kingdom*. Cambridge: Cambridge University Press.
——. 1992. 'Castes of Mind.' *Representations* 37:56-78.
——. 1995.'"Is vice versa?" Historical anthropologies and anthropological history.' In T. McDonald (ed.), *The historic turn in the human sciences*. Ann Arbor: University of Michigan Press.
——. n.d. 'The policing of tradition.' Unpublished manuscript.
Elmore, W.T. 1925 (1915). *Dravidian gods in modern Hinduism: a study of the local and village deities of southern India*. Madras: Christian Literature Society for India.
Ghurye, G.S. 1932. *Caste and race in India*. London: Kegan Paul.
——. 1950. *Caste and class in India*. Bombay: Popular Book Depot.
Hardgrave, R.L. 1965. *The Dravidian movement*. Bombay: Popular Prakashan.
Irschick, E.F. 1969. *Politics and social conflict in south India*. Berkeley: University of California Press.
Leopold, J. 1970. 'The Aryan theory of race.' *Indian Economic and Social History Review* 7:271-97.
Mani, L 1989. 'Contentious traditions: the debate on *sati* in colonial India.' In K. Sangari and S. Vaid (eds.), *Recasting women: essays in colonial history*. New Delhi: Kali for Women.
Presler, F.A. 1987. *Religion under bureaucracy: policy and administration for Hindu temples in south India*. Cambridge: Cambridge University Press.
Ramaswamy, S. 1992. 'Engendering language: the poetics and politics of Tamil identity.' Unpublished Ph.D. thesis, University of California, Berkeley.
Rudolph, L.I. and S. H. 1969. *The modernity of tradition: political development in India*. Chicago: University of Chicago Press.
Seal, A. 1968. *The emergence of Indian nationalism: competition and collaboration in the later nineteenth century*. Cambridge: Cambridge University Press.
Swaminatha Aiyar, R. 1975 (1922-3). *Dravidian theories*. Delhi: Motilal Banarssidas.
Thurston, E. 1906. *Ethnographic notes on southern India*. Madras: Government Press.
Trautmann, T.R. n.d. 'Aryans and British India.' Unpublished manuscript.
Visswanathan, E.S. 1983. *The political career of E.V. Ramaswami Naicker*. Madras: Ravi and Vasanth.